# Acknowledgements

My thanks are due to the following:

**Organisations**
Digital Equipment Corporation, for extracts from the XUI Style Guide
Acorn Computers Ltd.
Clares Micro Supplies

**People**
Professor K A Jukes, for encouragement and support
Colleagues in the CSM Department, Bristol Polytechnic, for advice and criticism
Sarah Teague and her colleagues at Ellis Horwood, for their patience
My family: Claire, Catherine and Charlotte, for their tolerance

# HUMAN–COMPUTER INTE
## Theory and Practice

WITHDRAWN

## University of Hertfordshire

# ELLIS HORWOOD SERIES IN COMPUTERS AND THEIR APPLICATIONS

*Series Editor:* IAN CHIVERS, Senior Analyst, The Computer Centre, King's College, London, and formerly Senior Programmer and Analyst, Imperial College of Science and Technology, University of London

# HUMAN–COMPUTER INTERACTION
## Theory and Practice

FRANK MADDIX
**Department of Computer Studies and Mathematics**
**Bristol Polytechnic**

**ELLIS HORWOOD**
NEW YORK   LONDON   TORONTO   SYDNEY   TOKYO   SINGAPORE

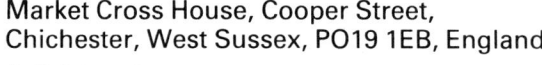
First published in 1990 by
**ELLIS HORWOOD LIMITED**
Market Cross House, Cooper Street,
Chichester, West Sussex, PO19 1EB, England

A division of
Simon & Schuster International Group
A Paramount Communications Company

Printed and bound in Great Britain
by Hartnolls, Bodmin, Cornwall

---

British Library Cataloguing in Publication Data

---

Maddix, Frank
Human–computer interaction; theory and practice. —
(Ellis Horwood series in computers and their
applications).
1. Man. Interactions with computer systems.
I. Title
004.019
ISBN 0–13–446238–6 (Library Edn.)
ISBN 0–13–446220–3 (Student Edn.)

---

Library of Congress Cataloging-in-Publication Data available

---

# Contents

# Preface

This book is aimed at everyone who believes that computer-based systems should be comprehensible, consistent and easy to use; and that improvements can, and must, be made by the people who are best placed to implement them: systems designers, software engineers, programmers and, above all, the users themselves. It is also aimed at those people who have a general or specific interest in HCI, possibly by being the innocent victim of a 'user-hostile' system. It does not undertake to be a comprehensive treatise of all aspects of HCI, but aims to provide a basis for further reading for the student, or as a stand-alone text in its own right.

The study of human-computer interaction has, as its central concern, the efficiency and quality of computer-based systems as perceived by the people who use them, whether from necessity or enjoyment. The quality of the interface may be judged directly (a systems designer might be able to provide specific criticisms); or indirectly (an end user might report a feeling of dissatisfaction, but be unable to pinpoint a specific cause).

There is an increasing realisation that attention to good HCI is not a fad or a technical gimmick, or even a 'feature'; major improvements in productivity can be realised by the thoughtful application of HCI principles. But just as good design cannot be 'injected' into a car or an aircraft after its manufacture, good HCI cannot be overlaid onto a computer application after its delivery to the user. A measure of the growing importance of HCI is that several major international standards organisations are currently developing HCI guidelines which will have the backing of law.

How, then, are good HCI principles learned and then applied to the design of applications? Ideally, there would be a body of knowledge that can be consulted by system designers who are seeking to improve the HCI aspects of their products; or by intending purchasers who wish to quantify the potential gains in productivity. A large and growing literature base does indeed exist; there are numerous learned journals and some excellent texts (recommendations for further reading are given at the end of each chapter).

However, HCI is a rapidly expanding area, and embodies activities which are stimulating and challenging in their diversity. Its appeal stems partly from the wide range of disciplines from which it draws its intellectual base - ergonomics, computer science, software engineering, psychology, cognitive science and Artificial Intelligence, to name but a few. Most existing texts reflect the specialist background of their author(s) to a great extent, whether that be systems design, psychology, ergonomics or (more rarely) computer science.

This book focuses on what has been called *praxis* - an appropriate and 'synergistic' blend of theory and practice. It is intended for people who want to combine an introduction to HCI principles with an appreciation of some of the practical problems encountered during the development of real systems. A layered approach has been taken, in which HCI has been treated as a communications problem between people and machines, and tackled in a similar way to computer communications.

In addition, therefore, to a comprehensive theoretical background, the reader will be introduced to the practicalities of planning HCI experiments, collecting and analysing data (and dealing with people), and designing small programs.

The structure of the book is as follows. Chapter 1 provides an overview of, and a rationale for, HCI. Chapter 2 introduces the 'layered' model and discusses some theoretical approaches. Chapter 3 introduces human factors, and Chapter 4 is concerned with the practical tools of HCI. Chapters 5 - 10 cover the main body of material, and Chapters 11 - 13 deal with issues related to HCI such as usability metrics and documentation. Chapter 14 considers some special issues, with a survey of new developments in hardware and software.  Chapter 15 concludes the book and includes sections on how the HCI community works and careers in HCI.

An important and often ignored issue, that of disabled users, is treated in Chapter 14.

This book does not set out to provide a full coverage in depth of a rapidly growing area such as HCI; it aims to foster an enthusiasm for, and understanding of, the subject which will stimulate readers to research further.

# 1 Introduction to HCI

*The failure of Systems Analysts and designers to make systems easily and comfortably usable by laymen is the most significant inhibiting factor in the future progress of the IT industry.*

*(V A J Maller, Editorial, Computing, June 1987)*

## Introduction

Computers, and the systems which contain them, are now part of our everyday life; yet the ways in which we interact with these systems are not fully understood, even by (or perhaps especially by) the people who design them for us. It has generally been assumed that people 'get along' somehow. This was acceptable as long as systems were relatively simple, or dedicated to one task (such as a payroll service). More recently, the systems have become immensely more complex: 'fly by wire' systems for aircraft, expert systems for medical diagnosis, etc. The interface to the human operators of these systems has of necessity become more complex, but not always more *comprehensible*. HCI has never been more relevant or necessary. This is reflected in the list of topics which have been selected for review in a recently launched abstracting journal[2]:

- User Interfaces

- Design guidelines and standards

- The development of interactive systems

- Documentation, user training, user support

- Usability measurement and testing

- Work organisation and social issues

- Requirements of special populations

- Cultural and international issues

- Safety and health aspects of computing

- Programming and software engineering

- Cognitive ergonomics and cognitive science

- Ergonomics of equipment and of the workplace

- Computers in training and education

- Computer graphics and hypermedia

- Computer assisted group work

- Knowledge based systems

- Aerospace and transportation systems

- Database and management information systems

- Decision support systems

Many of these topics are covered in this book.

In this chapter we will consider what HCI is, how it developed and how it relates to other disciplines concerned in the development of computer-based information systems.

## What is HCI?

HCI concerns itself with the domain of human-computer interaction, and all the issues associated with that activity: in other words, the interaction itself (as a process) and knowledge about that interaction. It is both an art and a science, and has also been has been variously labelled human-computer Interface, MMI (Man-Machine Interface), HSI (human-Systems Interface) and CHI (computer-human interaction). In spite of this variability in labelling of the subject, all HCI workers know exactly what HCI is and how they relate to it. Moreover, it should not be assumed that 'HCI' replaces the other acronyms mentioned above. The science of MMI, for example, has roots in Ergonomics, and offers solutions in those areas where people are interacting with machines such as nuclear power stations rather than computers. Of course, the distinction is becoming blurred as more and more complex plant is computerised. The goal of HCI is simple: to ensure that the systems produced by designers for people to use are comprehensible, consistent and usable. Its central concern is the good design of sociotechnical systems. However, the means employed are complex, and, appropriately for this kind of endeavour, the discipline of HCI draws its inspiration and technique from a broad range of subjects - psychology, Ergonomics, cognitive science, computer science and software engineering. It is evidently more than a concern for the interface itself, important though that is.

Like psychology, HCI has a body of theoretical information and a set of practical procedures. Ideally, one informs, and is informed by, the other. The extent to which this happens is governed largely by the professional standards adopted by the investigator.

One important distinction that must be made is between the terms Human-Computer *Interaction* and Human-Computer *Interface*. To quote Benyon and Murray[8]:

> *Interaction includes all aspects of the environment such as the working practices, office layout, provision of help and guidance, and so on.*

*The interface is the parts of the system with which the user comes into contact physically, perceptually or cognitively.*

## Sociotechnical systems

Marvin Minsky, who is a familiar figure in Artificial Intelligence circles, has characterised one of the fundamental problems of HCI - we know a good deal about computers, how they are put together, and how they behave; we know a reasonable amount about people, their cognitive abilities, and how they behave; but we lack knowledge of specific information about their behaviour, beliefs and emotions in the particular situation of sitting in front of a computer. Although we may suspect that often they would really rather be doing something else, we aren't absolutely certain about this - the very act of asking them may put ideas into their head. Minsky's Dumbells (Figure 1.1) illustrate this situation graphically.

HCI concerns itself in a broad sense with the 'thin' part of Minsky's Dumbells, both at an individual ('micro') and social ('macro') level. It could be characterised as a collection of disciplines which concerns itself with broadening this 'thin' region so that the understanding of both people and machines is well mapped and consistent.

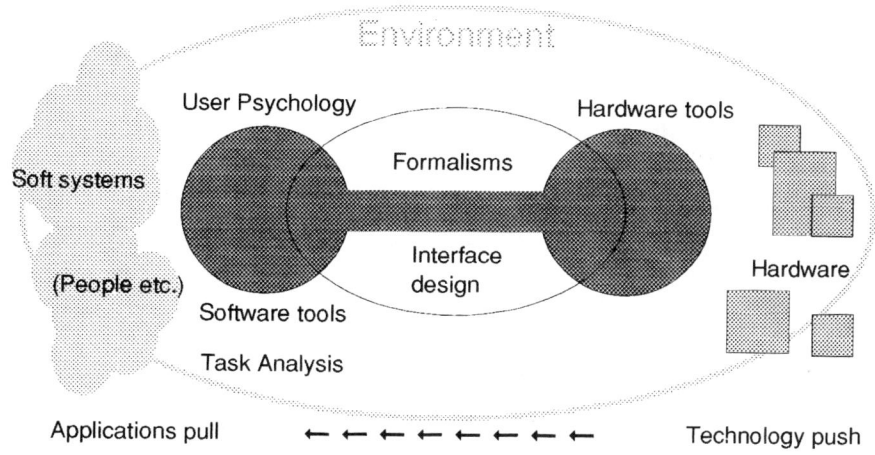

*Figure 1.1 Minsky's Dumbells*

## Development of HCI

There has always been a concern, on the part of some designers in the computer industry, that the‖users of computer systems are having a reasonably good experience with the products that have been designed for them.‖Unfortunately, it is arguable that these concerned designers are in a minority. Few justifications can be made on economic grounds for expending time and effort on improving the interface, although in retrospect it always seems worthwhile; there are few established ground rules for making such a case, and most systems analysts/designers are uneasy about dabbling in psychology.

Consequently, most designers (including the concerned ones) have been content to know that the menus are consistent, or the colours on the screen not too glaring, or the processing delay not too great, in the belief that their systems are working well vis-à-vis the user.

In spite of this, HCI has emerged as a useful discipline for a number of reasons. Some of these are listed below.

- The concern for 'time-and-motion' type studies in the past, although occasionally of limited effectiveness in the areas they purported to improve, led to some attention being paid to the behaviour of the staff in the data preparation room. An astute observer would have noticed a mismatch between what people were doing and what they had been 'designed' to do by the system, either on a quantitative (speed) basis or on a qualitative (behavioural) basis.

- As more and more people became employed in the data processing industry, the incidence of visual and other disorders increased significantly (so much so, that the TUC commissioned a survey on the effects of Visual Display Units (VDUs) in 19??). More recently, there has been some concern regarding 'Repetitive Strain Injury' (RSI) - a condition similar to arthritis which is thought to be a consequence of shock loading on the finger joints of users while typing. The damage is not only physical; a user who knows something is wrong with the system, but cannot express it, is likely to suffer some kind of cognitive stress, which may express itself as a headache or general feelings of anomie.

- Many 'system problems' emerged which were not directly related to the behaviour of the interface:

- The sheer volume of data entry operations has enabled significant cost-saving to be made as a result of some 'human factors' improvements.

Finally, a cynic might observe that the emergence of HCI has mirrored the increasing direct use of computers by middle and higher management in organisations, and could be viewed as a response by articulate members of this community to bad experiences at the keyboard.

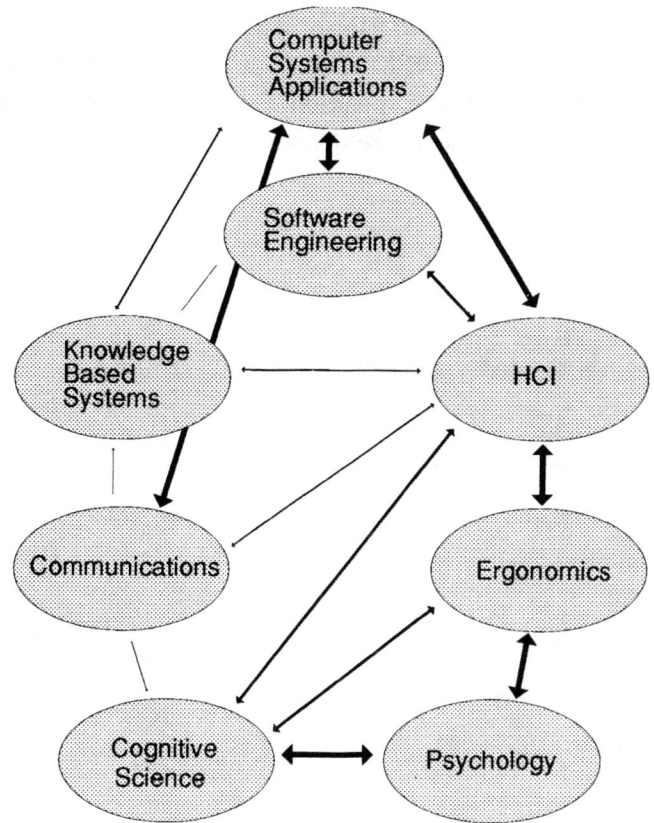

*Figure 1.2 Relationship of HCI with other disciplines*

## The place of HCI

Figure 1.2 illustrates how HCI relates to other important disciplines in computing. The link to software engineering is important, as it enables HCI to actively influence the software development process; but just as important is the link to cognitive science, as this provides the knowledge base of human factors used by theorists and practitioners.

## Scope of HCI

Figure 1.3 illustrates a possible diagram of how the scope of HCI, in terms of its activities, may be modelled - with two dimensions, *depth* (from shallow to deep) and *strength* (from weak to strong). A 'weak/broad' approach, for example, would be to feel that HCI was 'generally a good thing'. A 'strong/shallow' position would espouse the general incorporation of HCI into software design and development; a 'weak/

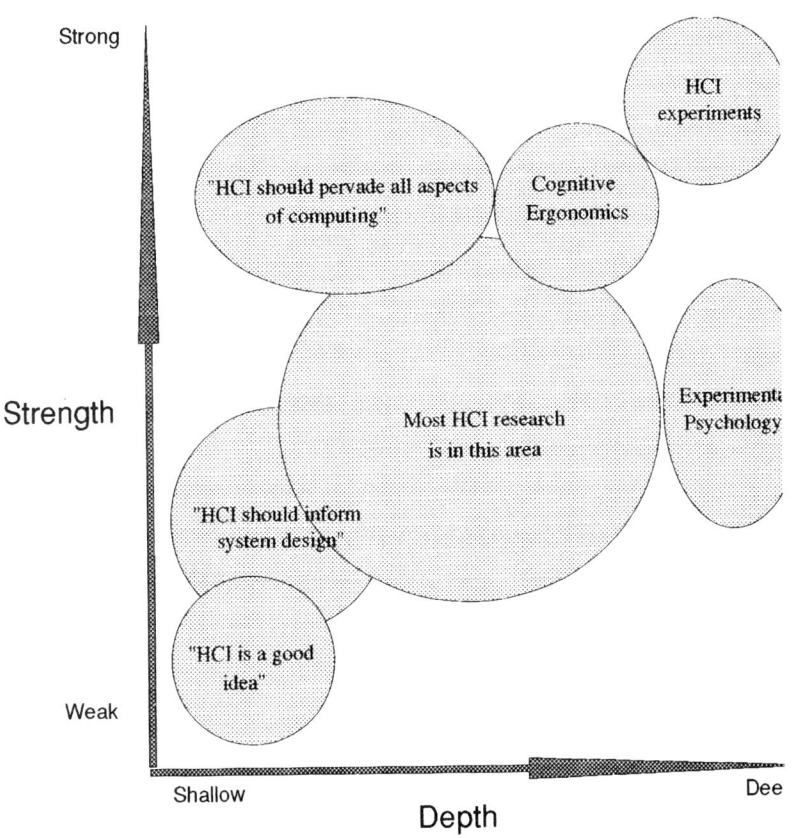

*Figure 1.3 The scope of HCI*

deep' position would hold that HCI, as well as being generally incorporated into systems, should be specifically researched for evidence of its appropriateness. Finally, a 'strong/deep' position would recommend that specific in-house HCI research and development was done, on an experimental basis, on various aspects of the HCI of the system. The last situation would probably be found in an academic or research institution.

Most HCI activities, and the material in this book, occur within the shaded circle in the figure.

## The 'DIY' model

There is another aspect to HCI, complementary to the above analysis. It is basically to do with the *necessity* of HCI with regard to a particular set of activities. For want of a better name, we will term it the *DIY model*, because it runs along the same dimensions as the classical DIY diagram (Figure 1.4).

The diagram helps to place the importance of any particular aspect of HCI. A good task model is obviously essential (structural/essential), and effort should be expended on this. On the other hand, it may not be worth spending a long time programming gold-plated buttons on windows (cosmetic/optional).

However, it should not be assumed that issues such as choosing the correct window colour are trivial.

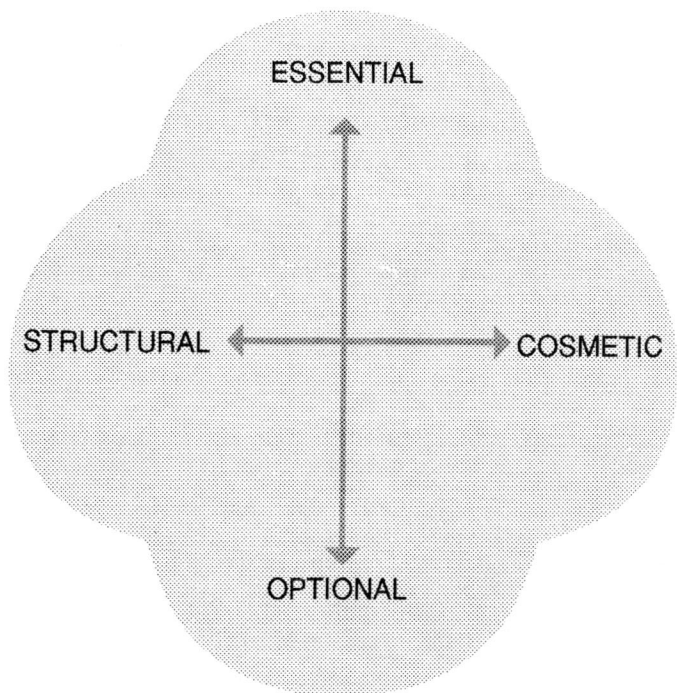

*Figure 1.4 The DIY model of HCI*

# Computers and people

### Computer-centred systems

Historically, computers have acted as centres for data gathering, processing and distribution. Because of the complex physical and logistical environment necessary to maintain such a large piece of equipment, and the associated organizational structure, the computer centre came to be seen as the 'natural' repository for information processing in an institution, even when the nature of this activity changed.

The process of turning all problems into a set of procedures, and programming them (or having them programmed) on a machine, became well understood and efficient, even if it was not always appropriate. Generally speaking, computer centres (at least in academic institutions) were specified and funded by the groups of users who would benefit most - aeronautical engineers, physicists etc.

Other potential users (psychologists, linguists, economists) often had an uphill struggle to make their needs comprehensible to the computer centre staff. The basic problem was that the machine-oriented, procedural methods of data processing which had evolved were generally inappropriate to the less structured data sets of these disciplines, and proprietary (i.e. 'off-the-shelf') packages were not generally available. A side effect of this was that workers in the 'softer' disciplines became greatly concerned with making their data amenable to computer analysis, sometimes with unfortunate consequences.

### A personal experience

When the author first used a mainframe computer system, in a university psychology department, the only access to it was via one of two devices: a teletype or a card punch. Both were large, heavy, noisy and unreliable; they were used mainly by the 'computer experts' in the department. The computer itself, and its support staff, was housed in its temple at the top of a hill. 'Jobs' were submitted with humility and trepidation via a deck of cards; occasionally, a card deck would be dropped, and would have to be rebuilt. (The sympathy of colleagues on such occasions provided a welcome human input to the computing process, and an excuse to visit a nearby pub in order to rebuild the deck in a calm atmosphere.)

Some days later the printout appeared. The elation experienced on seeing a 'correct' printout was generally out of all proportion to what had actually been achieved in real terms. The local publican was invariably the beneficiary on these occasions; indeed his theories on how a correct result had been achieved were as good as anyone else's.

There was, generally, little understanding of what was going on inside the system; copious notes were kept on the exact sequence to follow, and there was a certain amount of 'superstitious' behaviour, in which correct input was made with reference to some internal model of the system. This model was generally specious, and private, since to reveal it to the experts would be to invite ridicule.

The experts were friendly and patient, but not always able to explain things in simple terms. After a session with an expert, most users would be left with a feeling of inadequacy; in spite of the human contact with the advisory staff, most people felt that they had come into intimate contact with some kind of machine. This was, arguably, due to the machine-like terms to which it was necessary to reduce the problem description.

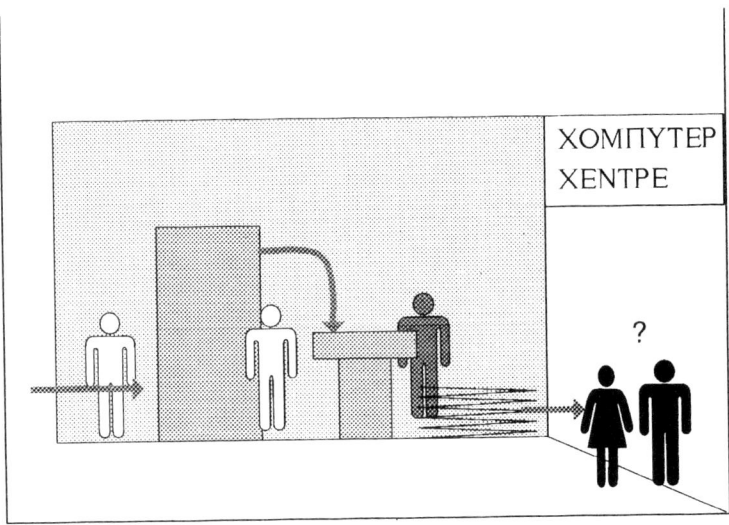

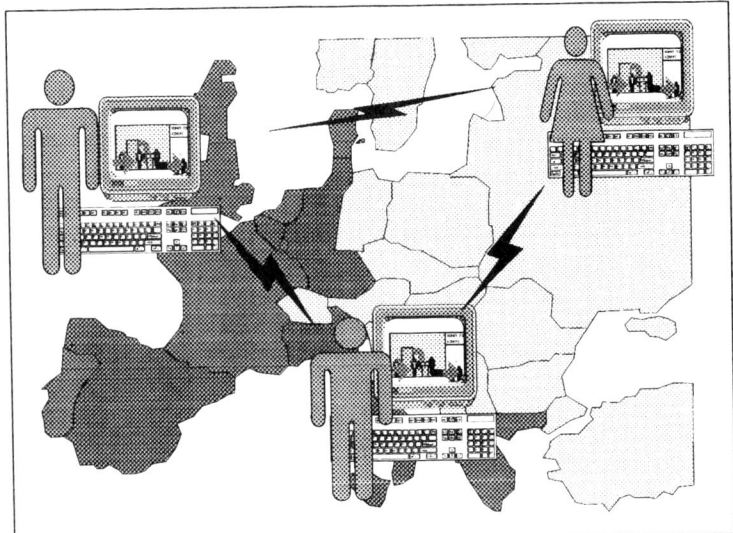

*Figure 1.5 Computer-centred versus people-centred systems*

### People-centred systems
For a variety of reasons, the 'system', and its interface, has been deferring
to, and moving towards, the user over the last few years (Figure 1.5)
Some of the reasons are:

- Smaller computers - minicomputers - came into use in scientific laboratories. The onus for software development was placed squarely on the shoulders of the end user, who often found the development facilities inadequate.

- The relationship between programmers and end-users changed. Many projects, both commercial and scientific, began to employ their 'own' programmer who, perforce, had to talk to other members of the project team. Very often, a good interface only emerged after a lot of wrangling about what the proposed system should, or should not, be expected to do.

- Users have become aware of how the interfaces to their applications ought to 'look and feel'. They no longer feel overawed about talking to applications designers, and are not prepared to tolerate an arcane or unhelpful interface.

- The nature of software has been changing - it is significant that the first spreadsheet program (Visicalc) was implemented on a microcomputer as a direct response to a well-articulated need by auditing professionals.

Whatever the reasons, there is no doubt that the user has a much greater window on his/her information, its processing is faster, and the ways in which it can be transformed are more than ever before. One symptom of this is the choice of multi-media workstations as the preferred environment for many information workers.

The development of the workstation environment could be regarded as the convergence of two trends: the personal computer, and the workstation commonly found in academic environments. The personal computer, which is quite common in a wide variety of working and domestic environments, has a well-written and well supported range of software available to the user; and the new generation of software author tends to have a degree in computer science or software engineering, experience in Unix and the C programming language, and will have well-formed ideas relating to the kind of working environment he/she expects to find. The rate of progress has been such that the high-end personal computer is increasingly undercut in price by the low-end workstation.

Moreover, advances in technology have meant that, not only can fast CPUs, memory and peripheral devices be put on the desktop for moderate cost, but also that procedures which require significant processing power (such as voice recognition, text scanning and the incorporation of video images) can be implemented. (Readers might be interested to know that the 'user' depicted in Figure 1.6 is the author's three year old daughter, whose picture was 'grabbed' from a video camera; and that the text on the 'fax' page was scanned in using a low-cost scanner. In each case, the image was 'cleaned up' using a painting package before final incorporation into the drawing).

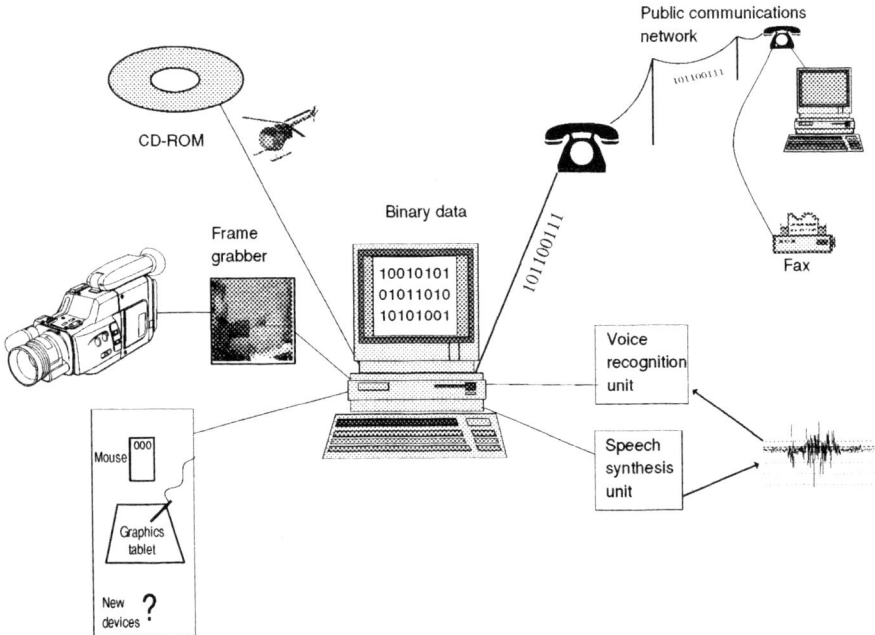

*Figure 1.6 Multi-media workstation: The workstation is a collection of advanced technology, with a powerful desktop computer at its core.*

incorporation into the drawing package used to generate the figures in this book).

Figure 1.6, referred to above, indicates how a typical multi-media workstation might be organised. (Note that 'workstation' refers to a collection of components rather than a single device like a computer). The proliferation of such workstations has resulted in the establishment of a new area in information systems, 'client-server' computing. As far as HCI is concerned, the benefits are considerable: most of the traditional restrictions on the user's liberty are removed or 'tamed', and the disadvantages (for example, the need for maintenance and security procedures on the part of the user) are outweighed by the benefits. (See Chapter 14 for a fuller discussion of these issues).

Generally (and this theme will be developed in Chapter 15), the status of the computer could be seen as moving from that of a *machine* to that of a *tool*, and possibly to that of an *instrument*. Boulter, in his book Turing's Man, puts it thus:

> *"The computer is in some ways a grand machine in the Western mechanical-dynamic tradition and in other ways a tool-in-hand to the ancient craft tradition. The best way to encourage the humane use of computers is to emphasize, wherever possible, the second heritage over the first, the tool over the machine."*

This duality (or uncertainty) of status may reflect our own ambivalence about the way in which we treat our information workers, the computer being in some way a reflection of our culture. Do we try to mould the computer into an analogue of the industrial machines of the past, or let it reach its own level? It looks as though the users are beginning to vote with their feet. If we do not address this problem seriously, and soon, we may not have a pool of people willing to turn their talents to information technology.

# Justification for HCI

There are basically two contrasting ways in which close attention to the HCI aspects of a new project or application can be justified - we will term these the *principled* and the *pragmatic* approaches. The first approach would espouse the adoption of good HCI out of a concern for the well-being of the user. However, although there is good evidence for enhanced operator satisfaction as a result of spending money on good HCI advice at the design stage, financial directors need more concrete evidence of the benefits, and take a pragmatic view.

Unfortunately, there is often a vested interest in justifying the choice of the original system, and so the wastage of time, or commission of errors, is often laid at the door of 'incompetent' operators, when it is the system, and its original designers, who should bear much of the responsibility.

### The *Scandinavian Model*

Where research has been done into the 'human factors' of computer-based systems, it is still often based on technological models rather than human or sociotechnical models.

In his paper "Are 'human factors' human?" [10] Nils Bjørn-Andersen has argued that all we are really doing in much 'human factors' research is to adapt the technology to so-called human weaknesses in order to reduce the resistance to using the technology. For example, the keyboard of a VDU may be made detachable so that a correct relationship can be obtained between operator, keyboard and screen. While this kind of improvement is undoubtedly important, Bjørn-Andersen maintains that we are often lulled into a false sense that 'all is well' with the system if the operators are uncomplaining, and that more deeply rooted problems are not tackled.

He further argues that, if it is to be a useful discipline, classical ergonomics needs to be subdivided into three categories: *workplace* ergonomics, *organizational* ergonomics and *societal* ergonomics.

While workplace ergonomics concerns itself with how the system might be improved physically with respect to its operators, organizational ergonomics concerns itself with the purpose of the system. Societal ergonomics addresses itself to the problems which arise when a society tackles the phenomenon of rapid growth in Information Technology in such areas as office automation.

Generally, then, HCI issues are considered to go far beyond a concern with the user interface. This is consistent with the commonly agreed philosophy in the HCI community, as stated in the first issue of its own journal[2]:

> *"...there are solutions in HCI that do not involve changing the interface at all.*
>
> *For example, some problems may be solved by providing training, or by changing the operators' tasks or the practices of their organisation."*

## Cost

Nobody now questions the value of good software engineering practice. However, it is an unfortunate demonstration of the central concern with financial constraints, rather than quality, that industry did not see the need for quality assurance in software until major errors had occurred, which were always 'unforeseen'. Perhaps the most famous is the missile alert in the United States in the 1960s, (as reported by Cantwell-Smith [14]) where an impending Russian attack was signalled, and the entire US defence system went to 'red'. The real cause? The moon was rising, causing substantial radar reflections, and this eventuality had not been foreseen.

In retrospect, it is easy to laugh at this omission. However, it is unlikely that the programmer/s in charge of that particular piece of software knew the full context in which it would be deployed.

## Standards

It looks as though the principled information technologist or data processing manager, interested in the well-being of users, will be disappointed in his/her dialogues with a strong pragmatist. Fortunately, the international standards organisations seem to be tackling the HCI domain seriously - there are emerging standards for all aspects of HCI, both at a low level (e.g. keyboard design) and a high level (cognitive loadings and stress levels).

The significant thing here is that the standards established as a result of the work of these committees will be backed, and enforced, by law.

## Studying HCI

### Thinking

Perhaps the most important activity, initially, is to get a 'mind set' for HCI. In the simplest case, this may involve reminding yourself to 'think HCI' every time you use a particular package, new or old. If you try to get into the habit of introspecting about what you are doing, and why, you will find that your observational and analytical skills will develop accordingly.

### Reading

Apart from the main journals, which are mentioned elsewhere in this chapter, there is a growing awareness of HCI in the general and popular computer press, and many well-written articles. Try to scan them, say, weekly.

### Doing

Talking to people is an inexpensive activity, and can yield a good deal of useful information. People often reveal more of their thoughts when talking to a friendly and interested companion (especially if they have been treated to a cup of coffee...).

Observing people while they work at computers is a fruitful (and occasionally amusing) activity if performed unobtrusively.

### Courses

There are an increasing number of courses in HCI, offered either as a main course (e.g. a Masters course) or as an option (e.g. on Systems Analysis or Information Technology courses). The Open University are planning to mount an HCI course in the UK in 1990.

## Resources

### *Literature*

There are an increasing number of textbooks concerned, directly or indirectly, with HCI. Some are written by information system designers of long standing (e.g. Sutcliffe), and some by 'recruits' from other disciplines, such as Ergonomics (e.g. Rasmussen).

The following books (listed in author alphabetical order) all provide a good introduction to HCI, each from a different perspective (see Appendix A for full details):

- Gaines & Shaw

- Rasmussen

- Shneiderman

- Smith & Green

- Sutcliffe

There are a number of journals concerned with HCI; again, an inspection of Appendix A will provide details. Journals such as the International Journal Of Man-Machine Studies are well-established; some, for example the new journal 'Interacting with Computers' (Butterworth) is the 'house journal' of the HCI community; the editorial team is mainly British, but contributions are international.

Many computer journals and magazines contain articles on HCI. *Byte* magazine is an authoritative source.

### Computer conferences

The HCI community has its own computer conferencing system, HICOM, which is hosted by Loughborough University of Technology. It runs on an industry-standard conferencing system, VAXNotes, and is available to all members of the HCI community, including students. There are several conferences, each containing many topics; each topic can be replied to. Users may add their own topics. Each conference has a moderator, who periodically scans it to ensure that the dialogue remains relevant, and that no immoderate language is used. As well as conferences on current issues, such as Interface design, object-oriented programming and multimedia, there are conferences on careers in HCI, reviews of current books, and some conferences which are just for fun. Appendix B contains three transcripts from typical HICOM conference sessions (the author pleads guilty to starting one of them).

Contributors can also access the system from abroad by logging in directly or by sending electronic mail through the international electronic mail system. In the UK, this is known as the *Joint Academic Network* (JANET) and there are also *gateways* to European networks such as the *European Academic Research Network* (EARN).

### Computer supported co-operative work (CSCW)

The HICOM system, described above, supports basic conferencing activities and this alone is a very useful service. It can be taken much further, however; many teams of workers undertake most of their work using a computer conference of some kind, and there are many advantages to be gained in working this way:

- No travel is involved.

- No meeting schedules have to be organised.

- As, by definition, everything is in writing, the decisions are soundly based.

- Part or all of the proceedings can be *downloaded* (transferred from the computer hosting the conference to the user's computer) for further inspection or for printing out.

Some very advanced systems have been developed for CSCW; a particular example is discussed in Chapter 15.

### *Software*

The student of HCI has a particular advantage: the raw material is available in quantity, in the form of people, computers and software. It is always possible to gain an insight by talking to people (they are generally glad of the temporary distraction). Most users have interesting things to say about the software package they are using, whether they are doing systems or applications work; so get into the habit of carrying a small notebook and record their comments.

If you are looking at a new software package, get into the habit of 'thinking HCI' as you examine it. Develop a facility for critical evaluation, and relate your criticisms to the various aspects of HCI discussed in this book.

## Summary

Taking HCI on board is becoming increasingly necessary as computer systems evolve into information systems and users become increasingly aware of the genuinely harmful nature of badly designed interfaces.

Soon, standards now being discussed and set will be enforceable by law.

## Further reading

As mentioned above, the recently-established journal of HCI, *Interacting with computers* (edited by Dan Diaper), is an authoritative and informed body of papers by HCI professionals and academic researchers. Relevant to this chapter is the introduction to the first issue:

Diaper, D. (1989) 'The discipline of HCI' (Editorial) in *Interacting with Computers* **1**,1, Butterworths, pp. 3-5.

# 2 Models of communication in HCI

## Introduction

A paper dart may be considered to be a good model of Concorde, from the point of view of function (to fly) and 'pure' design goals (a simple shape that flies). The model fails when other goals are addressed, such as the need to carry people. A bird is probably a better model in this sense, as it is capable of transporting living matter (itself), although the implementation is different (the bird's wings flap, and it does not need four Olympus engines). There are also some side effects generated by design choices, both significant (birds are much quieter) and not so significant (Concorde, when landing, looks somewhat like a duck performing the same operation, and has been caricatured as such). By the same token, the engineering drawings of Concorde and an anatomical diagram of a bird are also models, albeit static ones. Viewed from a distance, by a short-sighted person, they may be indistinguishable: a beak, two wings, and a tail.

Computer system designers are used to modelling of the 'boxes and arrows' variety (flowcharts) or more advanced techniques where a greater complexity needs to be represented (JSD, MASCOT, SSADM, object-oriented methodologies). As we shall see later, some of these techniques are used in HCI design activities.

Modelling, therefore, is a useful activity; indeed the processing going on inside the human brain during its day-to-day activities is largely a modelling process. We now turn to a consideration of models in HCI. We must face the fact that the limits of normal modelling procedures are, in many cases, being exceeded, particularly where complex adaptable interfaces are being considered. However, this is not a good reason for not trying. A good place to start might be an attempt to define a suitable model of HCI itself. A 'layered' approach is adopted, similar in concept to the way in which computer communications are modelled. This complexity reflects the fact that we are modelling a complex, dynamic interaction; although Concorde is not a simple thing, what it *does* is simple.

To provide theoretical underpinning to HCI work, two well-established models of human-computer interaction are studied; one is derived from work in psycholinguistics, and the other from a more down-to-earth engineering approach. Finally, an attempt to formalise a user model into a User Programming Language is described.

The underlying approach is that HCI is fundamentally an issue of communication between a person and a computer, and this communication needs to be adequately modelled.

## Layers of HCI

The task of interacting with a computer could be viewed very much as an act of communication, the aim being the successful transfer of 'meaningful' information between the participants, and the goal being an appropriate modification in behaviour. The user wishes to 'drive' the behaviour of the computer system; and the system's designer wishes to 'drive' the user, at a distance, via the system

This information transfer can be seen as taking place at a number of layers, each layer forming a reliable and 'transparent' transfer medium to the layer above, and providing structured information to the layer below. The actual methods used are not 'exported' outside a layer, and no data is shared apart from the data to be communicated. In our simple model of HCI, we are concerned with only 3 or 4 layers. Other workers such as Moran[47] and Rasmussen[57] have postulated a different number of layers, or suggested a different interpretation for each layer, but the idea is substantially the same. The kind of terminology used above will be familiar to readers who are interested in computer communications systems. In our HCI communication model, there are three layers: the *physical*, the *syntactic*, and the *semantic*. Note that this division is made from the point of view of clarity - it is not meant to indicate any sharp division of function (although there *is* a sharp division of function between the physical layer and the rest - it can be seen and felt; the other layers can only be conceptualised).

### Physical layer

At some level, the human being has to physically connect to the machine for the purpose of exchanging information. Ideally, this connection will 'match' the two components, much as a loudspeaker has to be matched to its amplifier for best results. A well-matched keyboard, for example, would possess the following desirable attributes:

- The keytops should be shaped to provide maximum comfort for the fingertips

- The keyboard should be 'dished' to accommodate the way in which the ends of the fingers move, that is, in a radius rather than in a straight line (lay one of your fingers sideways on your desk and trace out the path followed by the tip as you move it up and down)

- The travel between keys should be minimised

- The keypress pressure should not be too great nor too little

- The tactile 'profile' should be good

Much of this area has been well-researched by the ergonomics community. It is interesting that, in one study, typists reported that the IBM 'selectric' typewriter keyboard possessed the most attractive tactile profile. It would seem that the fingers 'like' to feel that they are operating some kind of mechanism.

By the same token, the display should be well-matched to the user's visual system at a low level. In other words, it should be well focused, steady, placed at the right distance for comfortable viewing. The choice of colours should be such that the eye does not have difficulty in accommodating from one to the other.

Additionally, there are many aspects of HCI at the physical level which are too often neglected. These include:

- Relative placement of keyboard and main unit of console

- Placement of peripheral devices such as removable disk units, printers etc.

In Chapter 5, we will consider in detail such factors as keyboard layout, key grouping etc.


**Syntactic layer**

Assuming that we have a reliable physical layer, we can use it to carry more structured information. This will range from simple two-key *chords* (CTRL + a key), through more complex *escape sequences* (ESC followed by one or more keys) to well-formed commands, such as might be typed to an operating system command-line interpreter in a file 'housekeeping' session.

To the extent that such key sequences (or messages) need to be acceptable to the application, we could say that we are concerned with the syntax of the messages at this layer. The syntax may be defined as the vehicle for a grammar which is acceptable to the application (and, hopefully to the user).

For example, the task of backing up all the files created after a certain date could be handled in a number of ways, depending on the operating system. In MSDOS, the user would type:

```
BACKUP *.* A:/S/D: 07-10-89
```

meaning, in plain English:

"Back up files in the current directory on the current drive to drive A; select only those files which were modified after 10th July 1989."

**Semantic layer**

This can be thought of as the layer at which the communication of meaning occurs. As before, the assumption is made that effective communication has occurred at the lower layers. The meaning is 'layered' onto the syntax, which is 'layered' onto the physical device. A psycholinguist might argue that this is a gross over-simplification; but William of Ockham's advice 'not to complicate unnecessarily' could be taken to heart here.

Figure 2.1 shows how a typical communication might take place for the example command discussed earlier, in terms of the three-layer model. We start at the 'top' layer (users ask 'what do I want to do?' when initiating a task, rather than asking 'what keys shall I press?' - although, with some users of the author's acquaintance, this may be debatable).

The intentionality (which in terms of its *deep structure* may be quite vague - 'I'd better backup those files, I suppose...' - can be seen as undergoing a functional decomposition into more formal chunks, which have to be ultimately mapped onto the legal syntax of the command line interpreter of the particular application which is being used. This may involve the consultation of manuals, or of online help systems, or 'asides' or telephone calls to colleagues. The resulting message has to be 'fixed' (possibly by writing it down) and a translation made into actual keypresses. A certain amount of time then elapses (which in itself could be psychologically important) while the computer system digests the message, performing a reverse process to that described above, and either carries out the command or issues an error message.

# Two further models of communication

Having established that certain issues in HCI can be interpreted as communications problems, we need to ask the question of what is going on in terms of the dynamic behaviour of each participant. Two models have proved useful; the first (Maass) is derived from the psycholinguistic study of social networks; the second (Rasmussen) stems from an attempt by engineers to make some sense of the behaviour of human beings as they operate complex plants.

As well as being useful models in their own right, they serve to illustrate the way in which HCI draws on a wide range of disciplines to

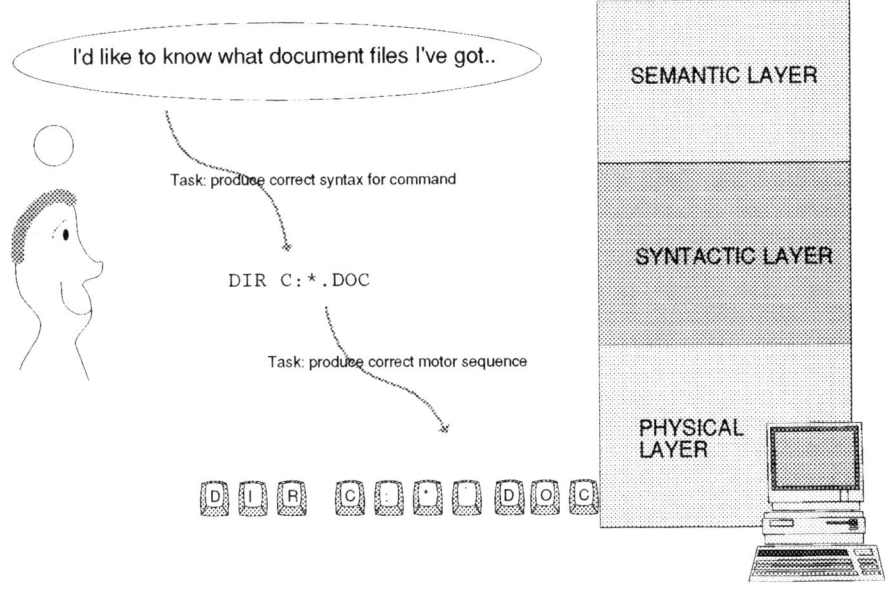

*Figure 2.1 Layered model of communication*

build its theories.

## Systems transparency

### *Channel/Agency Means/Activity networks*

These have been described by Maass [42] and are a development of a theoretical construct known as a Petri Net, after its inventor. Figure 2.2

illustrates the principle.

Partner 1 and Partner 2 have at least three things in common:

- A number of problem situations,

- A means of communication (the channel) through which messages are passed.

WORLD

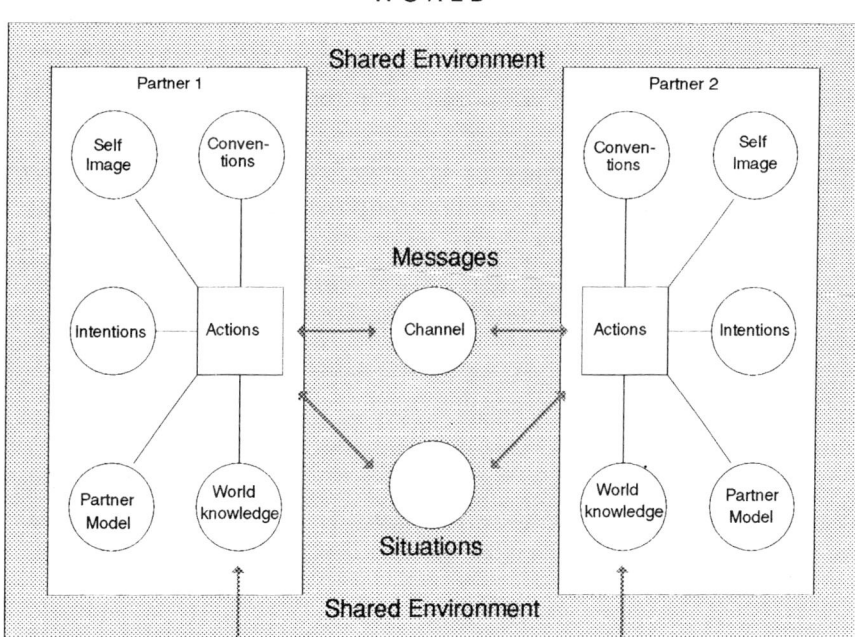

*Figure 2.2 Systems Transparency (after Maass, 1987)*

They each have, in addition, some 'private' information and procedures:

- *Conventions* about how the interaction should proceed

- *Intentions* about their partner

- A *self-image* which comprises the individual's orientation to the world

- A *Partner Model*

- *World knowledge* which constrains the interaction in various ways

- *Actions* which produce messages and act upon the world

The interaction begins by an intention on the part of Partner 1 (for instance, the user) that Partner 2 (for instance, the computer system) should perform some action (generally to the advantage of Partner 1). The action is realistic bearing in mind the partner model. An appropriate message is generated and passed via the communications channel. Partner 2 may perform the action or respond with a message. If the response signifies some problem, Partner 1 may have to modify its partner model, or conventions, or world knowledge, and generate a new message. A system (or partner) which appears to carry out intentions in a consistent and rational way, irrespective of the low-level implementation details, is said to be *transparent* .

Note that this interaction can also work the other way: the computer (viewed as a remote agency of the designer) can 'drive' the user (for example, by running a menu system). The study of communication in this way is known as *metacommunication.*

We can now consider the significance of this theory for HCI. Maass has listed the desirable characteristics of a transparent system. It:

- Does not hide its functions

- Does not obscure problems

- Is well-structured, consistent and comprehensible

- Ensures that its interface conforms with the user's 'picture'of it.

This could be regarded, directly, as a prescription for system designers. (Try substituting the word 'usable' for the word 'transparent' above).

Usability and functionality, then, are intimately related by transparency: a highly functional system which cannot communicate its abilities in an unambiguous way is effectively unusable; worse, it may be apparently usable but introduce subtle or unpredictable errors, which are only detected at a later stage. For example, a utility on a personal computer which backed up a hard disk to floppy disks on the basis of copying files modified after the last backup cycle was found to have a significant flaw: the same process worked when it was wished to restore a file, with the consequence that later versions of a file were not restored during a restore cycle. Changing the options on the operating system's copy utility, so that a file was copied irrespective of its date, solved the problem; but a large amount of data was, for a while, endangered.

The salient point is that the logic of the process was correct; the command line syntax was explicit and reasonable; but nevertheless the process was not *transparent*.

### The human as a system component

From a theoretical treatment of how two partners might interact, we turn to practical attempts to explore the relationship between humans and systems. These ideas often come from a tradition of control theory, which treats the user-system as a unified whole (with the user generally being regarded as a slow, noisy transfer function!)

The approach discussed here, developed by Rasmussen [56], differs from Maass' approach in that the user's cognitive functions are regarded as being useful, indeed central, to the operation of the system - it can be regarded as a subjective, not an objective, model. During normal functioning, the operator is considered to be a slow, somewhat flexible information processor; when the system begins to operate at or near to the limit of its design parameters, the inner mechanisms of the user become apparent.

Rasmussen has proposed two factors that operate within the user:

- *Conscious* - The information processing capacity (memory, perception, motor skills, etc.)

- *Subconscious* - The needs, drives, 'process feel', assumptions etc.

This, in turn, enabled Rasmussen to suggest a possible working model of what happens when a user interacts with a complex system, and how the various components are arranged. There are three aspects to Rasmussen's model:

- The operator can be regarded as being an integral part of the system - there is a common goal, and mutually understood control and information mechanisms (Figure 2.3)

- The operator functions by exercising *conscious* control processes which are informed by *unconscious* models of the system (Figure 2.4) .

- The various strategies of the operator are triggered into operation by the detection of a *mismatch* between the state of the system and the user's internal model (Figure 2.5).

As far as a working system is concerned, the crucial issue identified by Rasmussen is that we must understand the development, and maintenance, of *skilled performance* in humans. This can be briefly summarised in the following way, assuming that a new task is being learned:

- Large amounts of cognitive processing, and time, are devoted to learning the various aspects of the task, and to establishing the meaning of the various combinations of *signals* with respect to the state of the system. In this phase, large amounts of information are gathered (elicited) and built into appropriate knowledge bases.

- Certain procedures are retained as useful, others are discarded. Appropriate combinations of signals are accorded the status of *signs*. Cognitive capacity is diverted into building *heuristics* of the system.

- The processes mature; less cognitive capacity needs to be devoted to low-level aspects of understanding the system, control strategies move largely to the subconscious domain. In Rasmussens's terms,

> *"Characteristically, skilled performance rolls along without conscious attention or control. The total performance is smooth and integrated, and sense input is not selected or observed: the senses are only directed towards the aspects of the environment needed subconsciously to update and orient the internal map. The [person] looks rather than sees."*

This does not imply that low-level procedures are left to atrophy. They are still useful - in the same way that a reflex action is extremely useful in dangerous situations (such as sitting on a drawing pin). Equally, it should not be assumed that the high-level processes become inflexible - skilled drivers are capable of 'modulating' their performance to take account of new hazards. It is interesting to note the many reports from fatigued or injured fighter pilots that a 'ghost pilot' directed their actions so that they landed safely. This could well be a classic example of well-learned subconscious processes taking over in extreme conditions.

The full picture is illustrated in figure 2.6. Rasmussen describes three levels of performance:

- Skill based, triggered by signals and mediated internally by prototypical signs

- Rule based, triggered by signs, mediated by a rule base of some kind, with symbol development

- Knowledge based, triggered by symbols and mediated by a knowledge base of some kind, probably richly connected

The crucial test of such a schema occurs when an unforeseen situation arises. Ideally, the processes described above will work in reverse. Knowledge-based behaviour will inform the lower level processes (possibly using knowledge 'leakage' from other domains) and new hypotheses tested. With luck, one of these will work, and a new coping mechanism will be stamped in.

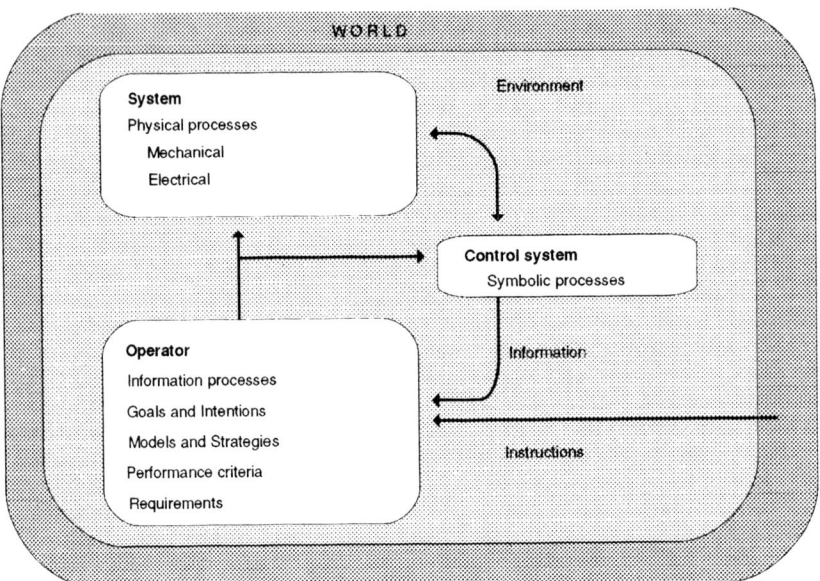

*Figure 2.3 The operator as a systems component (after Rasmussen,1983)*

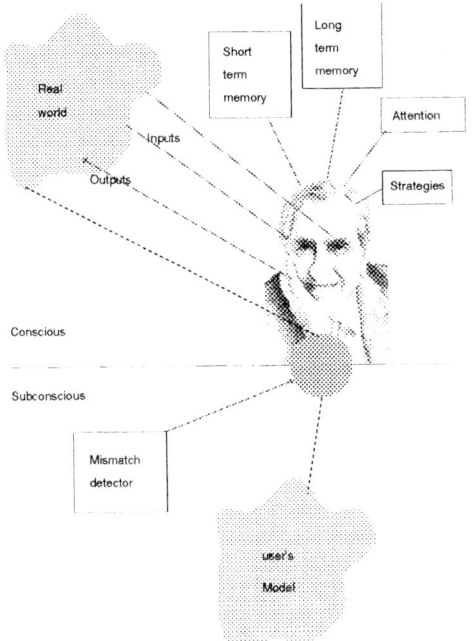

*Figure 2.4 Locus of conscious and unconscious processes in Rasmussen's model*

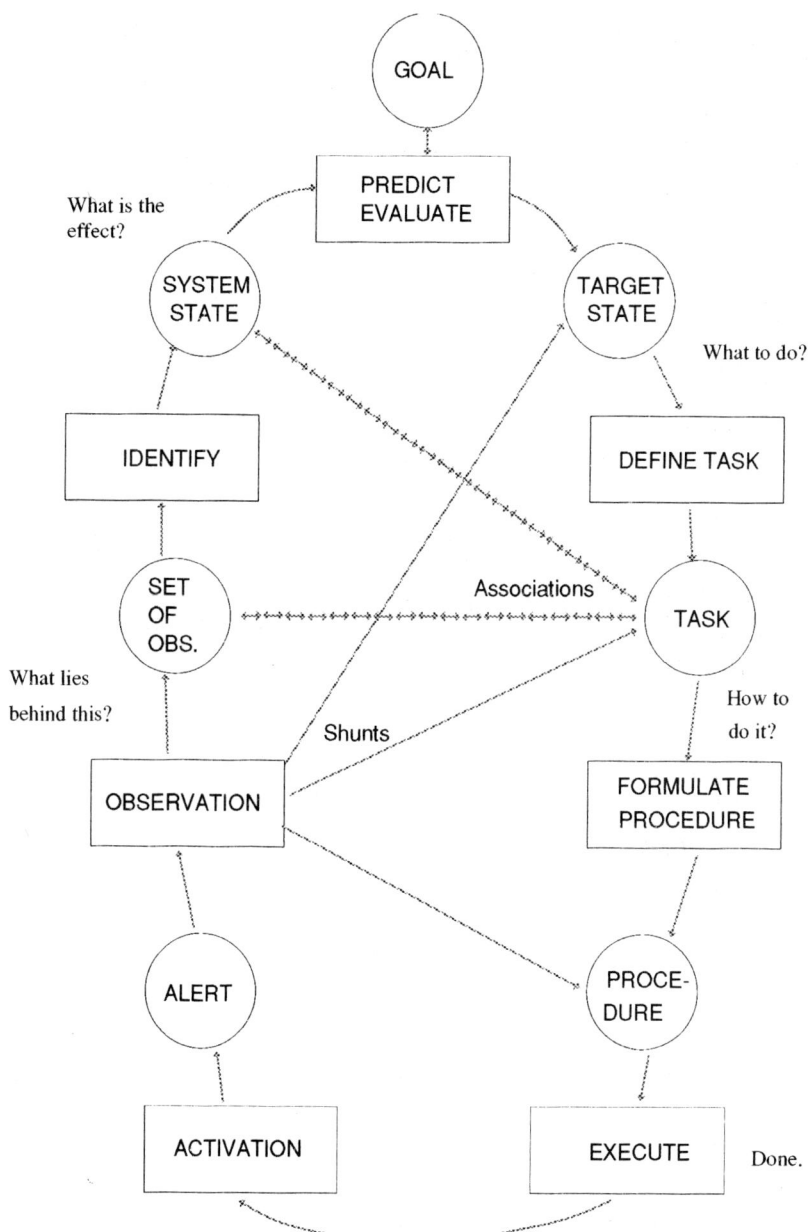

*Figure 2.5 The operator's activation/response cycle (after Rasmussen, 1980)*

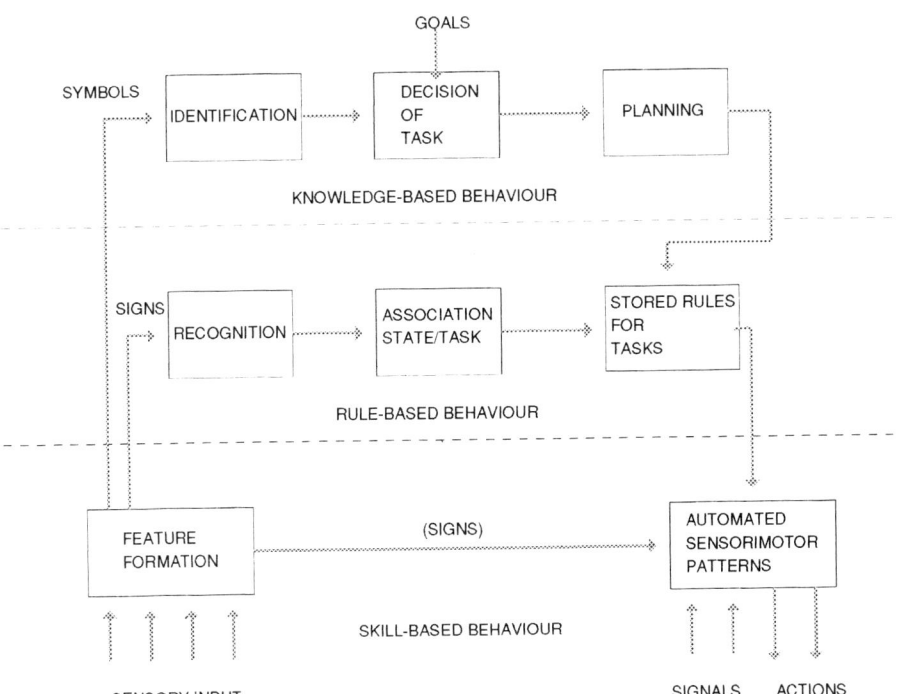

*Figure 2.6 Levels of performance of skilled human operators (after Rasmussen, 1983)*

Note that Rasmussen's distinction between *skill-based, rule-based and knowledge-based* layers corresponds conveniently with our earlier discussion of *physical, syntactic* and *semantic* layers, and in this context may be taken to be identical.

The essence of Rasmussen's model is best described by tracking an iteration. We will assume that a user is interacting with a typical package, such as a word processor. Starting at the bottom left-hand corner of Figure 2.5, let us assume that an error condition is encountered due to the user attempting to save a file to an error-prone floppy diskette in drive A.

The operating system will return an error code to the package, which will probably, in the first instance, cause the computer to give a beep. This is the **signal** which provides an initial **alert** to the user. At this point, the user will stop, possibly emit an expletive, and cast around for possible reasons for this interruption. Depending on the package, a more or less helpful **sign** will be provided in the form of a standard error message. In the worst case, this will be terse and unhelpful, such as:

```
I/O ERR ON A:(A)bort, (R)etry, (F)ail?
```

To the extent that this has little symbolic meaning to a naïve user, it cannot be regarded as a meaningful message, and does not provide many 'clues' as to further progress. Consequently the process of identifying the cause of the problem may become fairly elaborate at this point. The user's subvocal conversation might go as follows: "Presumably an ERR is an error. But what is an A:? And what is the consequence of (R)etrying or (F)ailing it? Presumably I am expected to respond with an A, an R or an F. But does F fail the whole session? Do I get back to my word processor if I press A or R? And should I use upper or lower case, or doesn't it matter? Should I hit the RETURN key?"

It looks as though there are two possible strategies for our naïve user:

- seek help from an 'expert'

- read the manual

This will enable him/her to continue round the cycle, hopefully retaining the knowledge that a floppy diskette should be kept in Drive A: at all times while running packages.

A package with a better thought-out interface might translate the raw operating system error message to read, say:

```
There is a problem saving the file on the disk in drive A.
Is there actually a diskette in the drive?
If there is, it may be faulty.
Try another, and press the ENTER key.
```

which, in most cases, will enable our user to proceed. Note that providing a **symbolic** message like this does not involve undue overheads in designing or programming the package, but puts the error dialogue at a high enough level to be useful. Generally speaking, facilitating this level of interaction (the knowledge-based, in Rasmussen's terms) benefits both naïve and experienced users, who generally need the same kind of information but differ in knowing the right questions to ask. The 'improved' message above achieves the same thing as the 'terse' message to an experienced user: a faulty diskette should be substituted. It also enables an inexperienced user to perform the same corrective action.

It avoids the meaningless dialogue about retrying, aborting or failing - if a diskette has developed a fault it is unlikely that retrying the operation will achieve anything, although the naïve user will not be aware of this; and the distinction between 'aborting' and 'failing' is not indicated.

## Other user models

Runciman and Hammond[59] have adopted a different approach. Taking the view that a rational model of a user should be predictable to the point of being *programmable*, they describe a *User Programming Language* (UPL). They conceive the UPL as being a language similar to Pascal - that is, modular, with a rich set of control structures and data types - but *constrained* to the known parameters of users. In other words, no operation specified by the UPL should be beyond the capacity of the average user to perform.

The following is a fragment of 'UPL', and represents a typical electronic mail processing procedure:

```
while first_number ≠ 0
          first_text
          if action_needed
                    note_action
                    acknowledge_first
                    delete_first
```

The simplicity of the language would seem to make this an attractive approach.

Runciman and Hammond go further than postulating a set of procedures which could embody a User Programming Language: they also specify a 'user architecture' on which that language could run (Figure 2.7).

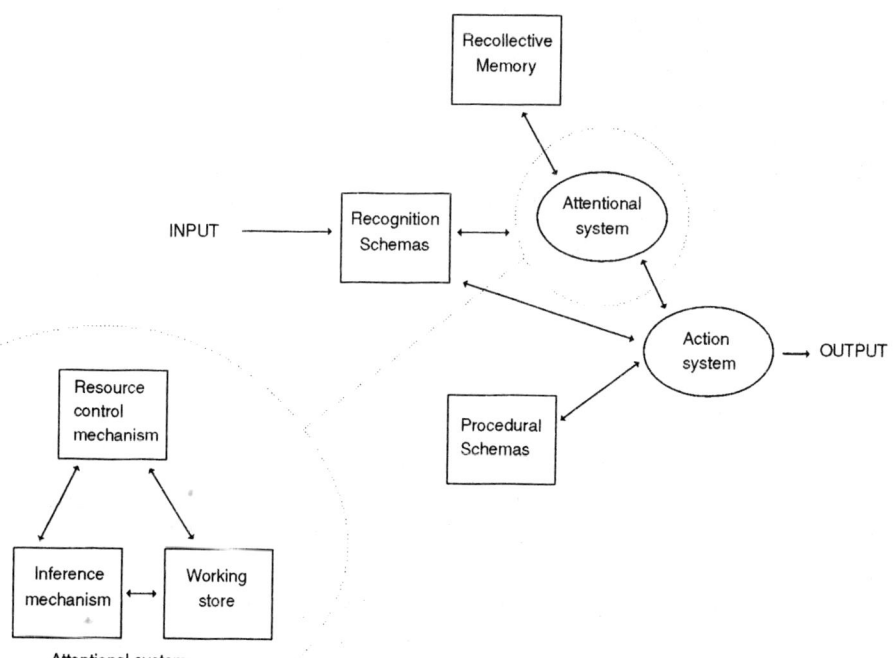

*Figure 2.7 Cognitive architecture of user model (after Runciman and Hammond)*

### *Usefulness of user models*

All the models we have discussed go some way towards capturing and predicting user behaviour. However, there are aspects of user performance which are not amenable to modelling in a 'boxes and arrows' way. In particular, the commission of *errors* is almost impossible to model in a coherent way. Errors can be committed for a variety of reasons: typographical errors while editing text, mistyping a command, and so on. It is important to distinguish between errors and *mistakes.* A mistake is an activity which is performed deliberately, but which later is perceived to be incorrect or undesirable. This is an error:

```
DLETE AFILE.DOC
```

but this is certainly a mistake, if unintended:

```
DELETE *.*
```

User models cannot predict the commission of errors or mistakes because they are based on *formalisms* derived from theory. To account for errors, we need to establish what kind of process causes them. The most satisfactory solution is to regard them as *stochastic* processes - that is, processes which occur randomly, but which are predictable up to a point. An example is the frequency of arrival of people at the end of a bus queue.

There are two ways of coping with errors:

- Assume that their commission occurs according to some simple mathematical model, and build in a random 'error generator' to the model

- Analyse, in some way, the error performance of real users and use the results of this analysis to *predict* the likely commission of errors, in terms of frequency of occurrence and type of error.

The latter approach, which is *atheoretical* - that is, depending on rules which are established purely on the basis of observed behaviour - is discussed in greater detail in Chapter 4.

## Summary

Modelling provides us with a view of a situation that we can discuss, modify and manipulate.

A layered approach is seen as appropriate for modelling the processes operating at the human-computer interface.

# 3 Information processing

*To be effective, the design must be based on compatible models of human information processes as well as the functions of the control system.*

*Jens Rasmussen*

## Introduction

The human-computer Interface is not a static entity. It is the channel through which all information passes between the user and the system. It is important to have a 'feel' for what information is, how it relates to data, and how it is processed by humans and machines at different levels, otherwise we cannot calculate the limits within which our systems will work.

In chapter 2 we discussed a framework for studying the communication between two entities; in this chapter we examine the 'raw material', i.e. what is communicated. We introduce basic information theory and relate it to the kind of information processing we know about, or would like to know about, in humans and machines. From this, we briefly examine data structures and processes in computers; and end with a discussion of the human cognitive processes in memory, attention and problem solving which are relevant to HCI.

## Information and Data

Imagine that you are sitting in a room with a friend. You are occupied with some task and ask 'Is it raining?'. Your friend informs you. We could say that you have received information. Now imagine that your friend makes the statement, unasked: 'It's raining!'. Could we still say that information had been passed? The answer would seem to be 'it all depends'. On what? On such things as whether you knew it was raining; whether the knowledge was important to you; and the situation. Your friend's statement would hardly be a startling revelation if, at the time it was made, you were standing in a pool of water clutching an umbrella.

Clearly, then, we need to establish when, exactly, we can use the term 'Information.' Is it the same as data? Consider the situation described above as an example. In the first case, it is clear that you did not know the state of the weather; your friend's answer resulted in a reduction of uncertainty. He/She did this by providing data, from which you extracted information. Imagine, now, that you friend unaccountably replies in ancient Greek. Data has been passed, but no information (unless you are fluent in that language). We need another concept, that of the protocol, to help us fully describe the situation. Lastly, we must consider the physical channel down which the data has been passed. If it distorts what it is passing on, then errors are likely to occur. The significance of error depends on the situation - a mistake by a Pentagon defence computer is likely to have a more profound effect than a mistake in your gas bill, although they may have occurred in the same way (i.e. in a 'bugged' computer program or data). The channel is also likely to have a limited capacity: it cannot pass data at a higher rate than it was designed for.

Information, then, needs certain conditions for its efficient transmission: the receiver must be in a state of uncertainty; both provider and receiver must share a common code; and errors must be, at least, detectable. *Information results in a change of state in the recipient.* (Review Chapter 2 if necessary to put this idea in context).

## Information transmission

We now focus on the 'nuts and bolts' of information transmission and representation. This will provide a sound basis of theory on which to build an understanding of information transmission in HCI.

In 1932, Fisher attempted to provide a measure of the amount of information that could be transmitted. He reasoned that, if a 'yes/no' answer provides a complete reduction of uncertainty, then the amount of information must be related to the 'uncertainty' of the answer. In statistical terms, the information transmitted is proportional to the *variance* of the input data. Totally random data, such as white noise (the sound made by escaping steam), provides no information at all. Two engineers Shannon and Weaver were interested (in 1948) in how quickly information could be transmitted through noisy channels such as telephone lines. They developed an equation which relates the bandwidth of a channel with the frequency and noise characteristics of a signal.

The derivation is not complex, and we will take it in easy stages. The importance to HCI is that it gives us a way of measuring the information handling capabilities of a number of things, including people. Firstly, we need to interpret the concept of information in terms of the number of choices we need to make. To establish, for example, which of eight cups has a bean under it, we need to ask three questions: Left hand four or right hand four? Then, when this is established: Left hand pair or right hand pair? Finally: Left hand or right hand cup? For sixteen cups, we would have to ask four questions; for thirty-two, eight; and so on.

In other words, the number of questions is the **log to the base 2** of the number of items to be discriminated between. As the answers to the questions are binary (yes/no) then we can say that they are equivalent to binary digits (one/zero) or **bits**. Thus, in solving the 'eight cups' problem, 3 **bits** of information has been transmitted.

Next, we need to understand the concepts of *signal* and *noise*. Holding a conversation at a noisy party is easy if people are prepared to shout in your ear, but impossible if they are six fect away. The *signal to noise ratio* is said to be low (even if the signal levels are very high). Conversely, it is possible to hear a quiet conversation in a sound-damped room, even if the participants are some distance away. The signal to noise ratio is high.

Finally we have the concept of *bandwidth*. This is the frequency range which the transmitting medium is capable of supporting. If you attempt to talk to a friend with your head in a bucket, the bandwidth available to both of you is severely restricted. The public telephone network is another example of a channel with restricted bandwidth. We will now derive Shannon and Weavers' formula.

Firstly, imagine a wheel, on a car or bicycle, complete with tyre valve, moving along a road (See Fig. 3.1).

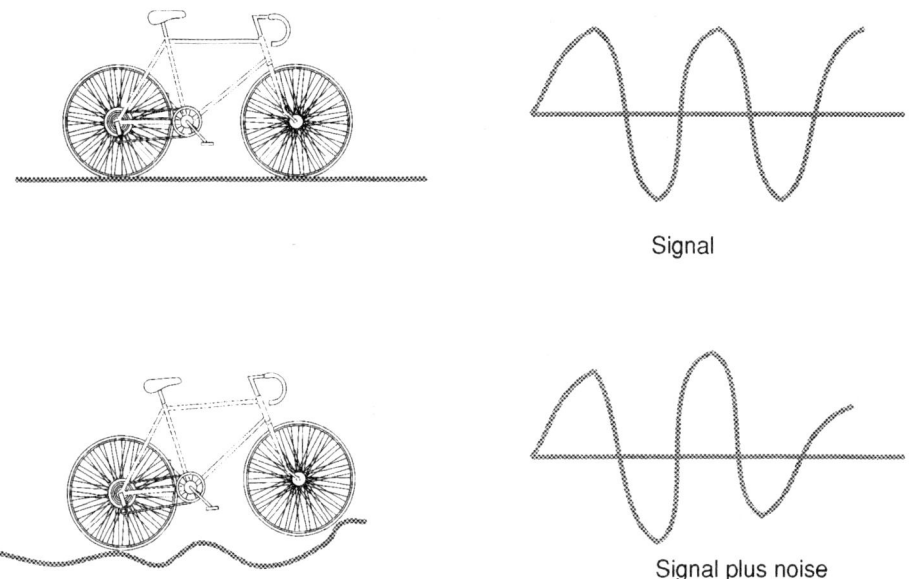

Signal

Signal plus noise

*Figure 3.1 Signal and noise*

If we plot the vertical distance of the tyre valve from the road against time, we get a sine wave (upper waveform). The maximum amplitude of the sine wave is determined by the size of the wheel, and the speed of the wheel determines the frequency. Sine waves are important because all sounds (indeed all continuously varying signals) consist of a mixture of sine waves of varying amplitudes and frequencies. (This was established by the mathematician Fourier). Imagine next that the cycle wheel is travelling over a bumpy road - noise has been introduced into the system (lower waveform).

Now consider a real waveform (say part of a speech signal). One way of turning it into a computer-digestible form is to measure (sample) the voltage at regular intervals. This process is known as digitising, or analogue to digital conversion. The more frequently we sample, the more accurate is the representation of the waveform in the computer. We can now ask our first important question - at what frequency do we have a perfect representation? This depends on the bandwidth of the channel (W), which may be thought of as the 'frequency response' of the channel. (Many readers will be familiar with the high quality output of a compact disc player. This quality is achieved at a sampling rate of about 44,000 per second - not very high by computer standards, but an increase in this rate would not be detectable by most human listeners).

There is no point in sampling at a frequency higher than twice the bandwidth, that is, at

2 * W samples per second, where W is the bandwidth.

Now consider Fig. 3.2. It represents the signal and noise in a waveform; it could represent a speech signal.

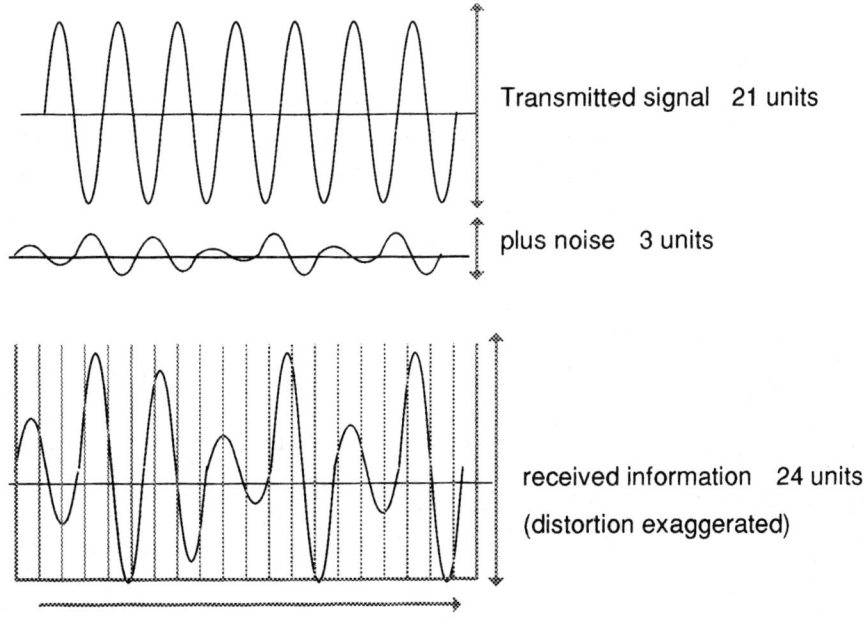

Figure 3.2 Signal and noise in a typical waveform

What is transmitted is the pure signal; what is received is the signal plus the noise. We now know two things about the channel:

1   The maximum noise value, and
2   The bandwidth.

Imagine that in this case, the maximum signal amplitude is 21 units and the maximum noise amplitude is 3. The maximum amplitude of signal + noise is thus 24. The maximum error must be the same as the noise, that is 3. Therefore there is no point in sampling at a precision of greater than 3 units. The number of categories (choices) is thus

$$(21 + 3) / 3 = 8.$$

choices, i.e. 3 bits per sample. In symbolic terms,

$$B = \log_2 (S + N) / N$$

bits per sample.

Now, at a sampling rate of 2 * W samples / sec, each sample is W / 2 seconds apart. If we wish to maximise the channel capacity T (so as not to overload the channel), then, since there are 2W samples per second, we can say

$$T = 2 * W * \log_2 (S + N) / N$$

bits per second.

It is convenient to measure power rather than the amplitude (telephone cables restrict the overall power, not amplitude, of the signal).

As power is directly proportional to the square of the amplitude, we take the square root of the formula to give us the power:

$$T = \sqrt{2 * W * \log_2 (S+N) / N}$$

This is Shannon and Weavers' result for the capacity of a noisy channel.

It is interesting to consider human speech in terms of information transmission in bits / second.

Fourier analysis (a way of analysing the frequencies present in a signal such as a voice waveform) gives us a maximum frequency range of 100 Hz - 10,000 Hz. For practical purposes, we do not need to use this entire range. Let us use a bandwidth of 5,000 Hz. If we assume a signal / noise ratio of 1000 : 1 (that is, a very high-quality channel), then

$$T = 2 * 5,000 * \log_2 (1000 + 1) / 1$$

$$= 50,000 \text{ bits per sec (approx)}.$$

If we lower the Signal/Noise ratio to 1000 : 4, then we can calculate that the required transmission rate is now 40,000 bits/sec. In other words, a small increase in the permissible noise level from 0.1% to 0.4% has reduced the required capacity (and cost) of the channel by 20%. If a noise (distortion) level of 10% is considered the maximum tolerable, then we can get away with a channel capacity of about 20,000 bits/sec. Although we need a channel capacity of up to 50,000 bits/sec to transmit human speech, the actual information rate (as far as meaningful messages are concerned) is only about 50 bits/sec. Thus there appears to be a redundancy factor of 1000 : 1 operating. This is the extent to which the system goes to minimise error or ambiguity in the message. It also enables a degree of error correction to be made 'on the fly'. This topic is covered in more detail in Chapter 6.

## Information theory and HCI

An understanding of how information 'behaves' is important at both low and high 'layers' in HCI. At the physical level, for example, it is important to know how many bits per second can be communicated by our chosen interface. We can then establish, for example:

- Whether the interface is as efficient as it could be

- Whether the information rate is too fast for human cognitive processes to cope

- Whether the error rate is tolerable

**Information in a visual display**

Edwards[22] has described an experiment conducted by Klemmer and Frick in 1953 (which indicates, incidentally, that the significance of information theory was appreciated at an early date). A single white dot appeared against a black background on a 40" by 40" screen. The subjects' task was to indicate, on a grid, where the dot had appeared. The amount of information conveyed to the subject could be determined by the grid resolution. Thus a 2 by 2 grid provided an 'input' of 2 bits; a 4 by 4, 4 bits; and so on.

The scores were recorded over a number of trials, and entered into a frequency matrix, and overall performance calculated as the relationship between input uncertainty (in bits per item) and error rate (measured as 'output bits'). If these are plotted, it can be seen that up to about 4 bits per item (i.e., a 1 in 16 choice) the efficiency is good. Over 4.4 bits per item, there is no increment in performance. Figure 3.3 is a graph of the results.

No change in performance occurred when grid lines were displayed together with the stimulus dots; but there was a significant increase when more than one stimulus dot was shown at a time (to 6.6 bits for 4 dots on a 3 by 3 display).

The message from Klemmer and Frick's experiment is quite clear. There is a constraint on the amount of information that can be transmitted in a single visual display, and it is pointless to devise more complex displays than this. If this information could be fed into a notional knowledge base, many over-elaborate screen designs would not see the light of day.

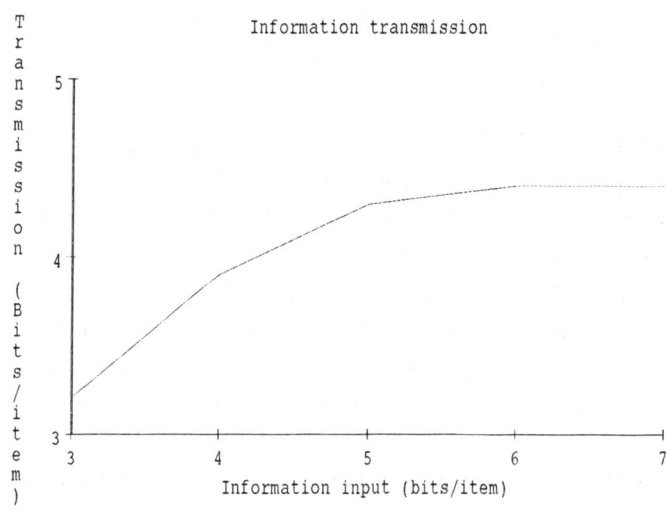

*Figure 3.3 Results from the experiment of Klemmer and Frick*

## Information processing in computers

One of the earliest recorded uses of a computer was during the second world war, when the German military communications were intercepted, and often successfully decoded, by the team of communications workers and cryptographers at Bletchley Park. Communications technology was far enough advanced to enable military users to transmit textual messages as radio signals.

The communications, which had been 'scrambled' electrically by a special device known as ENIGMA by applying a 'code of the day' to various dials on the apparatus, were intended to be unscrambled by a similar machine at the receiving end. The code itself was transmitted separately. German military efficiency and order being what it was, the critical code was often the first transmission of the day, a fact which did not go unnoticed at Bletchley Park.

Where there were no clues about the code, a 'brute force' method had to be used, where teams of human decoders would try various combinations of 'cracking' codes until one began to look promising. This was obviously very time-consuming, so electromechanical devices ('bombes') were used, and later electronic ones.

Thus the first application of computers was not scientific or commercial: what had been developed was a general-purpose symbolic manipulation device, which could handle information as a sequence of codes. This is important to bear in mind when we discuss the concept of 'data fusion' in the next section.

**Data fusion and technological convergence**
As mentioned above, the practice of encoding text as a stream of characters was well advanced in the 1940's (the American Standard Code for Information Interchange, ASCII, was developed in the 1930s). The art of analysing a problem, and translating it to a stored sequence of instructions, was well understood by the 1950s; and high-level languages to ease this translation process had been developed by the mid-1950s.

The technologically more demanding techniques of sampling analogue waveforms, such as speech, into a series of numeric codes, was more recent but developed rapidly as better hardware became available; and the technology of high-resolution graphics displays using television *(raster scan)* techniques has been most recent of all, but a rapid improver.

When computers became sufficiently small to be built into circuit boards, and powerful enough to enable significant processing to be done, a new generation of signal processing microprocessors was developed. In specialist applications such as pattern recognition, image analysis and voice input, they permitted a rapid development of cheap and robust specialist processing devices (for example in voice recognition and output).

The advances in computer performance (on a price/ performance/ cost basis) have continued, so that the typical desktop computer can now perform the functions that needed specialist devices of only two or three years ago. Additionally, communications technology has made equivalent advances.

We have a situation, therefore, where the rapid translation of information from one mode to another, together with processing power to perform significant transformations, is available locally. The consequence is that data of all kinds can be sampled, analysed, reworked, stored, transmitted and output in a variety of ways. This facility has been termed *data fusion.* The general phenomenon which characterises the symbiosis (syntechosis?) of computing and communications technologies has been termed *convergent technology,* and is really the essence of Information Technology.

Figure 3.4 illustrates the various ways in which information can be manipulated, even in a cheap personal computer. The picture of the house was scanned in using a video camera and a 'frame grabber', and is stored in the form of pixels (picture cells) each pixel comprising 16 grey scales. The car was drawn using an object-oriented drawing package. The voice was captured using an analogue-to-digital converter, and displayed using a sound manipulation package. The newspaper cutting was scanned in using a hand-held scanner. All this information is represented internally in the same way, as a series of 8-bit codes.

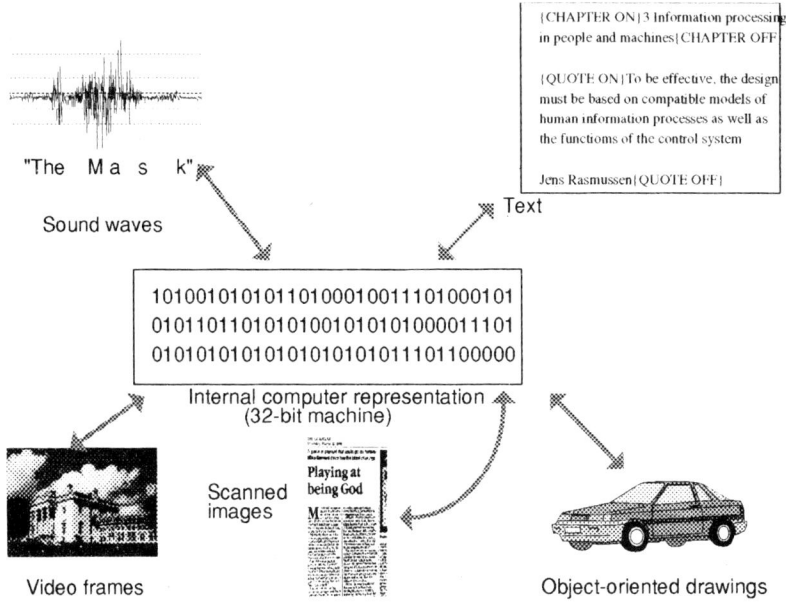

*Figure 3.4 Data fusion*

If we link the ability to manipulate information with increasingly powerful programming languages and data manipulation algorithms, we are well on the way to emulating any 'reality' we choose, whether it is acoustic, visual or textual. This task is made easier by making use of the new, more powerful, operating systems, which offer powerful *primitives* for the manipulation of data - Bezier curves for graphics, half-tone handling for printing, sound channel queueing etc.

(See Chapter 6 for a discussion of advanced input/output devices).

## Information processing in humans

At certain levels, we can say that human beings deal with information in forms that have been described in the section above - graphics, text, sound. However, our knowledge about the actual *processes* that go on in the human brain is much less complete - after all, the brain was not designed by humans, although it was arguably developed for their benefit. This represents a gap in our knowledge, considering that HCI is largely concerned with narrowing the gap of understanding between people and

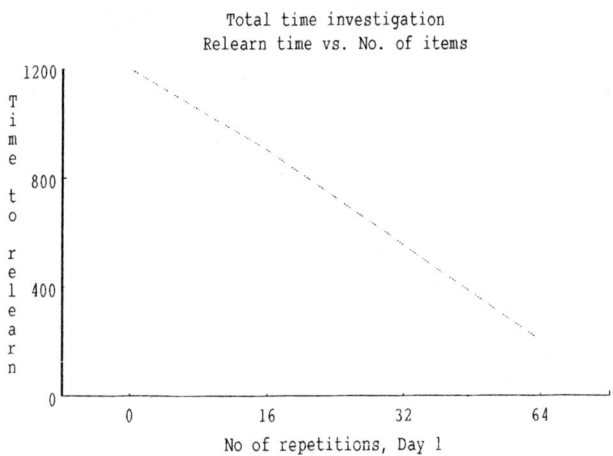

*Figure 3.5 Number of repetitions of original stimulus material plotted against the time taken to relearn the material after 24 hours (Ebbinghaus)*

computers. Fortunately, the science of psychology has long been concerned with the problems of human cognition and behaviour. In particular, HCI owes a lot to three branches of psychology: cognitive psychology, Ergonomics and Occupational psychology. The contribution of the latter two we can only acknowledge here, but it is useful to discuss the various aspects of human cognition in more detail.

## Memory

### *Memory for nonsense syllables*
Probably the first properly-controlled study of human memory was performed by Ebbinghaus[7a] in 1879. He was concerned, not with remembering, but forgetting - which may be regarded as the 'downside' of remembering. He used motivated subjects in controlled conditions and - so as to minimise any possible side-effect due to particular words - used nonsense syllables (such as *biv,dek* and *toj)* as his stimulus material. The results of a typical experiment are shown in Figure 3.5.

The results shown here caused Ebbinghaus to put forward a theory - the 'total time' theory - that the strength of a memory trace was proportional to the time taken in presenting the original material (in this case, the

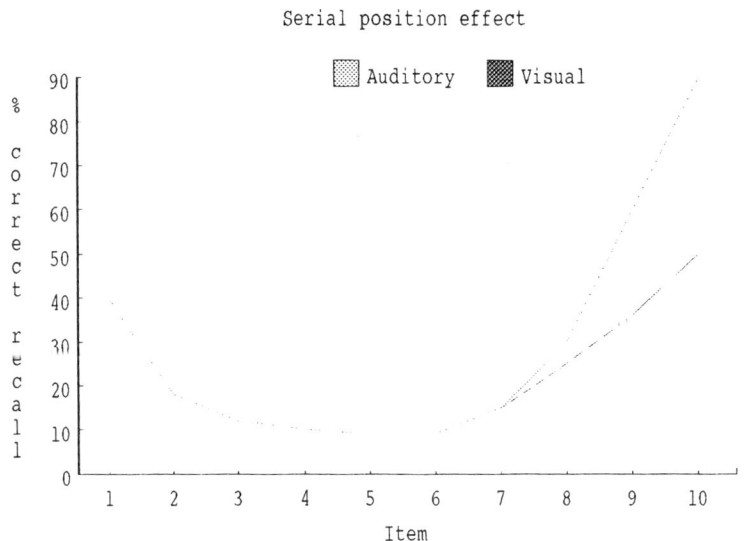

*Figure 3.6 Classical serial position curve for auditory and visual modalities*

number of repetitions). If the graph in figure 3.5 is inspected closely, it will be seen that the horizontal scale is not linear (the cynic would say that one way of obtaining a straight line is to tamper with the axes on the graph!) - it doubles for every division, and is therefore *logarithmic*.

Ebbinghaus also showed that, in terms of the rate of forgetting, the 'trace strength' of memory decays exponentially, rather like the charge on a capacitor or a musical note.

Ebbinghaus must be credited with pioneering the experimental approach to psychological research, and the 'decay' model was surprisingly persistent.

### Memory with context

A later worker, Bartlett[7a], criticised this approach. His claim was that Ebbinghaus' method had little to offer in terms of 'ecological validity';

the experiments were *stimulus bound* and hence invalid. Bartlett argued that, in real situations, people used context and *associations* to assist memory. His experiments were much more naturalistic, often involving the presentation of a story, with subjects' memory being tested for *meaning* rather than content.

### The serial position effect

Certain phenomena in human memory are well established, although not fully understood. From an operational point of view, this may not matter - after all, we use electricity without fully understanding what it is. The serial position effect is such a phenomenon, and is easy to demonstrate with a wide variety of stimulus material. Figure 3.6 illustrates it. Note that the shape of the curve is different between *auditory* and *visual* sensory modalities.

The stimulus was a list of digits, and subjects had to recall each digit in its correct position. The effect is remarkably similar for a wide variety of stimuli, for example the list of American presidents.

Evidently, this is a clue to some underlying process of information gathering and storage in the human brain, and it is unlikely to be a passive kind of store. It is well known, for example, that rehearsal (repetition) strengthens the memory trace, but does not guarantee permanent storage.

Two psychologists, Craik and Lockhart[7a], suggested in 1973 that the storage of an event was in some way related to the level of processing that the item had received - in other words, an item which has needed a large amount of processing capacity is likely to form a more persistent memory than an item which has not.

This notion led to the idea that there was some kind of active 'scratchpad' in memory (termed *working memory* by Baddeley and Hitch[7a]) which is shared between a variety of information processing tasks in the brain - perception, reasoning, pattern recognition etc. This is intuitively attractive, and is not unlike the situation in a complex windowed interface, with its scratchpad and multitasking.

There are some other aspects we should investigate before a full picture emerges, in particular we need to know what influences the memorising process.

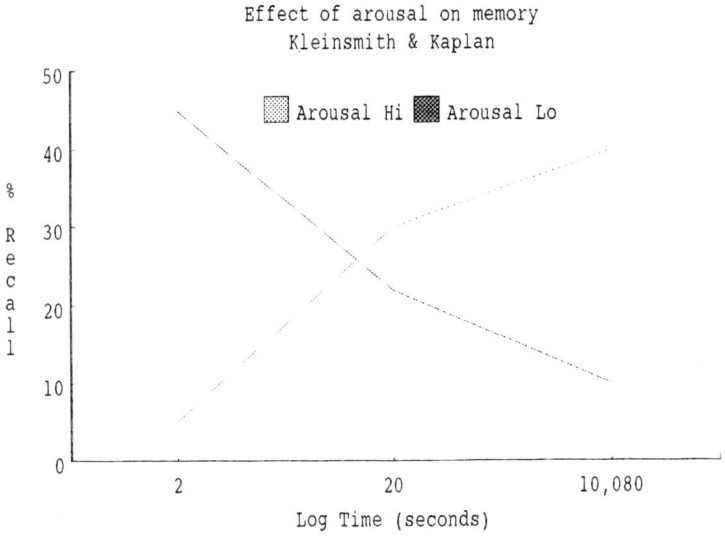

*Figure 3.7 Effect of arousal on memory. Notice the strong interaction between arousal and delay before recall.*

### Arousal

A sleeping person demonstrates a low level of arousal; a policeman arresting a violent person demonstrates a very high level. Extremely high arousal levels can impact on performance. What levels of arousal do people experience while computing, and how does it affect this kind of task?

An experiment by Kleinsmith and Kaplan demonstrates, in a striking way, that there is very little that is 'intuitive' about psychological findings. Figure 3.7 illustrates their experiment. There is a strong interaction between the degree of arousal and the delay before recall. In plain terms, a low degree of arousal is favoured at short delays, but this position is reversed at high arousal levels. It also seems counter-intuitive that items which are so poorly remembered at short delays should still somehow have got 'into the system'.

The 'kink' in the curve at the 20-second delay is interesting. It seems to indicate that something significant happens at this time, and this phenomenon has been interpreted by psychophysiologists as lending weight to the theory that information is transferred, at some stage, from a chemical state to a more permanent structural state.

### Practice effects

In HCI, we are interested in human memory from at least two points of view: memory for things and events, and memory for skills. If the process of skill acquisition can be made more efficient, then we have improved the user's experience (and maybe saved some time and money!) Baddeley and Longman were interested in how typing skills were acquired, and tested performance against four different training schedules. The significant finding was that the best training schedule comprised one-hour sessions. By 60 hours total training time, the performance was better than any of the other conditions *would ever be*. The worst condition (2 * 2) actually took the longest time, and had obviously 'flattened off'.

Baddeley and Longman also found that the best condition for training (1 * 1) also promoted the best *retention* of the learned skill.

It should be apparent by now that human memory, although it may be complex, is measurable in terms of its extent and persistence. The computer systems designer should be able to take these concepts on board in the quest for better HCI.

### How many kinds of memory?

The memory for a piece of music, or a poem, is subjectively different to the memory of a picture. But does this indicate a structural difference in the 'deep' storage of a memory? Many theorists maintain that what we perceive as a memory is largely a reconstructive process, and so it is possible that there may be an underlying commonality of process or structure.

An attempt was made by Atkinson and Shiffrin to develop a *unified* theory of memory, that postulated a single kind of storage mechanism.

**Attention**

A simple experiment will demonstrate the power of human attentional mechanisms. Take friend and a portable cassette recorder into a noisy place - a public house is ideal - and record a conversation. Although you are able to conduct a conversation quite easily in this noisy environment, the recorded version of the same conversation will be almost indecipherable due to the high levels of background noise. This is largely because humans are capable of *orienting* their perceptual and cognitive processes towards the major stimulus, and filtering out irrelevant noise.

Conversely, this *attentional* mechanism has its limits, and it is possible to overload (or underload) the perceptual sensors so that they are either incapable of making a discrimination or fail to register the input altogether.

Furthermore, the attentional processes have interesting dynamics over time. A stimulus which is repeated over time gradually loses its properties of 'attention-grabbing' and may be ignore altogether; some stimuli (such as a person's name spoken very quietly into one ear) have an unaccountably large effect.

The consequences of ignoring attentional failures can be drastic: over 400 incidents occur per year (in Britain) in which railway signals are passed at danger. The reason is that the preceding (amber) warning signals ring an alarm in the driver's cab which has to be manually cancelled, or the brakes are automatically applied. On a long journey, this procedure can become so automatic that the signal itself is not remembered, and the slowing of the train does not occur. Usually, the outcome is not fatal, as the final (red) signal stops the train automatically - but the system is not designed to stop a train from full speed, so there may not be room to stop in certain situations.

The consequences for HCI may be listed as follows:

- Visual error signals (for example, in a menu- or window-based system) should be arranged so that they occur in an otherwise uncluttered area on the screen. Generally, the presentation of a plain message on the bottom line of the screen will not be noticed unless it is made to flash.

- Well thought out auditory signals may be more effective than visual ones, especially if the possibilities of multiple channels or voice output are exploited (see Chapter 6).

## Problem solving

Problem solving tasks are often used in general psychology to test certain aspects of cognitive development: aptitude tests, 'intelligence' tests etc. Although there is much debate as to their relevance to general judgments of cognitive level (there are often severe cultural biases, for example) peoples' performance on problem-solving tasks can offer useful insights in specific areas such as troubleshooting, debugging, etc.

Performance may be measured in three ways: the time taken to complete a task (speed test); the maximum task difficulty that can be achieved (power test); or a simple recording of protocols (see Chapter 4); or a combination of these. For HCI, there does not yet seem to be extensive usage of problem solving as an analytical technique, but a number of justifications can be made for its inclusion in the HCI armoury:

- Efficient problem solving strategies can be exploited to improve learning curves for a package

- An understanding of the process of *concept attainment*, discussed below, can help software designers ensure that their products are fully understood

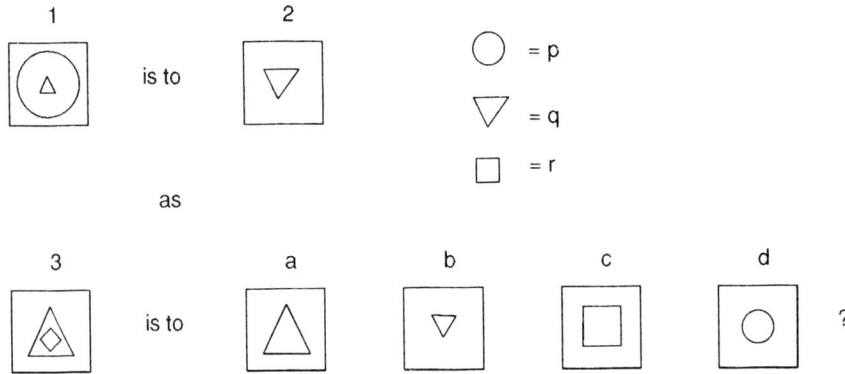

*Figure 3.8 Typical problem-solving task (courtesy Open University)*

### A typical task

Many readers will be familiar with the type of task illustrated in Figure 3.8. A moment's reflection enables us to identify **c** as the correct match. But how do we arrive at this conclusion? Is the process visual, logical or linguistic? Or does it vary between people? If a person devises a particular strategy, is he/she *more* likely or *less* likely to adopt alternatives, once they are pointed out? Is it possible to devise a 'universal' method which can be used in the design of complex applications, and which will best serve the user when the manuals cease to be of use in a complex situation?

One solution, which has been used in the development of artificial intelligence (AI) solutions to this kind of problem, is found by asking the question:

*Given a transformation between figures 1 and 2, which of the pairs 3:a, 3:b etc. give the most similar transformation?*

If the symbols within the figures are labelled as shown in Figure 3.8, then each figure can be represented linguistically as follows:

1 = q inside p
2 = q
3 = r inside q
a = q
b = q
c = r
d = p

Each pair is checked to see how the right-hand figure has been transformed form the left-hand figure:

1:2         p deleted
            q scaled by 2
            q rotated $60^{\circ}$

3:a         r deleted

3:b         q scaled by .5
            q rotated by $60^{\circ}$
3:c         q deleted
            r scaled by 2
            r rotated by $60^{\circ}$

3:d         q deleted
            r deleted

An inspection of the linguistic similarity between the various pairs reveals c to be the correct figure, even though there are differences of detail such as the exact angle of rotation.

   If all problem situations can be reduced to canonical forms like this, then we have a useful formalism for analysing and describing them. Arguably, however, such formalisms are not very good at prescribing *actions* in real situations.

*GPS*

Newell, Shaw and Simon devised a general-purpose problem solver (GPS) written in the LISP language. It typifies the *means-end analysis* approach to problem solving. It attempts to describe a problem situation in terms of a number of *states* - an *initial* state, a *goal* state and a number of *intermediate* states. The aim is to achieve the goal by changing the state of the system; this is done by applying an appropriate *operator*. The problem has been solved when the difference between the initial state and the goal state has been reduced to 0.

Initially, the operators are too global and non-specific to be of any use: 'fix the problem'. In the case of the non-booting computer described in Figure 3.9, the next step would be to establish an appropriate intermediate step in the booting process: **there must be a diskette in the drive**. This can be included as an intermediate state: **diskette in drive**. The problem now 'falls out' with a single intermediate state. This kind of solution may appear to be self-evident, but the example chosen is deliberately trivial and in a real situation there would be a number of alternative subgoals identified. For example, if the user did not know about the need for a diskette, a number of intermediate states involving documentation or advice-seeking could be needed.

Such analyses of problem situations can assist the HCI practitioner in identifying situations in which the user would be placed in a state where solution of a problem was actually impossible (in computer jargon, a *gotcha*). One of the most well-known 'gotchas' in the personal computer world occurs when a user has issued a command to format the hard disk drive, and receives the message:

```
Strike any key to continue
```

The user, grateful for this last chance to redeem his/her mistake, starts to type the **CTRL/ALT/DEL** key chord which, in practically all other circumstances, reboots (resets) the machine. In this case, however, the message means *exactly* what it says - any key. The only correct response is to switch off (*power down*) the machine.

These situations can arise not only at the applications interface, but in the course of normal computing activities. For example, writing data to a floppy diskette from a **copy** utility running on a PC is a routine activity in computing. If the target diskette is faulty, the operating system will signal an error and prompt the user:

```
(A)bort,(R)etry,(I)gnore?
```

Common sense would indicate that the offending diskette is replaced and the (R)etry operation selected. This is a *fatal error*; the diskette directory is not re-read into memory from the new diskette, and so the directory of the old diskette is used when the data is written to the new disk, with the consequence that the entire file structure of the new diskette is corrupted. If this fact were known to users, the solution path would be quite different, possibly involving the maintenance of 2 or 3 identical copies of the diskette.

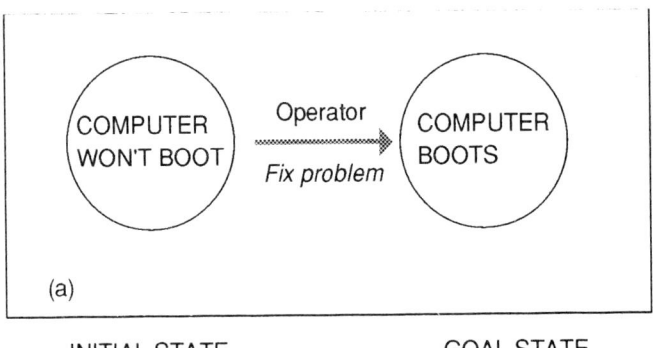

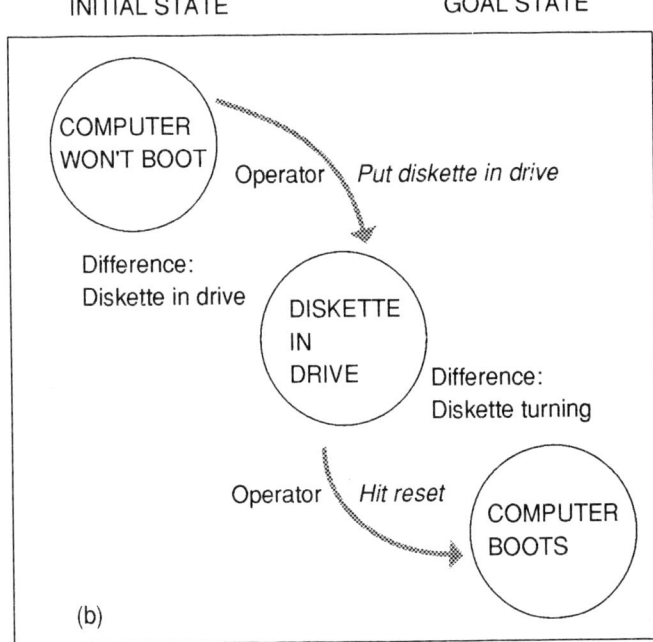

*Figure 3.9 GPS (From Newell, Shaw & Simon)*

## HCI and cognition

We now need to summarise what issues we need to identify from the area of cognition which are going to be useful in HCI. These may be listed as a number of questions:

- How do we organise the interface so that the known parameters of human memory, attention etc. are not violated?

- Can a knowledge of human cognition help bridge what has been called the *semantic gap*?

Figure 3.10 illustrates a conceptual view of this bridge-building process.

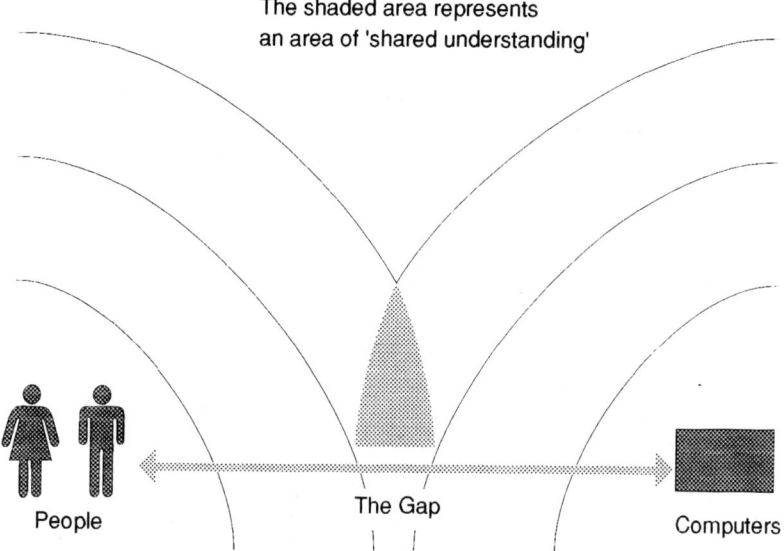

*Figure 3.10 Bridging the semantic gap.*

Low-level interaction involves little understanding and few skills are retained. As the interface improves in its ability to support true syntax, more skills and 'rules' are retained by the human user and understanding improves.

Finally, the 'spheres of understanding' overlap and we have true transparency. Some direct-manipulation systems may have achieved this in certain restricted domains.

## Summary

# 4 Information gathering in HCI

## Introduction

It is evident that studying the interaction between people and computers is of great theoretical as well as of practical interest. In this chapter we consider how the practical aspects might be pursued, and how useful information may be obtained about what is going on at the human-computer interface. Several aspects of data gathering are discussed: the use of appropriate programming languages, configurable applications, etc. In addition the issues of experimental design, statistical analysis and knowledge elicitation are introduced.

An important contrast should be made between *informal* and *formal* studies - the former provides information (sometimes in large quantities) which is of general interest, but unknown reliability. The latter type of study addresses a specific *hypothesis*, has rigorously designed and administercd experimental tasks, culminates with a statistical analysis of the data - and may not be very interesting at first glance. Both kinds of study have a place in HCI.

## The practicalities of studying HCI

The first reality to be faced by the serious student of HCI is that meeting people, putting them at their ease and (if necessary) practising a little temporary mild deception is the most important activity, far more important than being 'good with computers'. This latter quality is useful, but not essential.

The next most important reality is that people vary enormously in practically every aspect of their physical and psychological makeup. In spite of this, we need to establish general truths and make predictions about how an individual person might behave in front of a computer system.

## Information gathering methods

There are, broadly, two types of information that may be gathered from people: information which is volunteered consciously (such as opinions, feelings and judgments); and that which is provided by people via some kind of measurement (such as reaction time, skin resistance, choice selection etc.). Sometimes the two types of information are mixed in one study. The former type may be further subdivided into structured and unstructured methods - for example an interview may be totally open-ended or highly structured. Whether the information gathering is structured or not, there has to be some kind of protocol, or schedule, for analysing it - otherwise it is pointless to collect it.

### Questionnaires

A questionnaire has many advantages as a means of collecting information, among which are:

- It is cheap to administer in relatively large quantities

- Methods of analysis are well known and available as packages

- It is self-administered, freeing the experimenter's time

- Simple but well thought-out questionnaires can yield valuable information

There are certain disadvantages:

- People can be unenthusiastic or dilatory in their response

- It is restricted to the collection of subjective data

- A misunderstood question can invalidate the data for a whole subject

### Self-report techniques

Although a questionnaire is a form of self-report by the user, the form of that report is structured by the investigator; opportunities for expressing certain kinds of information are lost, and the technique does not permit the *individual* analysis of data which, in certain circumstances, may be useful. Finally, it offers no opportunity for the user to structure information in his/ her own way, or to provide information about *personal constructs*.

This problem has been attacked in the area of psychological tests, with the work of Kelly being paramount.

### *Personal Construct Theory (PCT)*

The basis of this theory is that a person's view of, and interpretation of, the world, is largely based on an internal set of constructs which are unique to that individual. These constructs can be deduced by administering a special kind of questionnaire which enables an investigator to elicit information about a person's set of constructs without the person being made directly aware of them.

The results are often surprising - for example a dislike of authority may be highly correlated with a dislike of a particular person, for example a parent.

As far as HCI is concerned, the technique is applicable in those areas where aspects of *affect* (emotion, attitudes) towards computer systems are being investigated.

### Online monitoring

If the HCI investigator is interested in collecting information of a 'harder' (more objective) kind, then there are many ways of collecting such data from users in an unobtrusive way. For example, if you are curious about the length of time it takes for a user to perform a certain task in terms of when particular keys are pressed, then the keystrokes could be directly monitored, as in the Playback system developed by IBM. This is straightforward in a simple terminal / host computer situation, as the connecting lead can just be diverted to another machine which monitors the interaction. If the computer concerned is a desktop machine, then the process becomes more complex, but more interesting things are possible. A similar system has been described in a paper by Morris et al. [49], and the technique is further discussed in Chapter 11 in the context of usability metrics.

The following techniques for monitoring are commonly in use:

- **Operating System traps:** Installing hidden routines which intercept normal operating system routines, in order to update a log file or to time some particular event. These routines are undetectable if properly written and installed. The concept is used in the popular 'pop-up' (Terminate and Stay Resident, TSR) utilities for PC-type computers, such as SideKick (an organiser-type utility). With true multitasking operating systems, use of this kind of technique is easier. The data can be analysed offline, or even while the test application is running.

- **Specific applications:** These are most conveniently programmed in a high level language, and, increasingly, implementations of HLLs are being provided with enhancements which permit easy access to operating system routines (see 'software tools' below).

- **Applications with configurable interfaces:** Many applications are provided with an interface that is configurable, such as the text editor EMACS - 'editing macros' - and the word processing package Sprint (TM). Such packages provide ways of altering the keyboard mappings, collecting often-used keystrokes together in *macros* and so on. Monitoring in this situation would be achieved by writing macros which incorporated data trapping routines as part of their operation. Configurable interfaces are discussed in greater depth in Chapter 7, and adaptive dialogues are discussed in Chapter 9.

- **Use of toolboxes:** These are increasingly being provided as enhancements to programming languages which enable certain facilities to be programmed at a very high level.

- **Specialist languages:** For certain kinds of investigation, it may be necessary to write a special-purpose language for handling presentations, data gathering etc.

## Possibilities

We are fortunate in having a boom in excellent software which looks as though it was designed to be configurable. Increasingly, operating systems are offering greater functionality from the point of view of interaction, handling different data types, and supporting the new kinds of message-passing application. In parallel with this, it seems as though diversity is emerging in the kind of hardware available. This is undoubtedly due to the proliferation of better and faster central processors - for example RISC (Reduced Instruction Set) computers which offer high performance with low complexity of construction. The manufacturers of such devices are aware that they will make no market headway without full support for standard operating systems, so the systems software development is heavily promoted (and possibly subsidised). This can only benefit the user, who generally does not care about the nature of the architecture.

It is reasonable to suppose, therefore, that HCI work will become easier and the test applications more robust. It is also reasonable to expect some HCI toolkits to emerge from third-party software suppliers.

## Experimental design

If the results of any quantitative measurements are to be meaningful, the investigator must be certain that they have been obtained under the correct conditions, as far as possible. This dictates that all experiments should conform to the following requirements:

- There should be a *control* condition against which all the experimental conditions are matched.

- Fatigue and practice effects should be anticipated and 'controlled out' of the experiment. For example, if it is known (or suspected) that people tend to slow down over time while doing a certain series of tests, then *half* the subjects should perform the tests in the reverse sequence so that this fatigue effect is balanced out.

- The difference between *within-* and *between-subjects* designs should be appreciated. There is often a greater   degree of variability between individuals than between different their performance on tasks they may be asked to perform.

- It should be remembered that adding an experimental condition *doubles* the amount of measurement to be performed, as all combinations of conditions have to be tested for. Generally, the experiment should be designed to be as simple as possible.

## Statistical analysis

Experiments should always be performed with the eventual statistical analysis in mind. This may be *descriptive* (the calculation of means, frequencies, histograms etc.), *inductive* (testing for significant differences between conditions) or both.

Testing may be as simple as testing between two means (averages) to see if they differ significantly (that is, more than would be predicted by chance) or as complex as an analysis of variance where the total variation in the data is accounted for, both between conditions and between subjects, together with any *interactions* between conditions and subjects.

In addition, there are two, distinctly different, approaches to statistical testing. *Nonparametric* tests make no assumption about how the data is distributed about a mean, and so data derived from, for example, frequency counts can be used; *parametric* tests assume that the data is normally distributed (as most biological data is) and are hence capable of maximising the information present in the data.

The basic problem of establishing the significance between two means is illustrated in Figure 4.1.

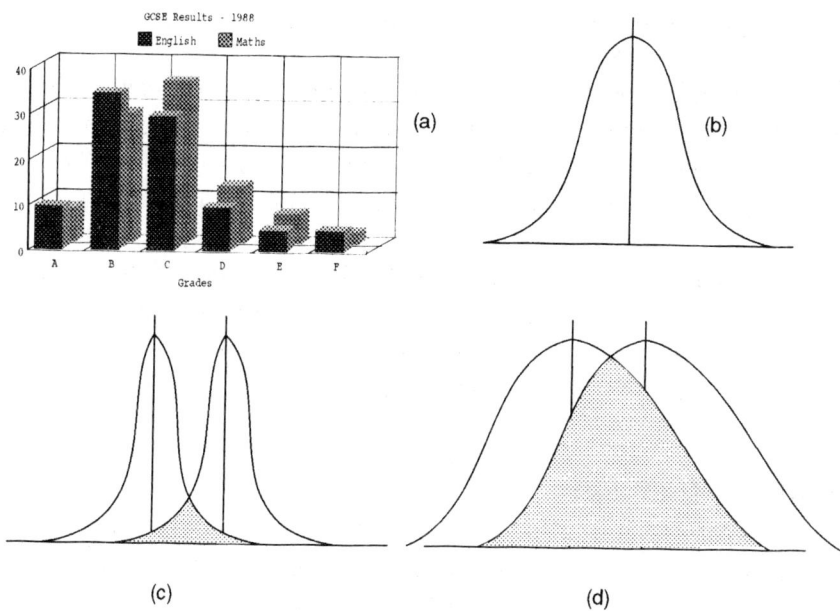

*Figure 4.1 Some normal distributions (Figure 4.1(a) courtesy Clares Micro Supplies)*

Figure 4.1(a) illustrates 'real' data (the percentage of GCSE examination scores obtained in each grade), plotted in the form of a bar chart. It will be observed that Grade C is the most frequent, with the higher and lower scores 'tailing off'. This particular data set is *skewed* so that the higher grades are favoured. This indicates some kind of bias in the data. This effect is quite common, and can be compensated for if not too extreme.

If many more measurements are taken, and a finer gradation used, the curve obtained smoothes out to a characteristic bell shape (4.1(b)) centred about the *mean* (average) value.

Given now that we may want to establish a difference between the means of two experimental groups, 4.1(c) and (d) show two possibilities. The difference between the means is in fact the same, but the *variability* of the data differs. Whereas the difference between the two populations is clear cut in (a), the difference might not be significant in (b). The shaded area indicates the amount of shared variability between the two sets of data.

**Statistical Packages**

The procedures necessary for the statistical analysis of data are not difficult to understand, but the calculations are extremely tedious, and ideally suited to computerisation. Fortunately, there are packages available which can perform all of the commonly used procedures. The most comprehensive is **SPSS** (statistical package for the social sciences) which provides for everything from simple frequency counts to factor analysis. Simpler packages such as **MINITAB** (a kind of statistical spreadsheet) are very useful for smaller data sets or less ambitious analyses.

# Knowledge elicitation

We need to gather, or elicit, knowledge about a variety of things relating to HCI, and we need to do it for at least two reasons:

- We want to plan an HCI experiment

- We want to design a system with 'good HCI'.

The procedures described above have great utility in extracting *normative* data - that is, measures of attributes such as response times, learning rates, etc., that can be seen to conform to a normally distributed pattern and where the measures are *robust*.

In HCI, we increasingly have a need for other kinds of information, which do not conform to a statistical model. For example, what model can predict the type of error a user will commit, and when? We need to go back to square one, and be involved not with information gathering, but with *knowledge elicitation* - information about how knowledge of a particular domain is stored and represented in the human brain (Conventionally, knowledge elicitation refers to the process of gathering knowledge from a human being for the specific purpose of gleaning an expert's knowledge for use in an Expert System).

There are basically two ways of eliciting knowledge: manually and automatically. The manual method involves a *knowledge engineer* trained in the techniques of abstracting an expert's knowledge. One application of this is in the **NoteCards** system, as described by Martin and McAleese[45]. Using a structured question/answer dialogue, the expert's semantic knowledge on a series of related concepts is extracted as a *concept map*. This information can be used directly, used as input to an expert system, or discussed with other experts.

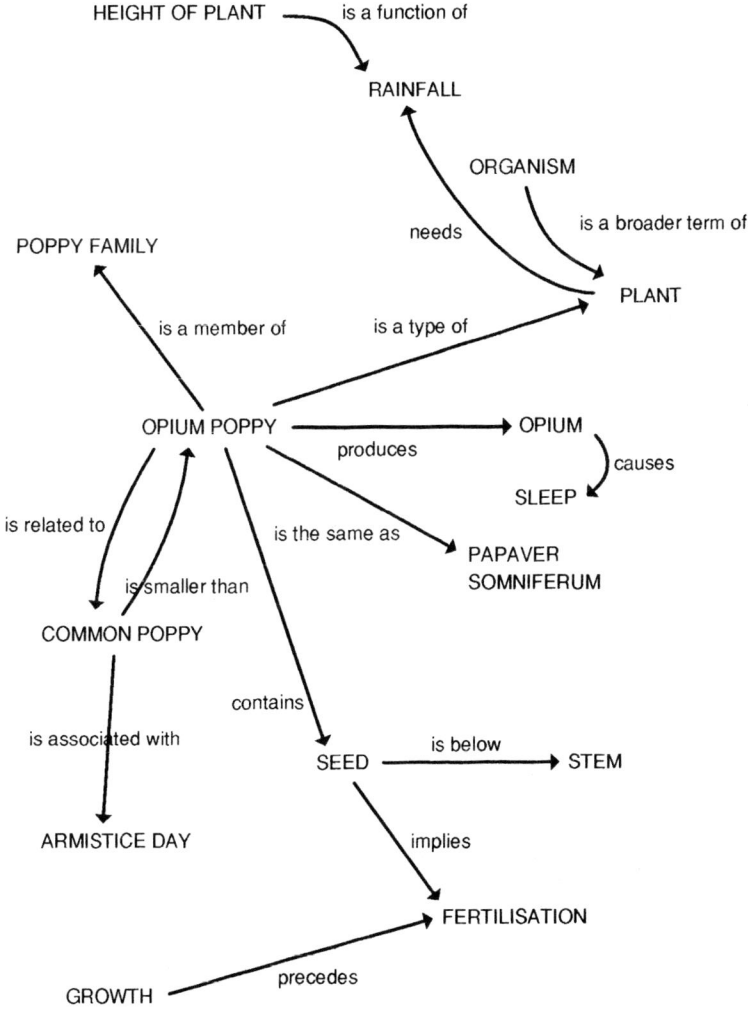

*Figure 4.2 Concept mapping as represented by the Notecards system (after Martin and McAleese, 1986)*

The automatic method involves some kind of *knowledge induction* - given a particular pattern of events or facts, the system attempts to reduce this data to a smaller number of rules which have some predictive power. A detailed description is beyond the scope of this book, but a brief discussion of one or two such systems would be helpful.

### Quinlan's ID3

ID3 stands for 'Interactive Dichotomiser Mark 3', and operates by attempting to reduce an arbitrary set of data about the relationships between certain specified entities into a set of rules implemented as a tree structure. Specifically, the amount of information provided by making a decision at each choice point is maximised (in Quinlan's terms, the *entropy* - measure of the disorder in a system - is minimised.)

Given a set of inputs, ID3 produces a set of rules (a rule base) which can be input to an expert system or used as a knowledge base in other ways.

### CART

This technique - 'classification and regression trees' - is similar in concept to ID3, but instead of a simple entropy calculation at each fork in the tree, a full regression analysis is performed. CART has been used in areas as diverse as EEG ('brainwave') diagnosis and the prediction of earthquakes.

### Genetic algorithms

Very often, decisions made on the evidence supplied by a rule base are *brittle* - they are not wrong, but, being based on information captured at a particular time, or on incomplete data, decisions may be inappropriately triggered when a particular combination of events matches a rule. To overcome this, a degree of *robustness* must be built into the system, and this is achieved by evolving the system over time with a selection of data from the real world.

Interestingly enough, providing some variability in the data can result in a better rule base. Performance in such systems is measured against some external criterion (such as a cost-error matrix) and more successful rule bases are allowed to stand. Occasionally, successful rules are allowed to recombine in a random way. This mechanism works quite well in nature, as evolution.

There are a number of variations on the genetic theme: such techniques as *simulated evolution*[23a], *simulated annealing* and *genetic hillclimbing* are in common use.

### Classifier systems

Holland[34a] has described a system which seems particularly attractive for building rule bases from real-time events such as those generated by people interacting with computers. Messages (events) from the real world are matched against a set of rules. If there is a match, then an action associated with each rule is performed. A match occurs if a message exactly corresponds with a rule, or if *some* criteria are matched on a 'wild card' basis. Generally, the action comprises merely the posting of a new message. Occasionally, the performance is evaluated and the rules with the most predictive power are 'promoted'. A genetic algorithm is then applied to the rules and their associated 'wild card' masks.

Using such a system, many quite complex situations reduce to no more than twenty rules (of the 'given *that* situation, *this* happens next') variety, but time must be allowed for the system to settle down.

Systems of the kind discussed above are particularly useful in such activities as task analysis and deriving interaction models for dialogue specification (see Chapter 9). By tending to 'filter out' variability in behaviour, and ignoring rare kinds of behaviour, they are better at 'sharpening' the available data than are statistical methods.

## Software tools

### Pascal

In its 'vanilla' form (that is, without any kind of enhancements to either the language or its environment), Pascal is a good teaching language but does not possess any features which render it suitable for HCI work - the ability to manipulate screen images, perform timings, set display colours etc. The reason for this is that these operations have, in the past, been hardware-dependent. However, improvements in operating systems have meant that many operations of this kind are now available as system calls (which only needs one new keyword to be defined), and in any case the proliferation of IBM-compatible personal computers has meant that the hardware configuration of millions of personal computers is identical, and so efficient routines can be written and accessed via libraries.

The Borland version of Pascal - Turbo Pascal - has been used successfully by the author to program a number of HCI experiments, one of which is described below.


**Prolog**
(In the following subsection, the implementation of Prolog under discussion is Turbo Prolog from Borland International).
Although developed primarily as a language for investigating symbolic maths, the general power of Prolog renders it suitable for a wide range of activities in HCI - knowledge elicitation, experiments, natural language interfaces etc.

Prolog is a non-procedural language - a Prolog program does not proceed by executing a sequence of procedures in an imperative way, but by seeking to establish the truth of a succession of *clauses*. For example, the clause

```
likes (frank,beer).
```

if entered as a 'fact', is installed into Prolog's 'database' of clauses. A subsequent 'enquiry' of the form

```
likes (frank,X).
```

returns the result

```
X=beer
no (more) results
```

In plain English, the Prolog interpreter is telling us two things: firstly, that the enquiry clause is 'true' in the sense that a match was obtained with an item in the database (both parameters were *instantiated*); and secondly (in fact, as a side-effect) that the variable X was instantiated to 'beer'.

This is not very exciting as it stands. But consider a clause with a similar form, but very different effect:

```
dir ("*.DOC", Filename).
```

when encountered as part of a Prolog database, it has the side-effect (on an MS-DOS machine running Turbo Prolog) of:

- Opening up a window containing a directory of matching filenames

- Providing the user with a cursor activated by the 'arrow' keys

- Returning the filename as a string, ready for further use, when the user presses the ENTER key.

As before, the clause returns 'true' if no error was encountered.

Similarly, the clause

```
edit ("A string").
```

invokes the entire resources of the system editor (including file loading and saving) to edit the string.

## Creating specific applications
In many situations, where simple measurements are to be made, it is possible to write a dedicated application in a suitable programming language. This could be used to present the various experimental conditions (with manual data recording); or it could perform some measurement as well, especially if the data set is simple, such as keypress timings or word list compilation.

**Configurable packages**
Many of the newer packages designed to run on personal computers (particularly

*Sprint*

## Task analysis

The experimental techniques outlined above are suitable for fundamental investigations into many aspects of HCI, but for certain areas, such as dialogue design and development, some higher-level activities must be carried out. Task analysis is one such activity, which encompasses a variety of techniques. All these techniques share a common goal: to derive a formal model for investigating how human tasks are (or may be) structured in the particular problem domain; and to use this model in the design of the computer-based tasks. Figure 4.3 shows how human and computer-based task may be identified and structured, but does not give us any ideas about how this arrangement was arrived at.

H: allocated to human operator
C: allocated to computer

Function: Check Customer Order

Repeat while orders
  H: enter customer number
  C: check customer number
  C: If no number assume customer & pass to accounts
  C: Check customer against credit-control list
  C: If customer on list send to credit control
  H: Check order value against credit limit
  C: If over limit send to credit control

Function: Enter Product Details

Repeat for products ordered
  H: Enter product code
  C: Check product code
  C: If in stock tick ex-stock column
  C: If not a stock item tick direct column
  C: Check product quantity
  C: If less than minimum quantity raise query note
  H: If over delivery limit and not a stock item raise bulk order

Function: Raise bulk order

Repeat for high quantity products ordered

  .
  .
  .
etc.

*Figure 4.3 Typical logical task allocation for an inventory system (after Sutcliffe, 1988)*

For a number of years, HCI workers have sought to develop models and methodologies for the process of task analysis. The importance of the area is reflected in the number of models developed; we only have space to discuss a few.

To get an idea of the task analysis philosophy, imagine the task of word processing. In the typical word processing package, there are many hundreds of individual functions, which may be accessed in a variety of ways. One important piece of information is the relative frequency with which various functions are used. This will have consequences for the dialogue design and the interface that the user eventually sees. If tasks are analysed by frequency, then we might see the following structure:

## MOST FREQUENT

Text entry

Special operations - deleting, inserting, cursor movement etc.

Block operations - move, copy, delete etc.

Changing text attributes - <u>underline</u>, **bold**, *italic*, ___all three___, etc.

Mode changing - for example, command mode for spell checking, word counting etc.

Loading new fonts

Special procedures such as printer installation, screen configuration

## LEAST FREQUENT

When designing the user interface, account will have to be taken of this task analysis. There is no point, for example, in having infrequently used operations available 'up front' on the display. The naive user would be confused, and the experienced user would be irritated. A possible solution might be as follows:

## MOST FREQUENT

Use the main alphanumeric keypad and display minimal information on a status line - for example, the line, column and page number.

Use the special keys available on the keyboard (see Chapter 5) - for example, the *Insert, Delete, Home, End* keys are available on the ANSI keyboard. For cursor movement, 'arrow' keys are available.

Alternatively, simple *key chords* - CONTROL/C, CONTROL/R - can be used. Or a pull-down or pop-up menu could be used, even on a non-WIMP system.

For changing text attributes, a combination of tasks will be used, depending on whether the text to be changed exists as a block, or the effect is to be applied from the next character entered.

Mode changing operations should use a 'significant' key, such as *Escape*. Tasks within the different modes will not need to be as memorable as the more frequent tasks, so a menu-driven approach could be used.

The least frequent tasks may not be accessible from the main user interface at all - for example, a separate *setup* or *install* package may be provided. If they are accessible from the main interface, then the user should be aware of their significance.

## LEAST FREQUENT

The important point is that the task analysis and the interface design should be compatible, and for the relatively simple tasks described above, a formal model of task analysis may suffice. To cope with more complex designs, some theoretical positions must be taken.

What is needed is a formal description of how *tasks* and *actions* interrelate - a grammar. Payne [54] has developed a *Task-Action Grammar*, which may be summarised as follows:

- Tasks are differentiated by *semantic* features - the user *means* to perform a task, with a meaningful goal.

- Tasks are mapped onto specific *action sequences* by means of a *feature grammar*.

- Easy to learn systems have simple grammars, and vice-versa.

Overall, the emphasis is on the way a user structures a task (rather than the way in which an applications programmer does).

An alternative (or rather complementary) view, which address itself more to the linkage between intentions and procedures, is the GOMS (Goals, Operators, Methods, Selection rules) model of Card et al [15]. Figures 4.4 and 4.5 illustrate it.

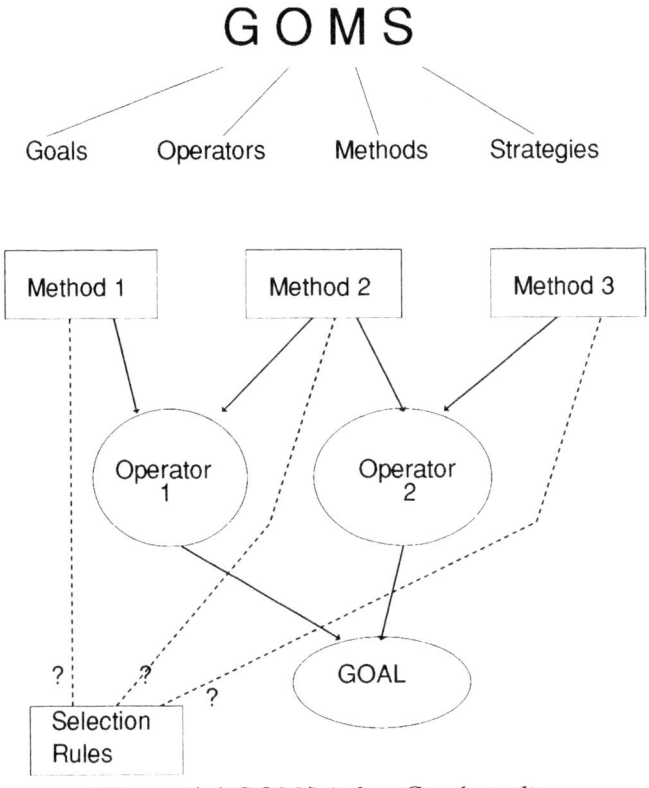

*Figure 4.4 GOMS (after Card et al)*

The GOMS procedure is as follows:

- Major goals are broken into *subgoals*; for example, replicating columns in a spreadsheet package could involve two subgoals - define the columns to be replicated, and define the range of columns to replicate into.

- Each subgoal is then 'attacked' by an *operator* using a *method*.

- If more than one method is appropriate for a subgoal, the most appropriate method is selected using a set of *rules*.

The process then iterates by further subdividing goals until they are amenable to attack by appropriate methods. Eventually, the goal is either achieved or not achieved.

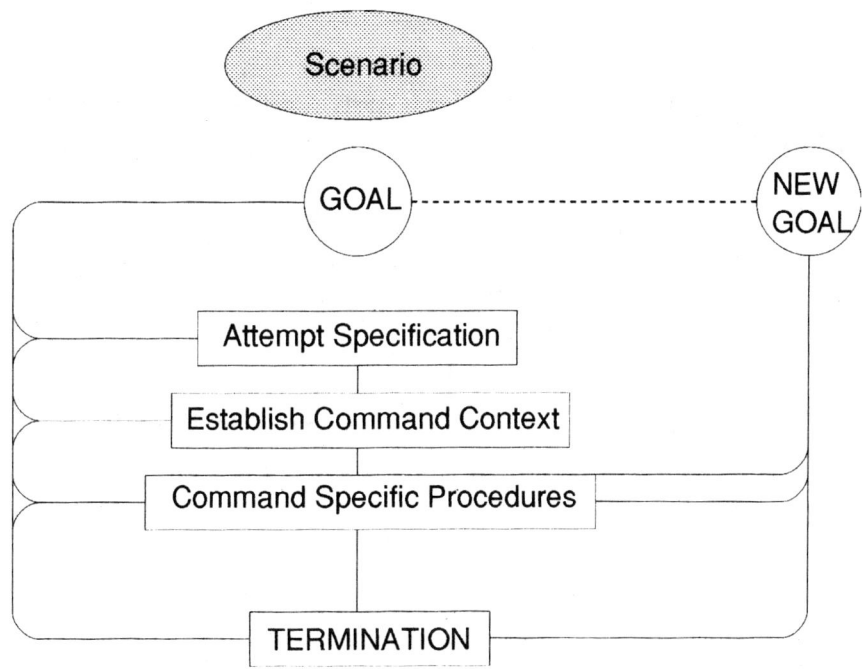

*Figure 4.5 GOMS procedure (after Wilson, Barnard and McClean)*

**Laddering**
This technique, illustrated in Figure 4.6, has been described by Shadbolt and Hayes; it is conceptually simple and of great practical utility in eliciting knowledge about tasks from people.

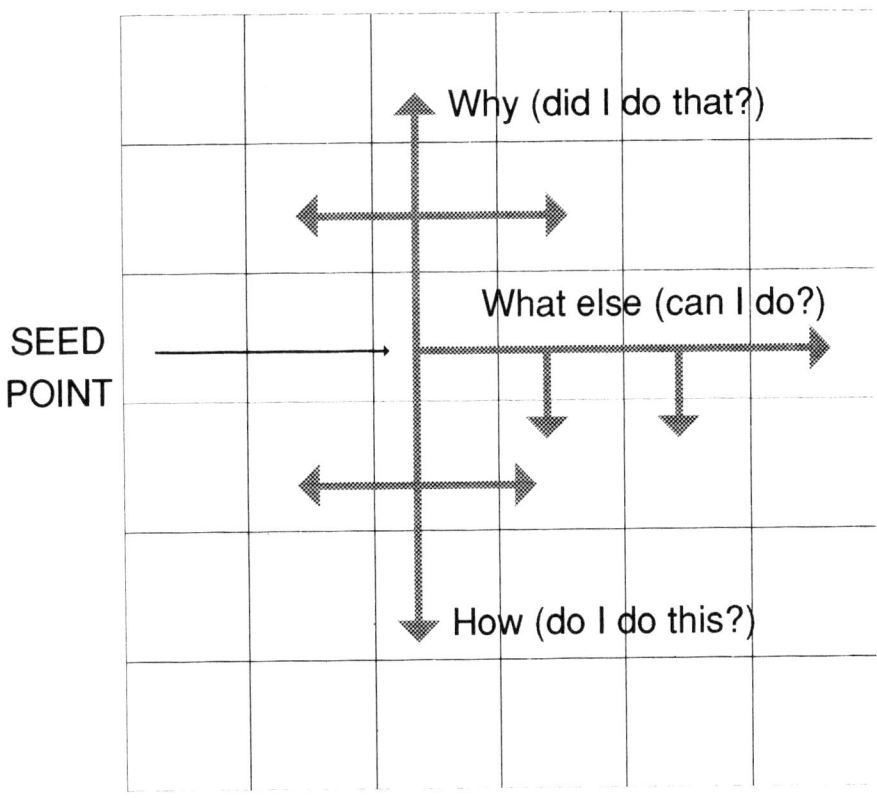

*Figure 4.6 Laddering (after Shadbolt & Hayes)*

It can be used to map the task structure for an existing manual task, or for a hypothetical interface, or for a real interface under development.

The 'ladder' is entered from an arbitrary point (the seed point). From the seed point, assuming that a particular task is being referenced, a number of questions can be asked:

- What **other** tasks is it possible to initiate at this level? (**left,right**)

- **Why** was this task initiated? (**up**)

- **How** is this task performed? (**down**)

A typical example would be the organisation of the tasks within, say, a
word-processing package on a PC. If we enter ladder at a point which is
located within 'cursor movement' operations, we could construct the
following ladder:

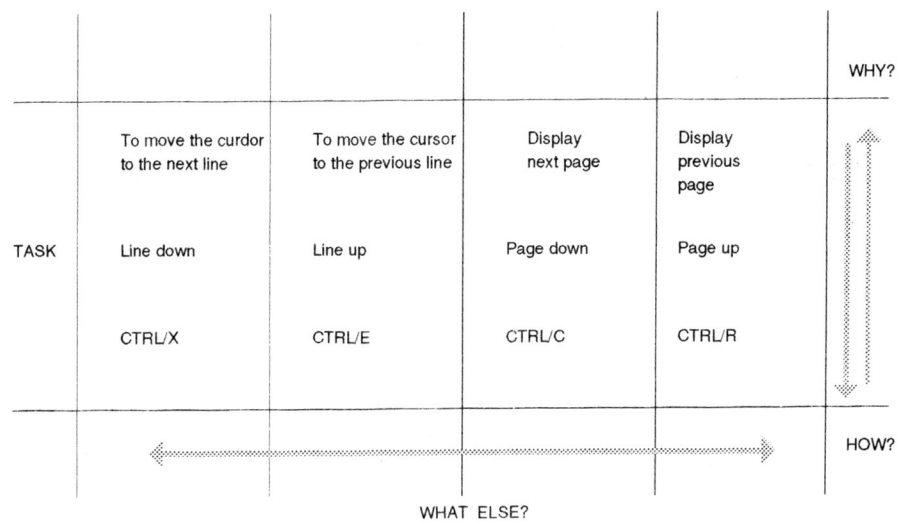

*Figure 4.7 4 cells of a 'ladder' matrix for a typical word
processing editor.*

One advantage of this technique is that the task structure of an application
can be presented graphically. Looking at the pattern presented by the
filled cells in the matrix, it is evident that a tall, thin appearance is
indicative of many levels of menus, with few operations at each level; on
the other hand a short, fat appearance shows the converse. Both extremes
should be avoided.

# 5 Physical input and output

*The keyboard is an extension of the fingers*

*Ben Shneiderman*

## Introduction

We have seen how HCI may be regarded as a communications problem -
that is, we have the notion of high-level messages being 'layered' onto a
lower-level transport mechanism. In this model, no layer is more
important than any other. The lowest, physical layer is encountered by all
users, and it must be reliable and well-matched to human characteristics.

In HCI, we are only concerned with 3 layers: the physical, the syntactic
and the semantic. (Several other 'layered' models exist - see Rasmussen
[57]).

In this chapter we are concerned with the various physical devices by
which input and output are performed: keyboards and displays (the most
common); graphics tablets and pointing devices (for specialised uses) and
new types of device (datagloves and head-up displays). Voice input/output
is discussed in Chapter 6.

Finally we discuss the importance of emerging international standards.

## Keyboards

The design of keyboards, in terms of layout, has remained basically the same since the middle of the last century, when the typewriter was invented. Major advances have been made, of course, in the general technology of keyboards. After problems with sticking keys, an engineer, Frederick Sholes, realised that if frequently-used letter keys were distributed over the keyboard, the slow mechanisms then available were not capable of keeping up with a fast typist. (It is amusing to note that this must be the first recorded instance of 'negative HCI engineering'; but we should not assume that the practice has ceased of functionally crippling the user to fit the machine - try the keyboard of certain 'laptop' personal computers.)

## The keys

Taken individually, a key is not a very interesting object. However, it is the sole physical interface between the system and the user, and its attributes are vitally important to the user's success in keying in data. It is therefore imperative that we ensure that the static and dynamic characteristics of the keys are well-matched to the known properties of the average 'user finger'.

### Static attributes

The shape and 'feel' of a key are important; after all, the vast bulk of information in a system has come via a keyboard of some sort. It is an interesting exercise to consider how much time is spent by, say, a data preparation clerk during a year in hitting keys with fingers.

Figure 5.1 illustrates another aspect of key design - which is often ignored in cheap devices - the 'scalloping' of each key, and the staggering of each row of keys so that the fingertips are accommodated comfortably and their natural radius of action is made use of.

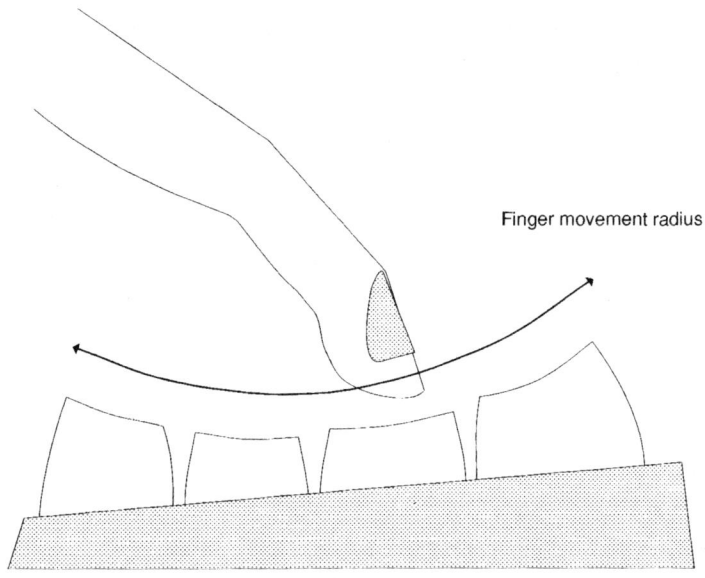

Finger movement radius

*Figure 5.1 Keyboard sculpturing*

### Dynamic attributes

Figure 5.2 shows a typical force/travel profile for a key. It illustrates graphically how the key behaves as it is depressed. At first, a steadily rising force is encountered. At a certain point, the key 'gives' and, given a constant force, will move rapidly to a new position. The keypress will be registered by the system at some point during this rapid travel. Further pressure does not have any further functional effect, but will serve to 'cushion' the remaining travel. It appears, from research carried out in the 1960s, that this positive 'give' is a desirable feature in a key, especially if accompanied by an acoustic 'click'. (This is exactly the situation that obtains in the IBM Selectric typewriter, which is an electromechanical device).

Most readers will be familiar with the simulated 'click' that some keyboards provide, perhaps in an effort to emulate the ideal situation in a low-cost way. It does certainly provide a positive indication that the key has been pressed, in the absence of any tactile feedback.

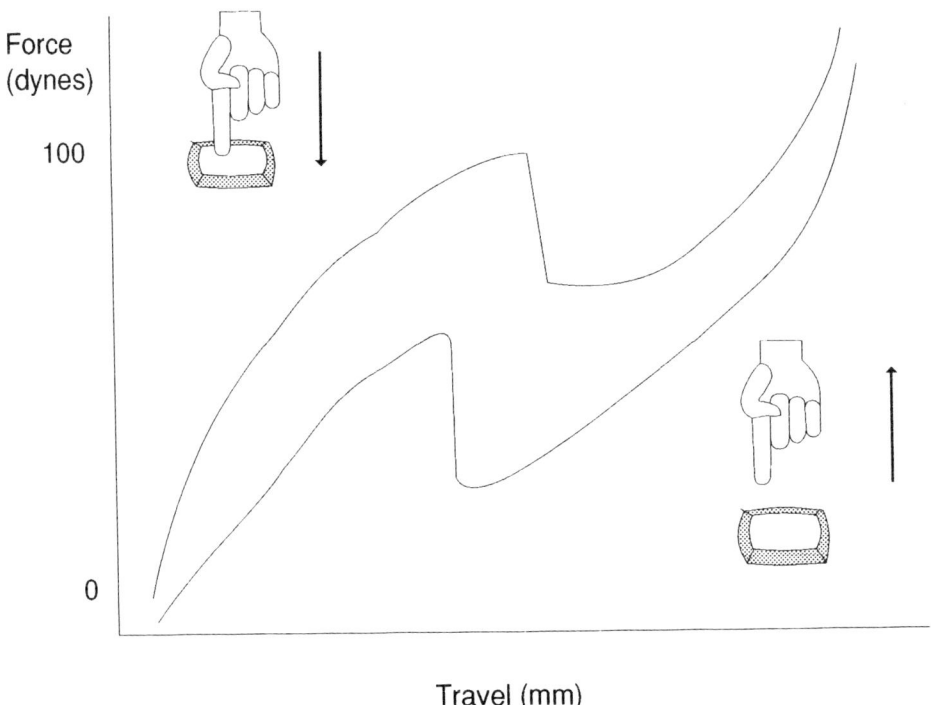

*Figure 5.2 Tactile profile of a typical key*

**Keyboard layout**

Figure 5.3 shows a typical modern keyboard as found on terminals, personal computers, and workstations. It conforms to the ANSI (American National Standards Institute) standard for keyboards. Keyboards of this type are to be found on most modern terminals and workstations, with small variations. The most obvious feature that distinguishes an ANSI keyboard from others is the arrangement of the programmable function keys in a row across the top. Apart from this, there are several functional groups of keys, the main group being the alphanumeric (alphabetic and numeric) keys. There are also several control keys which are used in text editing. Note that most control keys duplicate sequences which can be obtained by key 'chords' of an alpha key and the CONTROL key (for example, ESCAPE is CTRL/[, TAB is CTRL/I etc).

The function keys produce a sequence of 2 characters rather than a single ASCII code; a NULL (0) code first indicates that a function key has been pressed, and the next character to arrive signals the identity of the function key.

Escape key          Function keys          Miscellaneous  Status lights
                                           function keys

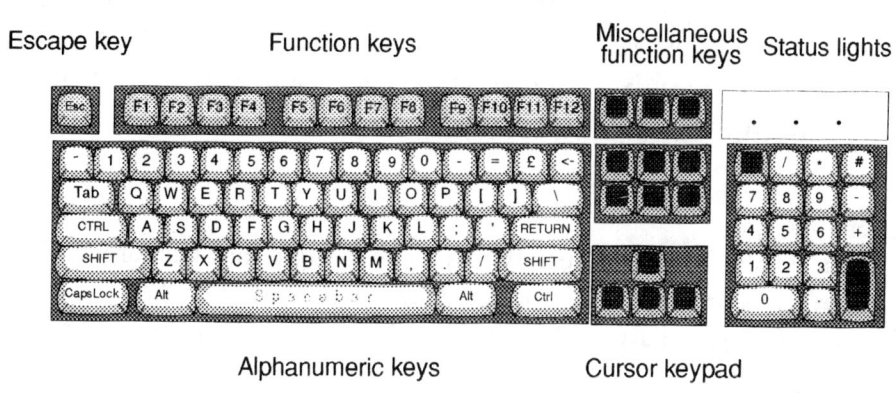

Alphanumeric keys              Cursor keypad

*Figure 5.3 ANSI standard keyboard*

# Non-QWERTY keyboards

As mentioned earlier, the 'qwerty' layout was designed to slow the keying rate of fast typists. Since technology now permits us to use any kind of layout, it is interesting to look at some of the alternative layouts which have been developed over the last few years.

## Dvorak

The design of this keyboard follows the observation that most words (at least in English and related languages) comprise an alternation of vowels and consonants. A large number of words(and sub-words) follow a 'trigram'  structure of Consonant - Vowel - Consonant (CVC) or, alternatively, Vowel - Consonant - Vowel (VCV).

By having the vowel letters on the left hand side, and the consonants predominantly on the right, the Dvorak layout encourages a natural 'rhythm' in the typing of words. Additionally, the use of a phonetic strategy (using the sound of the word to assist its typing) is made more efficient.

### Azerty

The keys are arranged in the normal alphabetical order. While not as arbitrary as the QWERTY layout, there does not seem to be much evidence that this layout assists typing. It is favoured in small alphanumeric keyboards as found on the increasingly popular electronic personal organisers.

### Other types

Over the years, many interesting keyboard designs have emerged. The **Maltron** keyboard maximises the mechanical efficiency of the fingers by arranging the keys in a way that fits both the horizontal and lateral arcs of movement.

The **Velotype** keyboard adopts the strategy of reducing the number of keys by making each key perform a multiple function. For common letters, the key alone is depressed. For less usual letters, a key chord is used.

The Quinkey (or MicroWriter) keyboard only has 5 keys, arranged in a way which lies naturally under the fingers and thumb. Letters are formed by making appropriate 'shapes' with various combinations of fingers and thumb. This keyboard is particularly suitable for people with restricted mobility.

## Other input devices

It is convenient to distinguish between input devices designed specifically for inputting text, and *pointing* devices.

**Text input**

Apart from voice input (discussed in Chapter 6), *written* input is coming under attention. For most people, handwriting is very much quicker than typing. However, handwriting analysis requires a great deal of processing power, especially if the recognition process is carried out 'on the fly' (that is, as the information is written). The way in which the letters are formed from strokes is much less variable than the shapes and sizes of letters as viewed statically. We now have adequate amounts of processing power to perform this task, and commercial devices are beginning to appear. perhaps the most exciting of these are the *active book* computers, which have no keyboard and a high-resolution liquid crystal display.

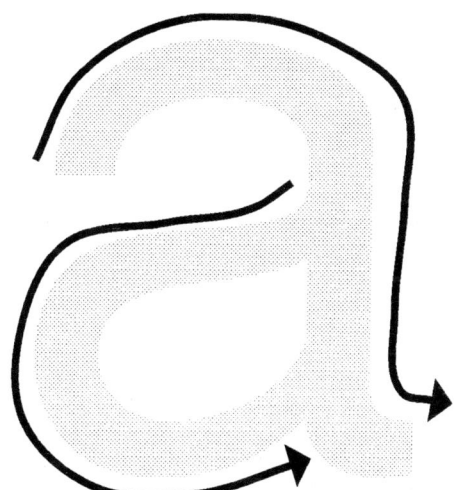

*Figure 5.4 Handwritten input - the significant information is in the stroke direction.*

**Pointing**

Although keyboards (or tablets, etc.) are the preferred device for new text input, this  is only one type of task involved in, say, word processing operations.  Blocks of text need to be moved, deleted or copied, and cursor operations   are often inconvenient and slow for this purpose. Several kinds of device have been developed which facilitate *direct manipulation* of a pointer. (See also Chapter 14 for a discussion of various pointing devices for disabled people.)

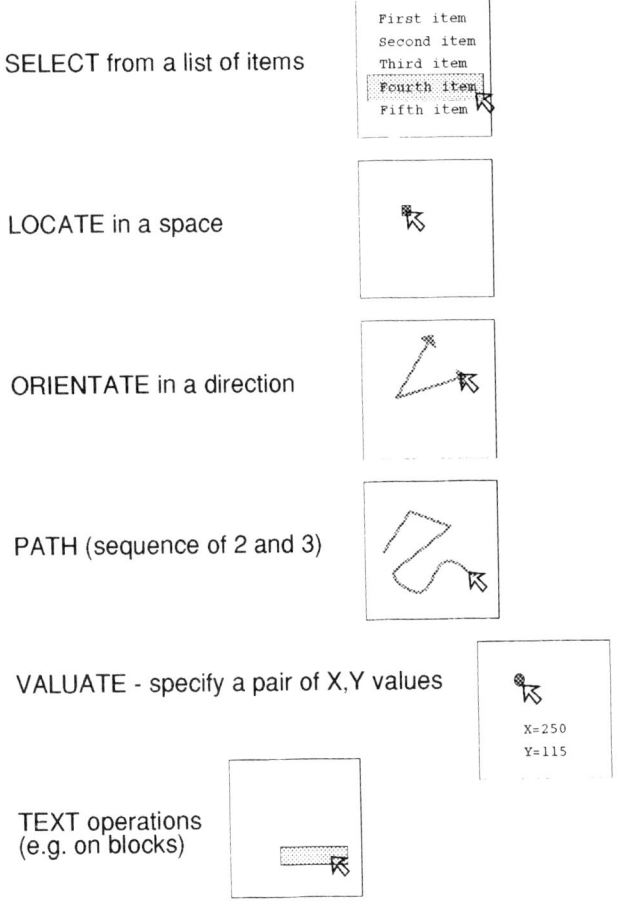

*Figure 5.5 Functions of pointing devices*

## Mice

Mice are now an integral part of 'WIMP'-based systems, and work by sending information to the host system about their horizontal and vertical positions. This is done incrementally, rather than by using absolute values. The mouse also incorporates one, two or three buttons which are used as selectors.

There do not seem to be any particular guidelines about how many buttons should be used - the Apple Macintosh makes do with only one, which performs all the selection operations listed in Figure 5.5. The Acorn Archimedes has three (Select, Menu and Adjust) which has the advantage that a menu can be called up wherever the mouse pointer happens to be on the screen. On the other hand, the Macintosh-style mouse is probably easier to adapt for, say, disabled people.

### *Ergonomics of mice*

The mouse device appears to be well-matched to the dynamics of human arm, wrist and finger movements. In fact, the arm plays very little part in moving the mouse, this being achieved largely by wrist movements. Large movements can be accomplished with high accuracy, a property of human limbs generally being that they can make large and rapid movements with no sacrifice of accuracy.

Edwards [22] has reported that a hand movement over a distance of 15" takes only 25% longer than a movement over 5". This is due to the dynamics of the movement taken as a whole, in which the more precise adjustments which occur as the hand approaches the target occupy a relatively high proportion of the total time. Another factor, also reported by Edwards, is that rapid tapping movements cannot be performed rapidly at rates of more than about 10 per second. This is significant when we consider that many operations of the 'activate' type (such as running a package) are performed by *double clicking* the mouse button.

### Trackerballs

Readers may be interested to know that the author procured a trackerball device to ensure that this section was informed by practical experience.

The trackerball itself is similar in size, feel and weight to a snooker ball, and is rotatable in any plane. The buttons (generally three) are located on the forward edge of the device. The main advantage of the device is that it does not have to be bodily moved like a mouse, and quite rapid movements can be made by 'spinning' the ball and braking it with the fingers. Fine control is also more precise than with a mouse (and, incidentally, applications such as flight simulators become more controllable).

The main drawback is that the typical 'click and drag' operation, common in window-based packages, is awkward to perform with a trackerball. Either a contortion has to be performed (using the thumb or forefinger to hold the button), or both hands have to be brought into operation, the left hand to hold the button and the right to spun the ball (in a right-handed person).

However, the author's experience with a trackerball was good enough for the device to find a permanent home next to the keyboard.

### Tablets
For more precise work, a mouse or a trackerball is not accurate enough - or some people may not like them. A *digitising tablet* offers an alternative. It is a rectangular surface which is sensitive to light pressure, such as from a stylus. An X-Y coordinate pair is returned continuously, which can be interpreted in the same way as a mouse movement, or used for precision work such as the tracing of a drawing.

### Performance of pointing devices
Figure 5.6 shows the relative positioning times for a key-driven cursor and a mouse-driven cursor.

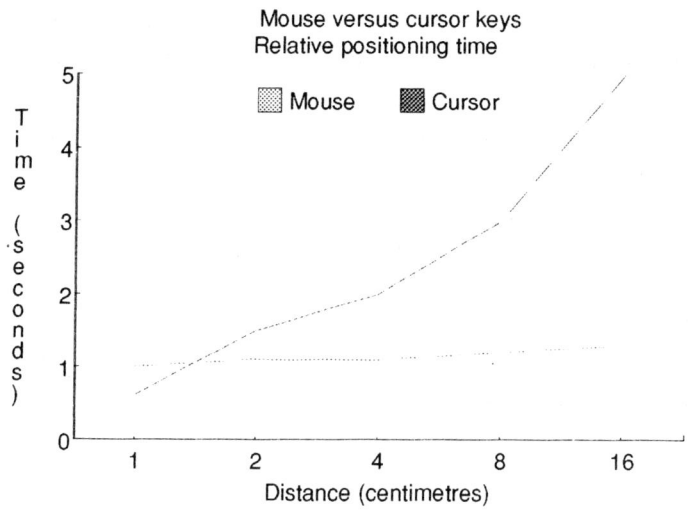

*Figure 5.6 Relative positioning times using mouse and cursor keys. Note that for the shortest distance, use of the cursor key is superior. (Card et al, 1978; From Shneiderman, 1987).*

For the shortest distances (less than 1.5 centimetres), the key-driven cursor is superior. In this experiment, the display used contained textual data, and so for a distance of 1 or 2 characters the keyboard gives a more positive and accurate movement.

## Output devices

### Displays

By far the most common output device is the raster-graphics (TV-type) display; that is, a colour or monochrome display driven by a single electron beam which is rapidly modulated to give the illusion of a solid display. Most displays nowadays are integral to the computer system that they serve, and share the same memory. Figure 5.7 shows the operation of a typical raster graphics display.

In a raster display, the electron beam is modulated according to the contents of an area of memory in the computer known as the video memory. In simple displays, a bit set indicates a colour (Red, Green or Blue); in more complex displays, each colour can have up to 256 levels (RGB Analogue). Resolution ranges from 320 by 256 points up to 1280 by 1024 points.

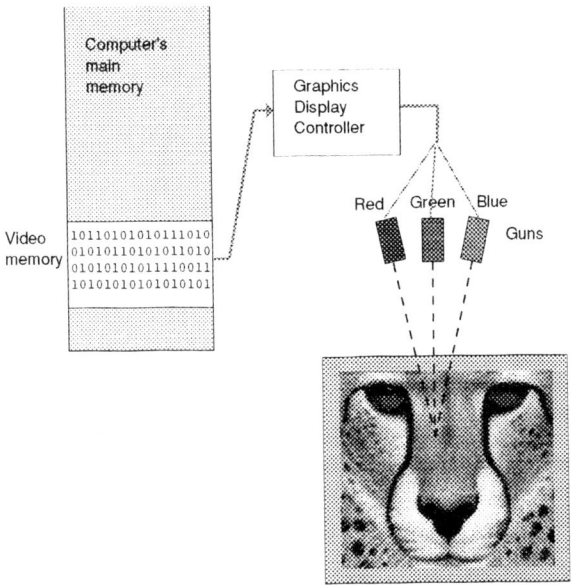

*Figure 5.7 Operation of a raster graphics display.*

In a typical system, the user will spend a great deal of time sitting in front of such a display, focusing on the text and graphics it produces. There are some points to note regarding legibility and fatigue:

- A monochrome monitor is less fatiguing than a normal colour monitor. The scan rate (in frames per second) is the same, but the phosphor is generally of a higher-persistence type so the image is more flicker-free.

- If a colour monitor is chosen, the multiple scan type is better. On a computer which offers multiple graphics modes, the user can experiment until a 'favourite' resolution is found. For example, the text for this book was edited using an Acorn Archimedes in Mode 82 (16 colours, 896 by 352 pixels, 57 Hz scan rate). For the author, this scan rate was flicker-free, but a drop to a 51Hz scan rate (mode 78) caused noticeable flicker. A 'boost' to Mode 83 (256 colours) caused a subtle improvement because the colours could be set up with great precision, the author's favourite being parchment text on a royal blue background. Later, the author discovered Mode 86 (16 colours, 832 by 336 pixels, 63Hz scan rate) which proved much steadier and fatigue-free.

- The very high resolution monochrome monitors beloved of Unix users are flicker-free at (70 - 90Hz) but some sizes of text font can be difficult to display without fatigue. The picture is so sharp that any 'jagged edges' can be perceived.

**Text display**

In the 'old days' (that is, about two years ago) the display of text was a fairly simple procedure. A character generator (generally in Read-Only Memory - ROM) provided the dot patterns needed to generate characters on the screen. Usually the characters were on a fairly coarse dot matrix, from 8 by 8 to 19 by 10. This latter pitch gave well-formed characters on an IBM PC monochrome display.

More recently, applications such as Desktop Publishing (DTP) have made much more stringent demands on displays. The problem is that text needs to be displayed in a wide range of fonts (styles) and sizes, yet the display resolution is fixed. At the same time, the fonts are much more complex than the simple 'system' fonts previously in use, and need more dots to achieve a realistic representation. Finally, if text in a given font is to be displayed in a wide range of sizes, possibly on the same page, then what is the definitive dot pitch for it to be displayed? Too small, and it will appear 'jagged' when made larger. Too large, and the computations needed become time-consuming.

### Outline fonts

The 'matrix size' problem discussed above can be overcome by storing a font (that is, the entire character set in a given style) as a set of *outlines*. Changing size then involves a recalculation (to a *bitmap*) in the resolution of the display device involved. There are advantages:

- The same font can be used for all display devices - screens and printers

- The font is always displayed in the maximum resolution that the device is capable of

The disadvantages are:

- Frequent changes of font or size involve substantial recalculation of the bitmaps - this can be avoided by reserving memory as a *cache* to store bitmaps so that they do not need to be recalculated, or by storing some precomputed bitmaps on disk for rapid access.

- On a slow computer (less than, say, 1 million instructions per second - MIPS) the recalculation can be slow, and refreshing a page can be a leisurely activity.

### Anti-aliasing

As mentioned earlier, there is a problem when attempting to display high-quality text on raster displays; at small sizes, the text appears 'lumpy', or *greeked* because the size of, say, an upright is not an exact multiple of the pixel resolution of the screen. This also renders the text less legible.

The problem is alleviated by *grey-shading* pixels. Figure 5.8 illustrates the technique.

The 'staircase' typically obtained when a sloping line is rendered on a low-resolution graphics device is 'softened' by grey-shading certain pixels. If you hold the book at arm's length, looking at Figure 5.8, and almost close your eyes, you will see the effect of the anti-aliasing (The effect is better if you look through a pinhole in a piece of card.)

This is approximately equivalent to seeing the text displayed at 6 points (1 point=1/72nd inch) on a colour screen of 850 by 350 pixels resolution, at which size it is just legible. On a monochrome screen it is not legible at all, because the shading operation cannot be performed, and the characters are 'Greeked'.

It is interesting to note that anti-aliased text on a medium resolution colour screen is often more legible, and less fatiguing, than normal text on a high resolution monochrome monitor, possibly because the eye-brain combination is trying to perform its own smoothing process on the monochrome image, and failing.

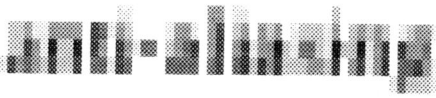

*Figure 5.8 Anti-aliased characters.*

### *Hinting*

This is not the whole story: even at 300 dots per inch resolution, as on a laser printer, characters do not look quite right. Because of very subtle perceptual effects, the characters look distorted. One solution, known to printers for hundreds of years, is *hinting* - a process whereby the shapes of letters are distorted by subtle thickening and adding 'blobs' in various places.

Overall, it is interesting how the typesetter's art has been accommodated by the technologist and the informed user to achieve a symbiosis. This is not restricted to desktop publishing - the film-maker's skills will soon be in demand by the multi-media authors, as will the sound recordist's.

## Novel devices

It is arguable that using the human hand to produce only 2-dimensional movements plus a button press, as in the case of a mouse, is a waste of resources. Each finger is capable of a wide range of movements, both singly and in combination. If this could be harnessed in a reliable way, then a much richer repertoire of input signals is available.

### The Dataglove

Perhaps this is the ultimate expression of a hand-operated device. Rather than capturing the gross movements of the hand and fingers (as, for example, with a mouse or joystick and buttons), the movement of the fingers relative to one another is translated by stretch sensors embedded in a close-fitting glove.

The number of degrees of freedom (i.e. possible range of movements) is greatly enhanced, and has significant consequences for the design of interfaces to complex systems. Assuming one glove per hand, the possible enhancements to an interface could be:

- enabling concurrent operations to be signalled by the movement of both hands

- subtle or delicate operations to be carried out

- complex operations could be signalled by combining movements from both hands: for example, a whole collection of objects such as files or 'folders' could be grasped by a two-handed motion, moved and then literally dropped in another place.

### Other devices

Many other kinds of device exist for performing input and output. The *joystring* (described by Foley[24]) consists of a short T-bar which is grasped in the palm of the hand, with strings attached (rather like a puppet). The relative movement of the strings produces signals in a variety of planes, which can be interpreted in a number of ways.

Additionally, servomotors attached to the strings can exert force on the user, and many force-feedback situations can be simulated.

Head-up displays, where the information is projected onto a transparent screen some distance ahead of operator, are familiar to pilots. They have been developed also for the computer user. If mounted directly in front of the eyes, with each screen providing half of a 3-dimensional image, a genuine *alternative reality* can be simulated. This has possibilities in a variety of areas - engineering, medicine, art, etc. In the United States, te National Aeronautics and Space Administration (NASA) has developed, at its Ames research centre, a complete alternative reality kit, with dataglove, voice recogniser and head-up display. Input can be by pointing, voice or gesture. In this way, a number of alternative realities (such as the repair of a space station in orbit) can be simulated, and human performance assessed without the expense of a space shuttle mission.

Some devices appear, at first scrutiny, to be rather silly. The *wobble-board* is a flat seat that is pivoted at its centre: input is achieved by moving the lower body around. For users with a mobility problem, however, it could be an ideal solution.

## Summary

The attention to detail evidenced by the various devices we have discussed in this chapter may seem unduly extreme; but it must be remembered that many people spend their entire working day in front of some kind of keyboard and some sort of display. The sad fact is that very few of these people are aware of the best way in which the input/output devices can be arranged or configured, and employers are equally uninformed.

In the 'old days', when the choice of display was limited to a slightly fuzzy green on black, there was some excuse for overlooking the problems that badly designed workstations could cause; but in these days of very high resolution colour displays, with literally millions of options, there is no excuse for putting users thorough the same torture. But the evidence is that we are still doing it.

# 6 Voice input and output

*Speech is the channel of the future*

*Nicholas Negroponte*

## Introduction

Although the keyboard seems to have been accepted as the standard I/O device for some time, and is assured of a future for some kinds of data capture, its suitability has to be reviewed in the light of 'user pull' and 'technological push' (for an explanation of these terms see Chapter 1).

Many users, if pressed, might report that they would prefer a more 'natural' mode of communication. Voice is certainly a more natural mode for human to human communication, so it seems reasonable to suppose that the human-computer interface would be improved by exploiting voice.

Shneiderman [62} has identified the following reasons for adopting a voice *input* strategy:

- The user's hands are busy

- Mobility is required (i.e. data entry on the move)

- The user's eyes are occupied

- Harsh conditions are encountered

Another reason for using voice input is that the user may not be able to operate a keyboard for reasons of disability.

The problems with voice as an input medium are, or have been, that:

- The algorithms necessary to recognise spoken sounds are complex

- The hardware is fairly specialised and expensive

- Users may have to adapt their behaviour in ways they find unacceptable, especially if simple voice recognition systems are used.

- The feature that most users would like, the ability to understand connected speech, is the most difficult to implement.

However, sufficient advances have been made over the past few years to warrant the serious examination of voice, and sound, as an I/O medium.

## Types of voice recognition system

Voice recognition (VR) systems may be broadly classified along two dimensions:

- Speaker dependent or speaker independent

- Isolated words or connected speech

This gives us four basic types of system to discuss, and it is convenient to do this in order of difficulty. Firstly, however, we need to consider how voice (and other) sounds are captured and stored in a computer system.

## Voice sampling

The first step in all VR interfaces is to sample the analogue waveform that constitutes the voice signal. Varying patterns of air pressure are picked up by a microphone and input to an analogue-to-digital converter (ADC). The result is a string (or vector) of binary numbers which represents the input waveform (see Chapter 3 for a basic introduction to information theory). Depending on the VR system in use, there may be further processing to transform the 'raw' waveform data into something more useful, such as a frequency-time-energy spectrum, or power spectrum, such as shown in figure 6.2. This is more useful for the more advanced methods. For simple systems, a more restricted set of features may be extracted, such as frequency over time or energy over time.

Figure 6.1 illustrates a sample of spoken speech, the words "The Mask".

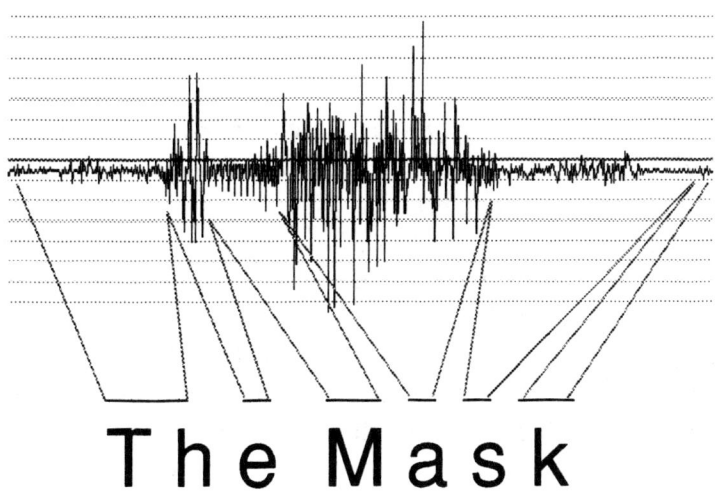

*Figure 6.1 A sampled speech waveform. The sample was taken using the "Armadeus" hardware and software package (courtesy Clares Micro Supplies)*

analogue waveform ⟶ A to D Converter

freq/time/energy
Spectrum ⟵ binary vector (input wave) ⟵

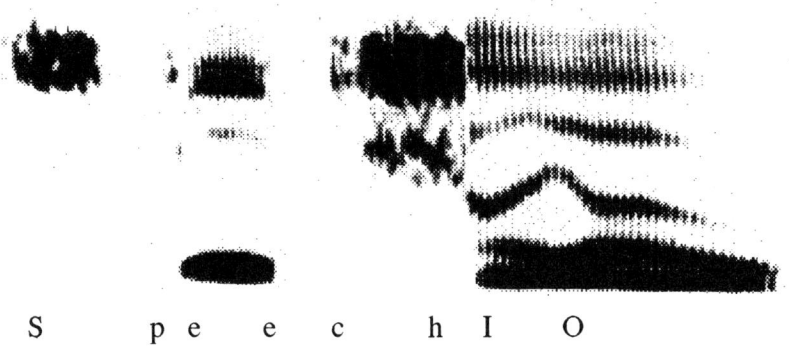

S     p e    e    c    h   I    O

*Figure 6.2 A frequency/time/energy (FTE) spectrum of the words 'Speech I/O'. (Courtesy Dr. R. Moore, Royal Signals and Radar Establishment)*

The most striking feature about the waveform is the disparity between the different amounts of *energy* allocated to different parts of the utterance. The '**a**' of 'mask' in figure 6.1 represents two orders of magnitude more energy than the '**k**', and occupies far more time, yet both are significant in recognising the utterance. This may be due to relative differences in the sensitivity of the ear to certain type of sound, but it is also known that speech is still quite comprehensible if all the vowel sounds are removed altogether.

It should be evident now why the task of disambiguating, say, the words **mask** and **mast** would be extremely difficult for a simple voice recognition system.

We will now review the major types of VR system.

## Speaker-dependent systems

### Isolated word recognition
Early VR systems adopted this strategy, which has the merits of relative

simplicity and of needing only unsophisticated hardware. After sampling, as discussed above, a simple time-varying feature (such as frequency or energy) is extracted. This feature vector is matched, in turn, against one of a number of templates held in memory. The template which gives the best match is judged to be the correct item. It is necessary to build some latitude into the matching process, as even with the same speaker uttering the same sound there is a natural variability - in the time taken to utter the voiced command, the pitch, etc. There are also well-documented *diurnal* (daily) variations - peoples' voices tend to be lower in the mornings and evenings, and higher at midday.

This variability is 'built into' each template by allowing a number of samples to be taken and the variability (in terms of a simple statistical measure such as the mean - or average) to be assessed. This is then taken into account when matching the samples. These systems require 'training' to the voice of a particular user, and are generally suited to applications making simple demands on the VR facility, such as the entry of numeric codes in a stocktaking system. In combination with other modes, such as direct manipulation, quite complex systems can be driven in a 'hands-off' manner as long as the restrictions of the system are recognised.

### *Performance of simple systems*

Although the ultimate performance of such systems is limited, careful arrangement of certain factors can make the best use of them:

- Careful design of the dialogue, in particular, the the choice path through a series of voice-driven menus. For example, allowing no more than 8 choices at each point, with each choice leading to 8 more, can give acceptable results.

- Careful choice of the words used at choice points. Some words are highly confusable - 'nine', 'five'.

## Speaker-independent systems

As mentioned above, there is a degree of variability in the human voice *within* people, but there is even more variability *between* people. The obvious difference is between male and female voices, and a more sophisticated statistical process is needed to discriminate between them. Alternatively, a greater number of templates can be stored, with 'male' and 'female' sets of templates being compared.

## Dynamic programming systems

The problem of variability has been identified as central to voice recognition systems, and a simple template matching approach has been discussed. This poses problems when extremes of length, pitch etc. have to be accommodated. One technique, which has been applied with success in a variety of problem domains, is *dynamic programming*. It is a technique which seeks to establish the minimum-cost difference between two waveforms. Imagine the various ways in which the word 'WINE' could be transformed to the word 'WATER' by changing one letter at a time. One of those ways will involve the least 'effort', that is, the minimum number of operations. The same problem occurs when trying to match an unknown word to a template. There are many ways in which they differ, but how can the least-cost difference be identified? With the large amounts of variability we are dealing with, it looks like a complex task.

Dynamic programming (which is a technique, not a programming language) provides a solution. Imagine that the samples and templates are stored as frequency-time-energy (FTE) spectra as shown in Figure 6.2. A simple way of matching them would be to perform a *cross-correlation* between the two, in which the frequency/energy spectra at each time-frame were compared. This would suffice if it were known that the samples were *synchronic* - that is, locked together in time, and that the same fundamental frequencies were present. The result from the correlation would then be a list, or vector, of 'distances' which could be summed to provide an overall measure.

If we accept that one sample may be time-shifted relative to another, it is evident that this simple scheme will not work. It is in fact necessary to match every frame in the sample with every frame in the template. But this, as it stands, does not benefit the recognition process. We merely end up with more figures. What we need is a way of checking the relative importance of each distance measure as we proceed through the data. This process of optimising each measure is central to dynamic programming.In detail, the process is as follows (readers who require more detail should refer to Moore [48]). For readers familiar to the procedure, the principle of dynamic programming is similar to the Critical Path Analysis technique used in project management.

Firstly, a distance matrix is built up by comparing frames in the sample and the template. The first ROW and the first COLUMN of this distance matrix is used to fill in the first row and column of a second matrix, the distance matrix. The rest of the cost matrix is filled in in the following way: each entry comprises a sum calculated by adding the corresponding value from the distance matrix to the *minimum* distance value from one of the three possible precursors (above, left, and above/left). At the same time, a pointer is set up from this cell to the co-ordinate of the cell from which the minimum value was taken. This process is continued until the cost matrix is full. What the contents of each cell of the cost matrix then represents is the 'least cost' route of getting to that cell.When the last cell of the cost matrix has been filled, the pointers are consulted, and a backtracking process carried out. As each cell is referenced (pointed to), the value of its contents is added to a sum. When the backtracking process is complete, the resulting sum represents the least-cost distance measure. This is repeated for all the templates in the system. The template with the lowest distance measure is taken to be the successful candidate. This process is illustrated graphically in Figure 6.3 (as described by Kavaler et al[39]). Note that in this diagram, the two words start in the lower left-hand corner, and the dynamic programming process proceeds rightwards and upwards.

## Connected speech recognition

The task of recognising connected speech is much more complex than the task of recognising a string of individual words. Take the well-known (and probably over-used) phrase "bread and butter". If asked to speak this phrase, few people will enunciate each word clearly. The most common rendition is "bread'n'butter" (if people are on their best behaviour) or, in extreme cases, "brembutta". The 'and' has disappeared completely, and if a FTE spectrum were examined it would be seen that changes have occurred to the first and last words in the phrase. This distortion (known as *prosody*) is probably due to such factors as (i) necessary adjustments in

PROSODY

the articulatory system to enable the free flow of speech, and (ii) a need to introduce some 'streamlining' of the message to make use of redundancies in the recipient's cognitive system - a Geordie will find it difficult to understand a Bristolian, but they are both speaking the same language. This is acceptable where the recipient is a human being, but provides an enormous computational load for a computer. It is extremely difficult, at the current state of psycholinguistics, to establish a formal method to cope with prosody. Each phrase introduces its own distortions.

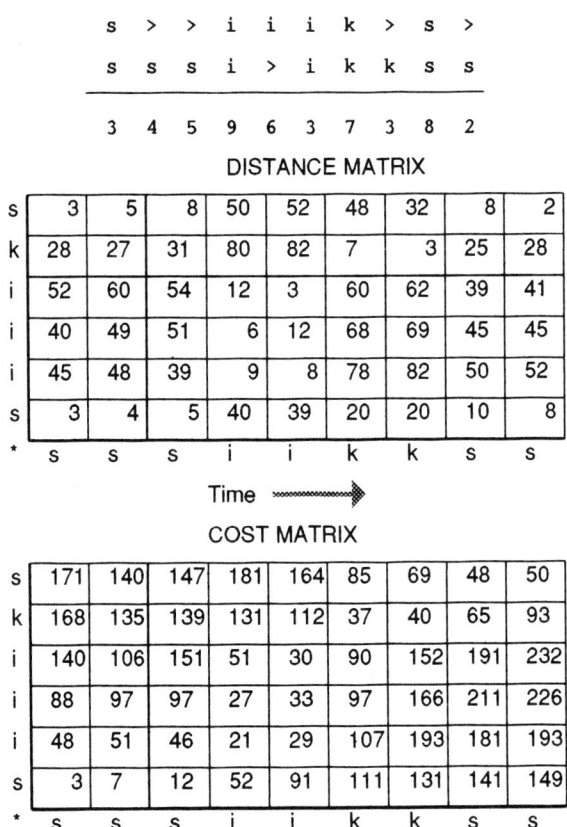

*Figure 6.3 Dynamic programming comparison of 'siiiks' and 'sssiikkss' (after Kavaler et al)*

One way to cope with prosody is to accept that the semantic units of a language are probably larger than the phonemes which comprise it, and to extend the vocabulary of a VR unit to accommodate phrases and even entire sentences.

The dynamic programming algorithm, described above can be extended to recognise whole phrases and sentences - all that is required is a larger matrix.

## More advanced VR systems

In real life, the recognition of spoken words is dependent on more than an analysis of the FTE spectra of voiced sounds. Other aspects, such as inflection, accent etc. are equally important as carriers of information. Conversely, a knowledge of the speech characteristics of a particular speaker could result in more efficient recognition. Additionally, in many specialised situations, jargon words may be used extensively, and a useful VR system would be 'tuned' to these.

One way of being less dependent on the physical characteristics of the sound alone would be for the VR system to have some 'knowledge' of, say, the user's accent and how it is likely to modify standard words. The words themselves could then be stored as a dictionary of pronunciation rules, which would not vary from speaker to speaker.

## A case study

The design of real systems requires more than just plugging a voice recognition card into a computer and modifying an application's interface.

A study carried out by Frankish et al[26] on a voice driven input to parcel sorting machines illustrates this very well. Normally, each parcel has to be manipulated into position by the postman, its address read, and one of about 50 keys pressed to assign the name and direct the parcel to the correct destination. Voice input was seen as providing promising improvements in both speed and error rate. A pilot study indicated that merely saying the names - 'Birmingham', 'Cambridge' - resulted in an unacceptable error rate (about 20% - too high for this application.) An alternative condition, using the ICAO (International Civil Aviation Organisation) code equivalents was therefore added. Typical codes might be 'Bravo One' or 'Charlie Two'. As these codes had been developed for high discriminability in noisy conditions, the expected error rate was low.

The results were analysed in terms of throughput (speed) and error rate, and are graphically displayed in Figure 6.4.

### Speed performance

Place names were superior to ICAO codes in terms of the number of postal codes per hour, although the difference is not as great as expected due to the fact that the ICAO codes were spoken more quickly. Contributory to the slow rate of the ICAO codes was the fact that the speech recognition apparatus was an isolated-word device rather than a connected-speech device. This imposed a delay between the parts of a 2-part code, which would have reduced the ICAO result by about 6 minutes compared with 1 minute for the placename condition.

### Error performance of VR equipment

In terms of correctly identified overall codes, there was a slight advantage for place names. If analysed in terms of the individual items, the recognition rate was the same. However, this concealed a superiority, in the ICAO vocabulary, of letters over numbers (it is only the letters which have been selected for maximum discriminability).

For the 2-part codes, the recognition performance is lower, as 2 correct responses have to be made for each code. As the ICAO condition contained a higher proportion of 2-part codes, there is an inbuilt bias to error. Moreover, the need to *segment* the codes (i.e., speak distinctly) to suit the isolated recogniser led to further errors when this was incorrectly done. Frankish et al recommended the use of a connected speech recogniser as a result of this finding.

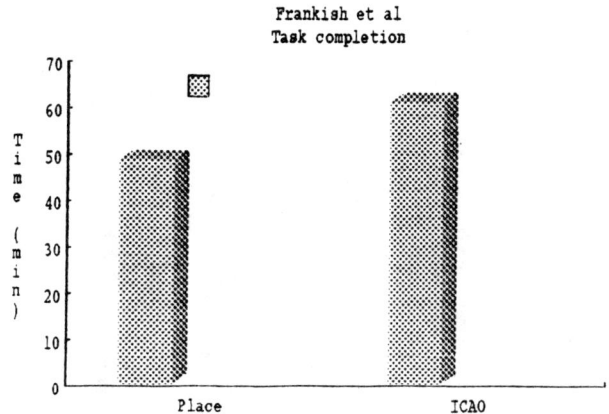

*Figure  6.4  (a)  Speed  performance  in  the  Frankish  et  al experiment*

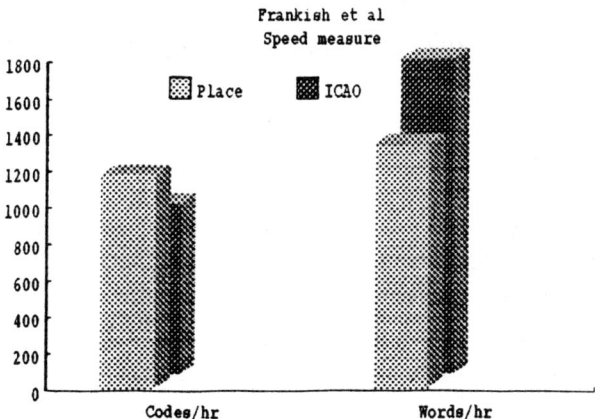

*Figure  6.4  (b)  Speed  performance  in  the  Frankish  et  al. experiment*

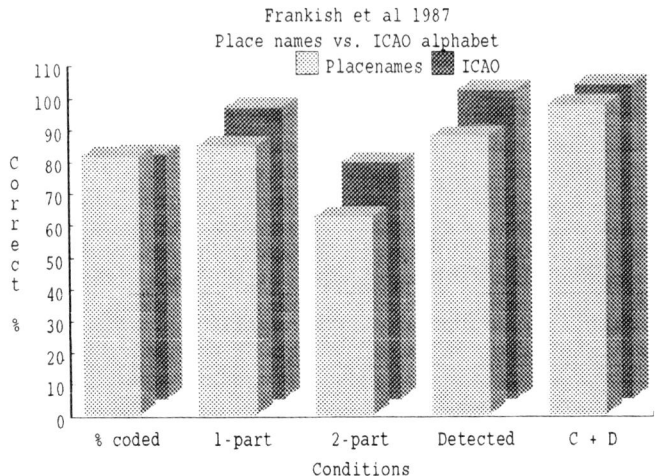

*Figure 6.4 (c) - Error performance in the Frankish et al experiment*

### Recognition performance

There are two types of recognition failure: *misrecognitions*, where a word is incorrectly identified as some other word in the vocabulary; and *detectable failures*, where no member of the vocabulary is recognised. Although the results showed that the overall failure rate was higher for the ICAO codes, the important measure in assessing the performance of this kind of system is the sum of correctly identified words *plus* identifiable errors. On this measure, there is a clear superiority of the ICAO code over place names - 99.6% as against 98.2, as shown in Fig 6.4(c).

### Conclusions

The basic issue is of vocabulary size and type versus performance. The ICAO code can be regarded as a special purpose vocabulary, of smaller size and greater discriminability than a normal vocabulary. Frankish et al stress that the effective design of systems incorporating voice recognisers cannot proceed without close attention to this issue.

## Voice output

The use of voice, or sound, for output has always been a feature of computing. Even a primitive 'beep' serves to alert a user to an error condition in a way which a visual message can not. Generally, little information is carried in a 'beep' - it is merely a signal (in Rasmussen's terms - see Chapter 3) and more information must be sought, which will probably be on the screen.

There are certain advantages in conveying more information in the auditory modality, now that the technology enables us to do so:

- humans are quite good at storing short-term auditory information and performing significant amounts of processing on it - visual information is more volatile

- The presentation of the error information in the same modality as the initial alert leads to fewer mistakes in identifying the source of the error - on the Apple Macintosh, for example, an agonised 'eek!' can be made to indicate certain error conditions. (In the author's experience, the novelty wears thin after about 5 errors - and, indeed, seriously worried an electrician who happened to be in the same room.)

- With more sophisticated sound systems, positional information can be conveyed. For example, with an 8-channel sound system, speakers could be positioned around the user's head so that auditory cues are provided which direct the attention to a particular part of the screen.

- Quite complex cues could be incorporated into the auditory message to indicate various error conditions - pitch, volume, timbre and duration could all be altered. A long, loud 'squawk' would be acted on more rapidly and assiduously than a short, quiet 'hoot'.

- Speech provides a new dimension, although its use should be carefully considered.

- Users with a visual handicap are better served by auditory signals.

**Speech synthesis**

The simplest, and most precise, method of achieving voice output is to perform digital to analogue conversion of the original encoded speech. This is acceptable if isolated fragments of speech, or indeed long stretches of speech or music, are to be output. For connected speech, however, the problems of organising and storing such large amounts of data become significant.

As we have seen earlier in this chapter, features can be extracted from speech and used in the recognition process. If this process is reversed, that is if features are used to drive a voice synthesis system, then there is a great saving on the amount of data needed (remembering that reasonable high-fidelity reproduction of the human voice requires about 50,000 bytes per second of data).

The most commonly used technique is known as Linear Predictive Coding. The sound to be produced is represented as a stream of time frames, each frame being a segment of a frequency-time-energy spectrum as discussed earlier. The spectrum itself could be derived naturally, or be synthesised. Each time frame contains information about the frequency of three or more *formants*. A formant is one of the fundamental frequencies that can be produced by the human voice, and is determined by physiological factors such as the configuration of the speaker's nasal cavity, etc. Other sounds are present in natural speech, and must be simulated to achieve a good effect: *fricative* sounds ('fff', 'sss', 'ch', 't'); *plosive* sounds ('p', 't'); *glottal stops* (uncommon in English, but the Cockney pronunciation of 'bottle' contains a glottal stop); and *nasal resonances* (which give the characteristic 'timbre' to a voice - few people have any difficulty distinguishing, say, Clive James from Melvyn Bragg).

The pattern of formants for various common voiced sounds is shown in Figure 6.5.

At each time frame, the appropriate levels and frequencies of each formant are applied to a system of sound generators and filters, as shown in figure 6.6. The result is speech, of a quality determined by:

- The frequency (and hence resolution) of the time frames

- The accuracy of the phonemic representation of the words

- The accuracy, and number, of the various filters

Another advantage of taking this approach is that much less data needs to be transmitted to maintain a normal rate of speech. The LPC technique is thus well suited for transmitting voice data over computer networks, for example in an X window client/server configuration (see chapter 8).

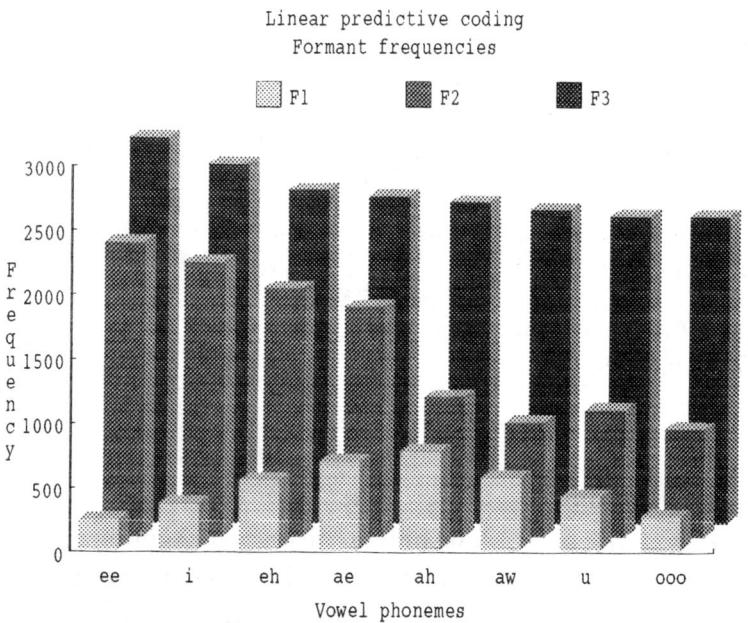

*Figure 6.5 Formant frequencies of some common phonemes (from Cater, 1983)*

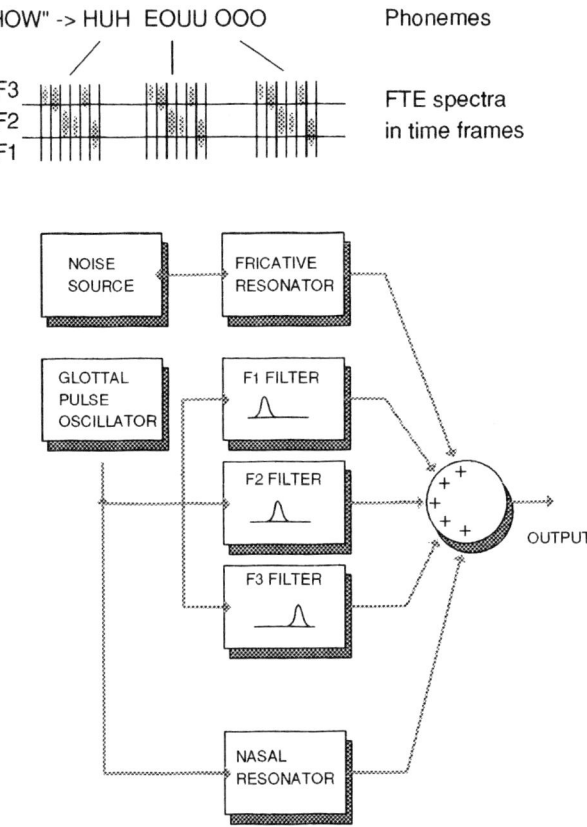

*Figure 6.6 Voice synthesis using Linear Predictive Coding (after Cater, 1983)*

## Voice communications

Conventionally, voice is transmitted using conventional analogue channels. However, this is quite inefficient, and can consume much of the available bandwidth when it is desired to mix voice and conventional data. For example, the 'kilostream' service of British Telecom runs at 64K bits per second; medium-quality transmission of speech can consume 50K bits per second. This does not leave much of the bandwidth (see chapter 3) for the data.

One obvious solution is to limit the information which is sent over the voice channel by using, for example, linear predictive coding (LPC) techniques for voice synthesis and sending only phoneme codes. This can result, however, in low-quality speech. Nevertheless, this basic notion of building some 'intelligence' into the receiving end could be extended so that high-quality speech could be produced.

Imagine that the advanced voice recognition system, discussed above, could be put into reverse. It would only need to receive the code for a word, which would be spoken according to the pronunciation rules held in the dictionary. Various accents or inflections could be added to add effect to the message, and this information could be incorporated with little overhead as a 'header'. These features could be incorporated on an additive basis and used as appropriate.

For example, troops in the field would be much more likely to respond rapidly to the clipped tones of Lord Montgomery of Alamein than if, say, Woody Allen were to be used as the medium. For greater efficiency still, regional variations could be incorporated - a Geordie soldier would be agreeably surprised if his commanding officer addressed him in the familiar tones of Walker rather than the drawl of Sandhurst.

## Summary

Voice input/output is essential in certain situations, and desirable in others. The technology is improving all the time, and the recognition of connected speech - and its direct transcription to text - will have major consequences in many areas, not just in computing, when it is perfected.

Meanwhile, the systems already in place can deliver adequate performance if certain guidelines are observed.

# 7 Interfaces

## Introduction

Although it is common to think of the 'interface' as the actual display with which the user interacts, it equally valid to regard, for example, programming languages themselves as interfaces, albeit of a less direct kind. Equally well, a visual display which emulates in some way a real control panel (such as a mimic screen in a power station) is an interface in which the various elements comprise the elements of the real interface - dials, switches etc.

Moreover, the software design process itself, in the form of the formalisms, syntax and semantics of the various program design methodologies, interact significantly with the designer's cognition with regard to the application being developed.

Finally, the operating system command interpreter itself may be regarded as a language, and as operating systems offer more and more functionality, the distinction between 'programming language' and 'operating system interface' will probably become less sharply defined.

## Command line interfaces

The command level of interaction forms an intermediate layer in terms of our 3-layer communications model of HCI. It should not be viewed as a more primitive precursor of visual interfaces, because, as we will see, the two can work together in building interfaces. Moreover, in certain situations, command languages are more appropriate. In spite of recent developments, command languages are still the way most people interact with a computer.

In this chapter the basic purposes and characteristics of programming languages and command languages are reviewed, followed by some examples from the real world.

## Purposes of a command language

The main purpose of a command language is to facilitate communication between a user and an application running on a computer system. Note that we do not distinguish here between *built-in*, or permanently resident, commands, and *transient* commands, which are loaded for the purpose of executing the command and are then discarded or overwritten. The syntax is (or should be) the same.

## Syntax

The syntax of a language can be defined in terms of the constraints it imposes on the various combinations that can be made using the elements of the language. This is true whether we are looking at a natural language (such as English) or a synthetic language (such as Esperanto). All computer command languages are by their nature synthetic. The purpose of a syntax is to enable a language to carry a rich enough set of messages so that useful work can be performed, yet remain simple enough to be memorable and usable.

Figure 7.1 illustrates the syntax of the command line interpreter (CLI) in MSDOS, a simple and popular operating system for personal computers. The main command appears first, possibly prefixed by a *pathname* which indicates which directory it is to be run from if it is a program. The rest of the command is known as the *command tail*, which provides information to the process constituting the command. For example, if it is a file handling command, then the filenames will have to be made 'known' to the command.

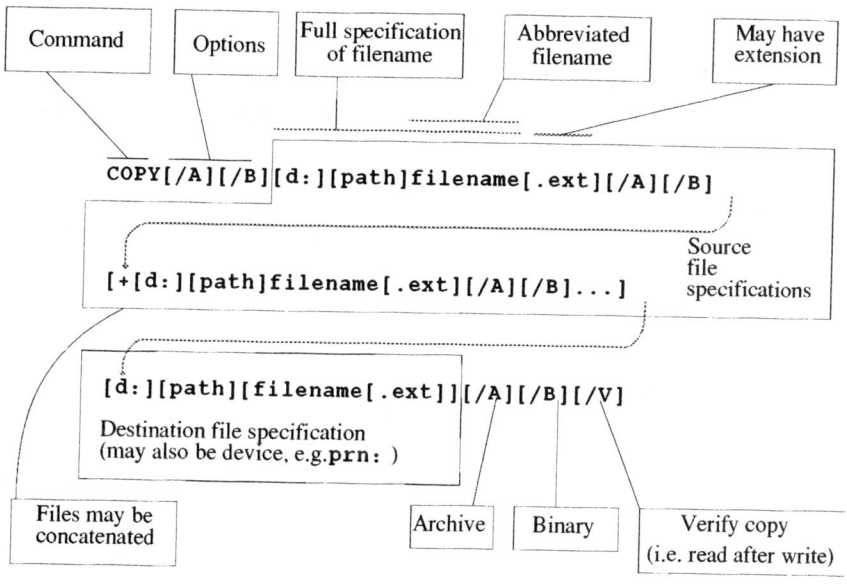

*Figure 7.1 MSDOS command-line interface (CLI) syntax for the COPY command*

## Batch languages

It is often convenient to redirect the input to a command line interpreter so that it comes from a file rather than directly from the user via the keyboard. In the simplest case, the language used will correspond exactly to the language used by the command line interpreter. More usually, it is enhanced to allow such constructs as looping, variables, conditional testing and so on. With a powerful *batch language*, entire applications can be written.

Many operating systems have raised the status of the batch language to a high level - particularly Unix, on which the *shell script* is a fully-featured language.

# Programming languages

Whatever kind of interaction the user has with the operating system, it is likely that a programming language will provide the interface between the problem domain and the underlying machine. It is important to understand the relationship between the various problem domains (science, commerce, linguistics, statistics, symbolic logic) and the languages that act as a vehicle for solutions.

In some cases, languages are so tightly matched to the exigencies of the problem domain that the two naturally go together - COBOL for commercial applications, CORAL-66 for real time applications, and so on. Occasionally, languages developed for a specific domain are discovered to have a general utility: Prolog was developed for solving problems in symbolic logic, but finds itself used ·in natural language analysis, databases, expert systems etc. In the long term, this could be regarded as a measure of the power of a language. Whatever the problem, and whatever the language, the user's task is to extract knowledge from the problem space and translate it into a form which is digestible by the chosen programming language. It is worth spending a little time considering some aspects of this process.

### Knowledge abstraction

Abbott[1] has characterised the typical programming language as an interface between a problem space and a solution space. The effectiveness of this interface depends on a number of factors, but Abbott has identified the problem of *knowledge abstraction* as being central in this context.

In the early days of computing, the programmer worked very closely with the machine, and the problem elements were transformed into machine code directly. As more useful concepts were developed, such as general subroutines and variables, the 'machine' that programmers were dealing with became more abstract (hence 'knowledge abstraction'), less machine-like and more expressive. It could be 'driven' from a sheet of paper, rather than front panel switches. In the case of scientific languages like FORTRAN, the domain syntax (scientific formulae) could be translated directly from written notation into machine language. For scientists, therefore, FORTRAN represented an efficient interface between their problems and the computer-based solutions.

Later, procedural languages were developed whose syntax conformed more closely with other domain requirements, most notably COBOL (common business-oriented language) which, surprisingly enough, was intended to enable businessmen to write their own programs. For some reason this idea did not catch on.

## 4GLs

The earliest way of interfacing to a computer was to enter binary instructions directly - true *machine code*. This has been termed, retrospectively, a first-generation language or '1GL'. The *assemblers* which enabled these codes to be expressed as simple mnemonics were 2GLs. Procedural languages such as FORTRAN, COBOL, Pascal and C have been termed 3GLs.

4GLs are much more domain specific. In brief, they act as 'application generators', either by compiling high-level statements in a domain-specific language to code in a 3GL or by executing as interpreters at run time (for more information on these topics, see Maddix and Morgan [43]).

## 5GLs

One drawback of conventional programming languages (including 4GLs) is their essential *procedurality*. All problems must be reduced to a set of procedures, a process which could be seen as damaging the knowledge structures extracted from the problem domain. For solutions which are naturally highly procedural - such as finite element analysis - this is not a problem. A difficulty does arise, however, when certain classes of problem are addressed. A classic example is the route-finding problem, where, given a matrix of cities and their distances apart, the user needs to know the shortest route from one to the other.

Using a conventional language, such as Pascal or C, it is necessary to maintain complex schemes of pointers so that the original problem is obscured. With a knowledge-based language such as Prolog, the problem can be expressed in more natural terms, and a domain specialist can easily become a proficient programmer.

# Domain-specific interfaces

Very often, computer systems are used to directly replace older technology, but, for a variety of reasons, it is not wished to dispense with the operating interface and procedures that went with the old system. One example would be a power station, but there are a number of reasons (including the need for absolute security) why the incorporation of computer-based interfaces has been slow. However, the importance of a clear, understandable interface has been highlighted recently by several unfortunate accidents (see chapter 13), and the industry is beginning to respond accordingly.

## Interfaces for operators

There are several advantages to using a computer-based interface in comparison with the conventional control panel:

- A virtual view can be obtained, where the display can be seen as 'scrolling' around a much bigger workspace.

- The view can be 'zoomed' in and out.

- Multiple views can be set up to suit the operator - each view would be in a separate window

- Reconfigurable display - various indicators can be set up with different parameters

- Logical grouping - operators can lay out the various controls and indicators to suit their preferences

- The performance of the interface can be 'tuned' in the light of operational experience.

- Online documentation - error or alert conditions can be expanded, or explanatory dialogues entered into

- Operators can interact by voice, text, or example when a situation arises.

- The inputs and outputs of the system (text, graphics etc.) can be imported and exported to/from standard packages such as spreadsheets, presentation graphics, and word processors.

- The state of the system can be continuously recorded so that an 'action replay' is possible in the event of a failure.

- Some degree of 'intelligent assistance' could be built in, for the detection of common patterns of events which may escape the human operator

- Various tests for operator alertness, fatigue levels, etc. could be incorporated.

- A simulation mode could be entered, in which the operator could investigate various 'hunches' about system behaviour.


**Interfaces for scientists**

Figure 7.2 shows a typical screen from the 'LabView' system developed by National Instruments. This interface (running in this case on an Apple Macintosh personal computer) enables the user to build  a complete emulation of the typical facilities to be found on laboratory instruments.

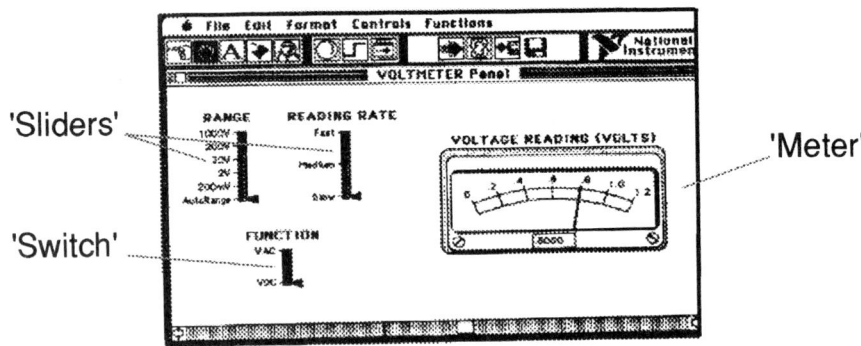

*Figure 7.2 A typical 'LabView' screen*

Note that the control and information interface uses familiar switches, sliders and dials. The user's view is of the instrument with which he/she is familiar, not of a computer. The computer-like aspects of the interface are restricted to the mouse (unless a touch screen is employed).

### Interfaces for designers and artists

With increasing computer power and display capabilities, and the incorporation of very sophisticated graphics procedures at a low level (for example, within the computer's operating system), professionals in disciplines such as architecture, graphic design, engineering etc. find it natural to use computers for their work.

The requirement for the interface is quite simple: it must emulate paper, pens, rulers and erasers (for the draughtsman); or paper, brushes, paint and, possibly, a damp rag (for the artist). The illusion must be preserved in spite of the fact that the results must be viewed, on relatively low-resolution displays, as patterns of small dots.

It is convenient to distinguish between *painting*-type applications and *drawing*-type applications, although sometimes the two are combined in one package.

### Painting applications

Painting packages work by conveying an illusion of common painting operations - brushing, spraying etc. Various brush shapes can be chosen, and the spray gun can be adjusted for 'spread' and 'force'. A range of colours can also be specified. More advanced packages allow graded colours and 'smudging' of areas so that, for example, a smudgy charcoal picture can be produced.

The interface itself consists of two elements: a pointing and selection device (usually a mouse) and a *tool selection* menu. A typical screen is shown in Figure 7.3.

*Figure 7.3 Typical painting application showing work area, colour selection menu and tool selection menu (courtesy Acorn Computers Ltd.)*

### Drawing applications

Whereas a painting package works with coloured pixels, drawing packages are 'object-oriented' - that is, the drawing comprises objects which are defined in terms of *paths* - straight or curved lines with start and end points, sometimes connected together. If an enclosed shape is defined, it can be *filled* with a variety of colours or shades.

After the shapes have been defined, they can be edited, resized, grouped together, copied etc.

The advantage of this path-based approach is that all objects are represented internally as sequences of lines and vectors, so the resolution of the final work is independent of the resolution of the display device, and can always be rendered in the maximum resolution of which a device is capable.

The interface again consists of two elements - a pointing device and a tool selector - but the functions are different and more complex. For example, the start of a straight line can be fixed to an origin, and the end point fixed by stretching (*rubberbanding*) it using the pointer and releasing a button. When the line is fixed, it can be moved or copied as a complete object. In this case, the pointing device is being used in a different *mode*.

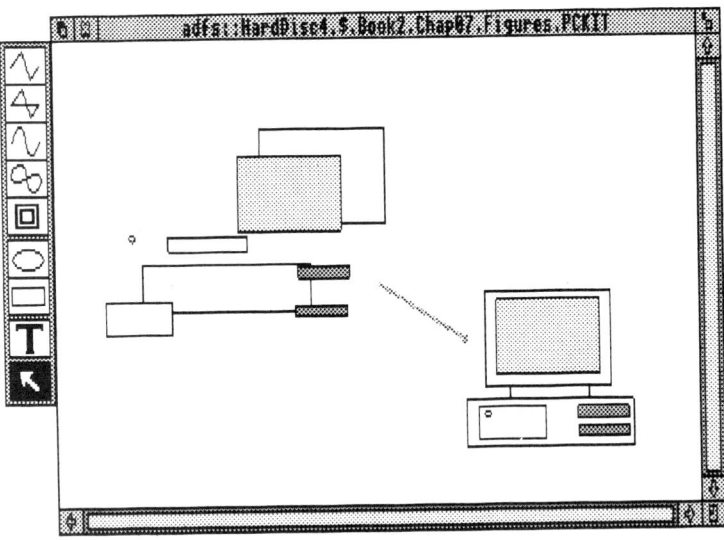

*Figure 7.4 Typical object-oriented drawing package interface showing range of primitive objects (courtesy Acorn Computers Ltd.)*

## Interfaces for musicians

Although computers have been used to 'compose' and play music, the alternative methods were generally found to be preferable as far as composers were concerned. The great disadvantage of traditional methods is that you often need an orchestra (or at least a soloist) to hear the results, and musical manuscripts are difficult to edit.

Computers powerful enough to provide musical editing and replay facilities have only emerged recently, and interfaces are still very much under development. However, Figure 7.5 gives an idea of what we could expect to see.

*Figure 7.5 Typical music editor interface (courtesy Acorn Computers Ltd.)*

## Interfaces for medical workers

Many surgical procedures require a high precision of operation with a 'hold' capability - it is one thing to delicately uncover a nerve or artery, and quite another to hold it absolutely still while some operation is performed. A computer-driven scalpel, or laser, could be interfaced via a dataglove (see Chapter 5) and the area of interest observed either directly or via a high-resolution colour display. The latter solution has the additional advantage that 3-dimensional images could be produced by such techniques as nuclear magnetic resonance (NMR) or positron emission tomography (PET) which are both capable of producing sectional views of an area.

An added advantage of this method is that some 'intelligence' could be incorporated into the system so that certain hazardous situations could be monitored for and be signalled.

Computer assistance in this area is in its infancy and we can expect exciting developments in the future.

### Interfaces for programmers

A full discussion of the various tools available for software development and maintenance is outside the scope of this book. Generally speaking, activities such as CASE (computer assisted software engineering) are fully supported by sophisticated interfaces (note that 'sophisticated' is not synonymous with 'perfect').

It is useful, however, to discuss two aspects of interfacing which are of concern to programmers - *integrated environments* and *debuggers*.

#### Integrated environments

Software development can be a very time-consuming task, mainly because the typical edit/ compile/ test/ debug cycle is performed by different packages which have to be called up separately, and the options set appropriately. This not only takes up time, but places a considerable cognitive load on the programmer, whose brain should ideally be fully devoted to the task of programming. The main problem is retaining a 'picture' of the source code, together with its latest amendments, during periods when it is not visible on the screen.

What is needed is the ability to retain the source code on screen, together with the editor, while the program is compiled, linked and run. this is the facility offered on the increasingly popular integrated environments such as **Microsoft C** (Microsoft), **Turbo C, Turbo Pascal** (Borland), **Zortech C++** and **Topspeed Modula-2** (JPI). Later versions of most of these products have built-in tracers and debuggers, which allow the code to be run a line at a time, variables inspected and so on.

Using an integrated environment dramatically cuts development time for small and medium-scale projects, where, arguably, there is more recourse to a rapid prototyping style of software development.

### *Debuggers*

Although, theoretically, no program should ever need debugging - the code should be perfect by design - programs that run first time are the exception. A debugger is then used which runs the compiled code in a controlled manner and provides information about machine registers, memory contents and so on. Simple debuggers cannot use any of the symbolic information present in the original source code: it is lost after compilation and linking.

A *symbolic debugger* is capable of retrieving the original variable names and displaying the data in a meaningful way - as a real number, or as a string, etc. It is also capable of displaying the machine registers directly, showing the compiled machine code together with the source code, and stepping or running it until some condition is met.

With windowed systems, a number of various 'views' can be displayed simultaneously - processor registers, input/output port values, memory and source code - so that the programmer has a complete 'picture' down to machine level if this is necessary.

### Transparency

There is a common aim in the use of domain-specific interfaces: the achievement of *transparency*. The closer the interface is matched in appearance and behaviour to the operator's cognitive model, the more likely it is that the operator's existing experience will transfer positively, and that new procedures will be incorporated effectively (see chapter 2).

In this way, we can conceive of the operator as interacting with the system *through* the interface, rather than interacting *with* the interface directly. This view does have its attendant dangers, which have been identified by Bench-Capon and McEnery[9]. The transparency obtained by a correct modelling of the user must be thought through very carefully if the system is to be genuinely transparent. In particular, domain knowledge or expertise in the user must be correctly judged. Bench-Capon and McEnery quote the example of an Ada program which prompts:

```
Enter three real numbers:
```

For the interaction to be successful, the operator must know three things:

- The numbers must be entered in the form 2.0 (2 will fail).

- Spaces will act as separators between numbers

- The input is terminated by pressing the <RETURN> key.

The programmer's assumption about the level of knowledge possessed by the user has avoided complex explanations; but

> *"it is the programmer, not the system, which is doing the modelling"*

This is acceptable in simple systems. But where expert systems, or AI (artificial intelligence) based systems are in use, the user may be tempted to ascribe a spurious intelligence to the system, and believe that it is the interface which is driving the dialogue rather than the programmer. In this situation, there is a strong likelihood of misunderstandings developing. This is especially likely when natural language interfaces are being considered; we must be sure that the interface designer's art does not triumph at the expense of the user's understanding. As the old countryman observed when his neighbour trained a dog to walk across the surface of a river to retrieve a stick: "Carn't 'e zwim, then?"

## Modes

The tuning knob of a radio has a different effect if the wavechange switch is set to 'FM' than if it is set to 'AM'. This is an example of a *moded* control. Similarly, the key **a** on a computer keyboard may have a number of different meanings in an editor, depending on the mode the editor is in:

- producing the letter **a** in text

- selecting **append** in command mode

- selecting an option from a menu

- using the letter **a** as part of a filename

Are modes good or bad? It could be argued that they are good, as they permit a small number of devices, each with a small range of adjustments, to cover a wide range of selections. On the other hand, the cognitive load necessary to master and retain the appropriate combinations may be higher than if a 'one-to-one' strategy were adopted.

Johnson[38] has investigated the use of modes in a wide variety of *non-*computer devices, prompted by a lack of unanimity amongst HCI workers as to what comprised 'moded' systems. Starting with the informal definition of Poller and Garter - a system has modes if the effect of a given user action is not always the same - Johnson reviewed the 'modality' of such devices as slide projectors, cars, cameras, food processors, typewriters and firearms. His aim was to glean some ideas about the *designed* use of modes, and to assess how the computing world could benefit.

For example, early mass-market cameras avoided mode errors by having such a simple functionality that no errors were possible - if the camera was pointing in more or less the right direction, and there was enough light, you got a picture. The complex interactions between focus, aperture, film speed and shutter speed were simply not there. More recently, the cameras themselves have become so intelligent (with automatic focusing, film speed adjustment, motorised advance, etc.) that mode errors (although possible if the camera is manually overridden) cannot occur. The advantage to the beginner is that he/she is protected from mode errors; a more experienced user can begin to experiment in creativity *by making deliberate mode errors.*

Overall, modes were used with more or less success depending on the application, but there was little evidence that the experience gained had mapped across to the computer world. In fact, as more everyday devices become driven by embedded computers, it is possible that conventional control interfaces will become entirely 'soft'.

Johnson concludes:

> *"We are witnessing an age in which computer design practice, still immature, threatens to cause a regression in the design of "non-computer" devices, with unfortunate results."*

## Other interface topics

### Cross-domain interfaces

As we have seen, interfaces can be matched closely to the preferences of different kinds of user. This also applies to users who do not have a concept of a computer 'interface' as such to their domain - for example, economists. In these situations, it is worth considering whether other users, in different disciplines, have ready-made interfaces which might be useful (a mainframe computer once used by the author had a 'usage meter' which indicated the load on the system. It always indicated 100%).

To get back to our example (the economist), we could ask what kind of indicators and controls would be useful in, say, modelling an economy: levels of wage settlement could be set directly by *sliders*, rather than being typed in as figures; levels of inflation and unemployment could be directly viewed as a *meter* or bar chart display; *buttons* could be pressed to simulate unpredictable phenomena such as wars; and so on.

In short, whenever parameters can be viewed as continuously variable they can be set by controls of the type we have discussed above.

### Adaptable interfaces

An examination of the way in which people structure their behaviour while learning to operate an application shows that certain familiar operations are executed more and more rapidly as the user gains experience with the system. If these operations involve several steps, such as a series of menu selections, the user may become aware of the need for some kind of 'short-cut'. Initially, this may be implemented by delaying menu display for, say, half a second so that a rapid series of keypresses avoids unwanted menus 'popping up'. Another way, as we will see in Chapter 9, is to provide 'hot keys'. Together with some facility for altering the key bindings, package interfaces can certainly be adapted to the preferences of a particular user.

However, the possibility of such customisation may not be apparent to a learning user, or its significance not be appreciated; or, alternatively, the user may go through an orgy of reconfiguration, only to find later that many of the changes were undesirable.

### Adaptive interfaces

An adaptive interface may be regarded as a special kind of adaptable interface which has the capacity to adapt *itself*. This topic is considered in detail in Chapter 9.

## Further reading

"Human interaction with computers", edited by H.T. Smith & T.R.G. Green - especially Part 3.

# 8 Visual interfaces

*The computer too is a prehensile tool, and it encourages an almost tactile approach to solving problems. Through its circuitry, the human operator "manipulates" ... information, probes ... files to examine their contents, builds data structures and tears them down...*

*J. David Boulter*

## Introduction

Human beings maintain a strongly spatial view of the world. If this were not the case, then atlases would not exist, and road signs located ahead of roundabouts would be entirely linguistic rather than mostly diagrammatic. For most people, this sense of space is mediated by the visual sense, or modality, but it can also be mediated by acoustic or tactile modalities. People who have been blind from birth negotiate the rooms in their own homes successfully, and can manage in an unfamiliar room after one or two 'passes'. Thus although we will be referring *visual* interfaces by convention, it may be more proper to use the word *spatial* in this context. The visual metaphor will be referred to when discussing the lower (physical) layers of a DM (direct manipulation) interface, reserving the specific use of the term *direct manipulation* for the task-oriented aspects of the technique.

In this chapter we will discuss the basic principles, and some examples, of direct manipulation interfaces. This kind of interface has come into some prominence recently, as it forms an attractive way of insulating a naive user from an operating system, or file structure, while still enabling him/her to perform relatively complex tasks.

## Justification for the visual metaphor

You will have gathered from Chapter 7 that the efficient and powerful use of a command-line interface (CLI) requires a considerable investment of time and cognitive effort on the part of the user. Indeed, many users never get beyond the simple 'turnkey' system which makes use of a simple batch file running on a conventional operating system. Many do not need to, of course, but it must be the case that many users are unaware of the basic facilities offered by an operating system for the purposes of file maintenance and general housekeeping. (On one application package in the author's experience, for example, backing up the data files took all night because they were being copied 80 bytes at a time - escaping from the package and using the operating system **copy** command to perform the equivalent operation took 15 minutes). The main reason for not adopting this method was that the operating system was something unknown and mysterious, that users did not tamper with.

### Visual information

The visual presentation of information has long been accepted as a superior alternative to, say, lists of figures. The list in Figure 8.1, for example, indicates the sales and profits figures for ten computer companies in the U.S. Fortune 500 list.

| Company | Sales ($m) | Profits($m) |
|---------|-----------|-------------|
| IBM | 63,438 | 3,758 |
| DEC | 12,866 | 1,073 |
| HP | 11,899 | 829 |
| Unisys | 10,097 | -639 |
| NCR | 5,956 | 412 |
| Apple | 5,284 | 454 |
| Wang | 3,078 | -424 |
| CDC | 2,952 | -680 |
| Compaq | 2,876 | 333 |
| Amdahl | 2,154 | 153 |

*Figure 8.1 Financial information as a table*

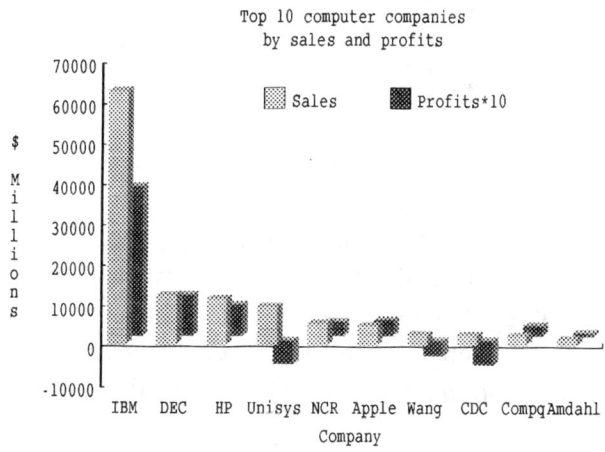

*Figure 8.2 Financial information as a graph*

As you can observe, the information presented visually (rather than textually):

- has more immediate impact

- is more memorable

- enables more rapid reviews to be made

- allows more rapid decisions to be made

## Icons

Experience seems to indicate that icons work better than spoken or written language to convey many kinds of information.\\Certainly, the icons illustrated in Figure 8.3 are fairly unambiguous in their significance, possibly because they evoke 'rich' associations with familiar actions, and so succeed in 'packaging' objects and activities together. But what about more complex activities, which have no equivalent associations, such as copying one file to another, or deleting a file? We need to know what approach to adopt to design an appropriate icon. We could adopt a complex approach - build a new visual dialogue system - or a simple approach - find a suitable analogue and use it, even if it stretches the analogy to some extent. Most visual interface designers seem to have taken the latter approach. Perhaps the best known example is the well-known 'wastebasket' as used by the Xerox Star workstation, and later the Apple Macintosh computer. Deleting a file then becomes a natural sequence of **selecting** an object, **dragging** it to the wastebasket icon and **releasing** it. The analogy is continued in the Macintosh system by 'keeping' the files in the wastebasket, from whence they can be retrieved at a later stage if necessary. On many other DM systems, the files are deleted straight away.

This process does not work quite as well if more complex operations are to be performed, or if the proposed operation has to be qualified in some way (only copying files that have been modified, for example). In this case, an option would have to be set in a **copy** menu before the operation was attempted; or a special keypress could be combined with the mouse operation. However, the iconic approach does seem to have built-in attractions which makes it preferable for many users - perhaps the majority.

Note that the precise meaning of an icon is sometimes attributed by consensus, or association, rather than some intrinsic quality. Very often, the meaning is ambiguous until some context is provided. For example, the umbrella symbol in Figure 8.3 could indicate 'keep dry' if printed on the side of a packing case, or 'umbrellas for sale' if seen outside a stall at a market. The 'No Smoking' icon has its meaning partly ascribed by association with the 'No Entry' roadsign. The alternative 'keep dry' sign, if seen on a map, could indicate a path through some trees.

| Telephone | Fragile | High Voltage |
| --- | --- | --- |
| Keep Dry | Avoid Magnets | No Smoking |
| Keep Dry | Poison | Radiation |

*Figure 8.3 Some Icons*

Chang [18] has described a taxonomy, devised by Lodding, which classifies icons into three categories: the *representational*, such as the umbrella above; the *abstract*, such as the 'fragile' symbol; and the *arbitrary*, such as the 'radiation' symbol. The advantage of the representational icon is its lack of ambiguity in a particular context; the disadvantage is its highly specific meaning, which is not 'portable' to other contexts. By the same token, a more arbitrary icon may be more general in the range of meanings attributable to it (e.g. to indicate a generic range of actions rather than a specific action) but suffer by being less memorable. As there is no commonly accepted set of icons to indicate particular meanings, there is an evolutionary aspect to the selection of particular icons. For example, the selection of a 'filing-cabinet' representation of a disk file directory was arguably appropriate when the aim of visual interface designers was to provide a symbol that office workers would relate to; but some offices now exist without any filing cabinets at all, so what should icon should be used? And presumably one day paper may become a rarity in most offices. What would then be the icon for 'wastebasketing' an item? Possibly, as the kinds of data handled by the electronic office become more diverse (video, voice etc.) a more abstract metaphor would be appropriate, indicating the type of data rather than the type of container.

One solution is to 'package' the application together with its data files such that a generic icon is used. The RISC-OS operating system, used on the Acorn Archimedes computer, adopts the strategy of maintaining an application as a directory, containing all necessary 'boot' and 'run' files. Data files 'belonging' to this application have a similar appearance:

Associated data file

Application directory
contains:

Associated data file

Application directory
contains:

Visual representations, then, are culturally strongly anchored and are convenient to use. We turn now to how this can be exploited with the new technology available to us. The most obvious manifestation of the visual metaphor is in the rapid and profuse development of systems based on windows, icons, menus and pointers - WIMP systems.

## WIMP systems in operation

Current WIMP systems, employing as they do a combination of advanced hardware and  software, are a tribute to the intelligent collaboration of people  involved in the diverse fields of hardware design, software design and  psychology. The credit is due largely to the Palo Alto Research

Centre (PARC) of the Xerox corporation, where the STAR office automation system was developed. This forms the basis of most of the currently available WIMP-based systems, and the Xerox corporation should be commended for its altruistic, if somewhat uncommercial, approach to the exploitation of its discoveries.

The operation of a WIMP system is clear and unambiguous. Objects (files, programs) in the system are represented by icons in a window. A window may act as a 'parent' to other windows ('children') who inherit the basic characteristics of their parent. All the windows are situated on a *desktop*. Several different windows may be open at once, and windows may be moved, resized, opened and closed. Objects (which may be files or devices) may be activated by selecting with the pointer (generally mouse-driven) and double-clicking; or they can be moved about in the window. Alternatively, a special kind of icon, with selectable items (a menu) can be pulled down from a menu bar at the top of the desktop.

Operations such as file copying are achieved by selecting and dragging one icon over another; and all applications have to be written in a way which makes best use of the resources available.

The underlying operating system is similar in many ways to a conventional one (with, for example, a normal range of file handling services), but has many enhancements to enable the various windowed operations to be handled. Output, for example, would not be to just a screen, but to a uniquely identified virtual workstation. Input operations have to handle events such as the entry of a pointer into a window, or a resize operation. The operating system handles this by treating every event as a message. Applications can wait for, and interpret, these messages and act accordingly. One consequence is that applications programs have to look after the management of their windows in addition to their normal input/output. This is generally managed by placing a call to the window manager polling routine in a 'tight loop' of the application.

An extensive set of graphics primitives is also implemented - for example: lines, circles, arcs, filled polygons and so on.

The significance of this desktop metaphor for the design of systems cannot be overestimated. As far as the user is concerned, the following benefits are conferred:

- There is a good match between the 'mental model' of the system and its physical appearance.

- Syntax errors are eliminated, so the only complexity lies with  the application not with the system interface.

- Most importantly, this kind of system provides a generic  interface which can be made common to all applications. See the discussion of Open Look later in this chapter.

For the designer, the advantages include:

- rapid development, especially of the user interface

- a 'prototyping' ability so that  certain aspects can be fine-tuned, possibly to individual end-user requirements

- an easy migration to the system, as the  facilities are available from any high-level language which  supports operating system calls.

## Cognitive aspects of WIMP systems

It may be intuitively evident that direct-manipulation systems are 'better' in some way than, say, command-line interfaces; but the reasons may not be obvious.

The main point is that the operative word is *manipulation*. This involves more than seeing an object on the screen; it involves manipulation - in Bolter's terms , *grasping* the object in the same way that we 'grasp' a concept [13]. This ability to see, pick, grasp, move and drop an object arguably provides a perfect match between the user's model of a system and the operations necessary to control it.

Further, the way in which windows and their associated events can be conceptualised and realised means that an object-oriented approach to the design and programming of such systems is natural and productive (see Chapter 13).

It is apparent that the use of a DM system cuts out much unnecessary syntactic overgrowth, and in some way enables the user to directly 'drive' the semantic layer for certain operations.

Shneiderman [62] has made a distinction between *semantic* and *syntactic* modes of memory and learning, illustrated in Figure 8.4

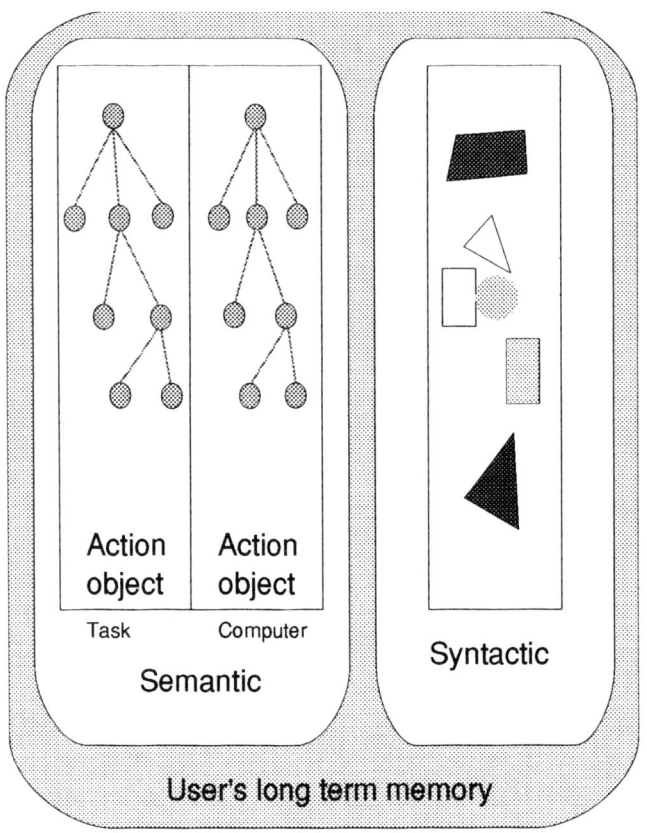

*Figure 8.4 Semantic and Syntactic aspects of users' memory for tasks*

## Layered approach to visual interfaces

Recently, developments in hardware and software technology have converged in the domain of advanced graphics and associated software. High resolution graphics displays need complex software, and hence a good deal of computing power, to drive them. The complexity of the software has, in turn, stimulated the establishment of international standards for interface design and development. In discussing how the various elements interact, it is convenient once again to adopt a *layered* approach.

At the lowest, physical, layer, we are concerned with handling a screenful of bits, or picture elements (*pels*, or *pixels*). Such an array of bits is termed a *pixrect*, and there may be more than one pixrect in a display, organised as 'planes'. Operations at this level are usually built in to the operating system, in the case of the newer workstations such as the Apple Macintosh and Acorn Archimedes, or as an overlay onto an existing operating system (such as Microsoft Windows running on MS-DOS). The most advanced workstations (such as the Hewlett-Packard 9000 300 series) have dedicated graphics processors to handle these 'bit plane' operations. The most common, and resource-intensive, operations are of the 'bit block transfer' variety, commonly termed 'bit blitting'. This is the operation that would be performed, for example, if a window was uncovered by another window, and had to redraw part of itself.

At a higher layer, the concern is how the various areas on the screen are managed in a logical and systematic way so that, for example, an area which is partly overlaid by another graphic object can be reconstructed without having to consult the application.

Finally, the primitive window operations must be presented in a functional way so that, for example, windows can be presented as having their own coordinate systems and so that window events (such as mouse clicks and keypresses) can be signalled.

This is the layer that an applications program 'sees', normally via a library of Applications Program Interface (API )functions such as the X window library, XLib, which is discussed in the next section. All the input and output operations, as well as the management of the window interface, are managed by the application and the window manager between them. The API is also the layer that the user 'sees' from the other side, usually in the form of a set of system calls accessed in the same way as normal operating system calls. (For a discussion on operating system calls in general, see *Systems Software* by F Maddix & G Morgan, Ellis Horwood, 1989.)

**Intermediate level operations in X Window**
The X Window system (which is essentially a set of protocols rather than

a software package) was developed by the Massachusetts Institute of Technology some years ago. It was made available in the public domain (that is, free) with the intention that interested developers would review, implement and develop it. To this end, release 10.4 of X Window was 'frozen' for a year. The commercial release of X (11.3 at the time of writing) has been adopted by a wide variety of vendors.

The significant feature of X is that the activities of supporting an application and of managing the windows belonging to the application have been separated into two functional parts, the *client* (which comprises the application and its X library) and the *server* (which controls the graphics drivers and input/output generally for a particular workstation).

The communication between the X client and the X server is in the form of messages, which follow a strict protocol, the X protocol. Generally, the transfer of large amounts of information, such as bitmaps, is avoided as this tends to 'jam' the communications medium, and is, in most cases, unnecessary.

There are several important consequences to this careful planning:

- The client and server can exist in different machines

- The client and server can communicate via a network

- There is total hardware independence, and cross-platform operation is therefore feasible.

Other significant features are:

- A client can have any number of windows open, not necessarily on the same server

- The system lends itself naturally to object-oriented technique

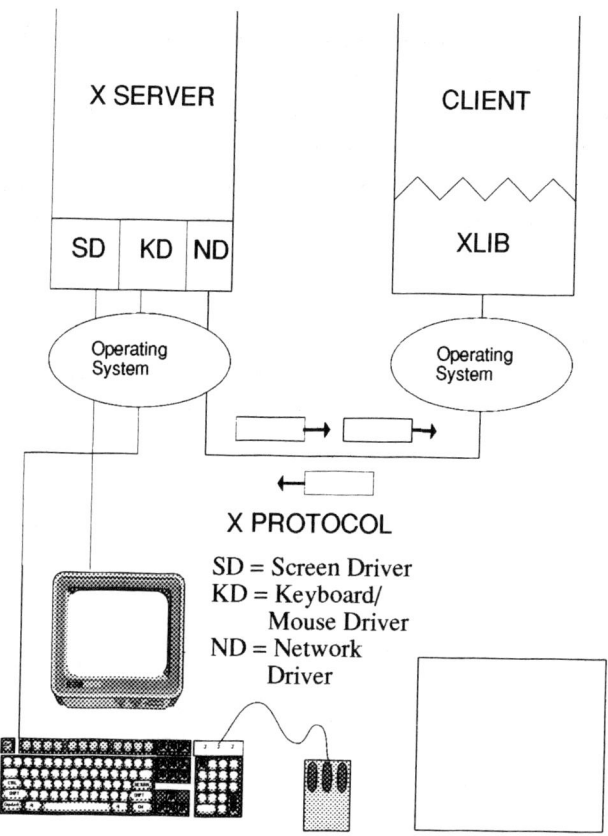

*Figure 8.5 X Window organisation*

## How an application uses X Window

### Window set up

The first task of an application is to make a connection to the appropriate X server, generally by making a network call. Note that an application (client) can be in communication with any number of X servers, so that, for example, an application could provide user information on one workstation while also providing debugging information on another.

The next task for the client is to call upon the selected X server to set up the initial window/s. Windows are requested of an appropriate size, colour, and location. At this time, the *attributes* of a window are also determined - whether it is to be resizeable, movable, 'hideable' and so on.

### Events - mouse and keyboard

The next task is to determine which *events* shall be passed back to the application by the X window manager. This is determined by setting a bit in an *event mask* which is sent to the server. When an event (such as a mouse click or keypress) occurs, the appropriate *callback routine* is entered. The list of callback routines is sent via a separate X library call.

### Basic application operation (main loop)

In a correctly written X application, the main program 'loop' is merely a call to the X event handler, from which the main program never returns (one of the callback routines is an exit handler).

While the application runs, various events will be fielded and the appropriate callback routine will be entered. Note that an event can be quite a complex thing to handle. For example, if an application has several windows open, and a different process opens a large window which obscures the original windows, then upon closing the large window certain parts of the originals may need to be redrawn. The X server does not know which ones, so it returns as an adjunct to an event a list of rectangles that have been obscured. If the client application can be certain that nothing needs to be regenerated in the newly uncovered window, the X server can be instructed to do this automatically, thus saving considerable processing time in the application and reducing the network load.

### High level operations in X Window: widgets

Many applications programmers do not wish to use the XLib interface at the low level described above. They reason that there is too much of an overhead in managing the windows and associated events, and that development effort ought to go on building better applications, not mastering a complex interface. Consequently, many system vendors provide *toolkits* to make this task easier. For reasons which we may never be told (although it may be a contraction of *window gadgets*), these toolkits are generally referred to as *widget* sets.

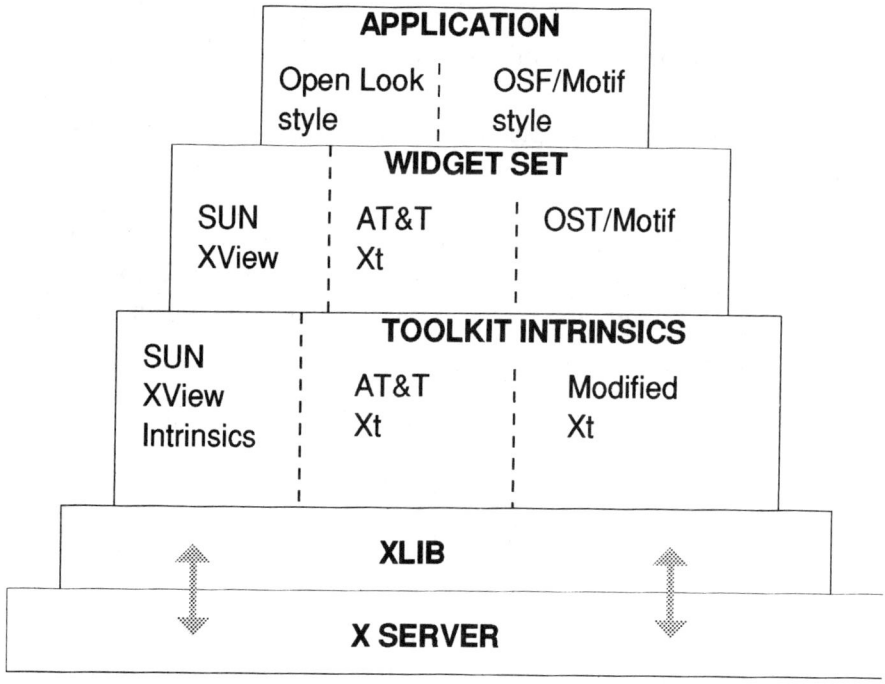

*Figure 8.6 Layers of X Window*

**Interface building tools**
As the reader will have gathered from reading the sections above, there is a large overhead involved in setting up a windowing system. This impacts on productivity, and it is in everyone's interest to get applications running correctly (and reliably) in the shortest time possible.

Consequently, most of the major computer vendors provide X widget toolkits, together with recommended 'look and feel' standards: Digital Equipment Corporation (DEC) provides its X User Interface (XUI) which has been adopted by the Open Software Foundation (OSF) as being 'Motif-conformant'. XUI is also licensed by Hewlett Packard and by SCO for its Open Desktop, and additionally defines the standard for the Presentation Manager graphical user interface (GUI) for the OS/2 operating system. This covers the majority of high-end personal computer workstations. The alternative Open Look toolkit is supported by AT&T and Sun Microsystems, both providers of 'serious' Unix-based workstations.

Whichever standard is adopted, using a widget toolkit confers the following advantages:

- There is a much higher level of interaction with the X Window system: the *event* from the Xlib interface (e.g. 'the mouse pointer has entered this rectangle') is replaced by a *reason* ('this menu item has been selected').

- It is an appropriate level to define the 'look and feel' of a family of interfaces

- There is less opportunity for making errors, as code is re-used in much bigger chunks)

- There is more consistency across applications from the same 'stable'.

**Standards**

As mentioned above, there are two major classes of interface, which we will refer to as 'XUI' and 'Open Look'. Although the basic functionality is the same across the two, there are differences in how that functionality is made available to the user - the 'look and feel'.

It is instructive to examine the design goals of one of the main contenders, Open Look. It is a safe assumption that Motif will have a similar set of goals.

*Open Look design goals*

The design goals of Open Look have been summarised by Hoeber[34] as follows. The goals are in bold type, and some comments are appended:

- **Create an open standard** (so that hardware platforms from different vendors may be used to support windowing interfaces)

- **Design an excellent user interface** (the precise meaning of 'excellent' is unclear, but would hopefully involve some user judgments of excellence in an interface)

- **Make the interface work for a variety of applications** (having established a common standard for a GUI, applications vendors should be encouraged to use it. This approach works, as evidenced by applications written for the Apple Macintosh)

- **Complement Unix power** (Unix is the preferred platform for advanced GUIs, because of its mature multitasking multiuser architecture)

- **Get vendors to adopt it**

- **Harmonize with other user interfaces** (However excellent an Applications Program Interface, nobody will use it if it is perceived to be 'out on a limb').

- **Avoid legal clouds!** (In the United States, the list of who sued whom over the 'look and feel' issue of windowed interfaces reads like the family history section of the book of Genesis.)

- **Make it portable**

These are general design goals; the important issue is how these goals translate into specifics for systems designers and applications writers. It is instructive to study one particular example, DEC's XUI style guide. (The author is grateful to Digital Equipment Corporation for allowing extracts from their *XUI style guide* to be paraphrased).

### Portable window libraries

Although there appear to be considerable efforts to achieve a standard windowed system, it is not yet true that the various systems offer a consistent interface, either at the API or at the user level. A programmer who has developed applications in GEM, or Windows, is unlikely to be able to transport much of that experience when moving to, say, OS/2, or the Apple Macintosh environment, or X Window. However, the fact is that all windowed systems offer a similar set of features and services - a protocol for setting up and manipulating windows and their contents, and a mechanism for handling events.

It should be possible, therefore, to devise a common subset of features which would enable an application to be *portable* across various windowing systems. This could be implemented as a library and a specific 'back-end' selected at link time to generate code for the selected environment.

## Summary

The visual metaphor is now strongly rooted in user culture. It is seen to be direct, unambiguous and reliable, and it enables transparent interfaces and dialogues to be written.

Standards have been implemented in a rigorous and professional way, and, although a windowed interface requires large overheads, and programmers to develop a new style, the provision of libraries and toolkits eases the task.

## Further reading

There is a large, and increasing, body of literature on windowed systems in general and on X Window in particular:

*X Window applications programming*, Eric F. Johnson and Kevin Reichard, MIS Press 1989

# 9 Dialogues

## Introduction

If my car is serviced and I am dissatisfied with the results, I might ring the service agents and give my opinions regarding their competence. If I do not give them an opportunity to reply then I am engaging in a monologue. If I allow a space for a reply and dismiss their comments out of hand, then it is still a monologue. If I take note of what they say and moderate my verbal behaviour accordingly, then we have the beginnings of a dialogue.

Dialogues and interfaces are often confused; the first thing we need to establish is the relationship between them:

- An *interface* is a channel of communication between two partners in an interaction (see Chapter 2)

- A *dialogue* is a conversation between the partners, carried on via the interface, in which the behaviour of one partner modifies the other. Ideally, the dialogue enables the satisfactory resolution of some problem.

- Dialogues can range from the very simple and highly constrained (as in a simple menu-driven system) to highly complex and open-ended (a rich command language or WIMP system).

Note that:

- In the HCI domain, one partner is generally the computer - but there are some good reasons (see chapter 7) to adopt the working assumption that one of the partners can be the *designer* of the application that is being run. This aspect could become increasingly significant if, for example, applications packages offer an 'online help' facility where a software support team, or indeed the package designer, can be dialled directly by the package.

- Referring to our layered model of HCI (see chapter 2), we can visualise the dialogue as being layered onto, and 'carried' by, the interface. A bad interface can ruin a good dialogue, but a good dialogue does not improve an interface, although it may make better use of it and render it to be judged more usable as a consequence.

Users rarely judge dialogues, they judge interfaces, although their experience may be largely determined by remembered episodes within the dialogue. Interfaces can be seen and compared, whereas dialogues are unseen and rarely repeated exactly. Consequently, it is in everyone's interest to understand dialogues, their development and maintenance. If there is some truth in the assertion that 'the interface is the system', then it is certainly true that it is the quality of the dialogue that forms the user's lasting impression of the system.

In this chapter, we will discuss the following issues relating to dialogues:

- Analysis and design of dialogues

- Dialogue specification

There is a relationship between the design of dialogues in HCI and natural language dialogues; many of the analysis techniques and grammars are similar. The reader might like to read this chapter in conjunction with Chapter 11 on natural language processing.

## Analysis and design of dialogues

Although the analysis of dialogues could be regarded as a branch of task analysis, it is probably the least investigated area in the early stages of system design. The main reason must be that systems analysts are trained in the techniques of program design, not psycholinguistics.

The consequence is that much dialogue design is based on an incomplete understanding of what kinds of interaction might take place between a typical user and the proposed system. For example, here is a typical interaction, described by Pinsky[55], between an inexperienced user and a form-filling application. The purpose of the application is to update a database of individuals who are classified according to profession and economic activity. If any of the information on the form is incomplete (such as an unknown code), an attempt is made to establish it by searching the database: (operator input **underlined**, verbal protocol in *italics*):

**profession = inspector, business frauds**

(the economic activity has already been coded as: '9004 external administrative services other than economic or financial')

```
PIVOT WORD 'INSPECTOR', SECTION SUPERVISOR (PUBLIC DUTIES)

-INSPECTORS, POSTAL                      ENTER C-FP21
-INSPECTORS, TREASURY, CUSTOMS, TAX      ENTER C-FP22
-INSPECTORS, STATE (VERY RARE)           ENTER C-FP11
-INSPECTORS, CIVIL AVIATION              ENTER C-TD02
-OTHERS                                  ENTER C-FP24
```

*"Ah! It's 'others'"*

**profession = FP24**

```
FP24 OTHER PERSONNEL UNDER CATEGORY B OF PUBLIC OFFICE
(ADMINISTRATIVE SECRETARIES; INSPECTORS, WORK, TRADE...)
```

*"..." (Silence)*

(Researcher: Does that surprise you?)

*"No... but, after all! A moment ago it said 'others' and then... Still, if that's the way it works! One has to read it in relationship with the message just received. Is that it? No, because read like that it is 'other personnel under Category B'. One asks oneself 'What's going on here!' Still, one must remember that...(others?) Exactly!"*

We are left with the impression that the final word of this protocol is a pious hope rather than a true indication of understanding. After all, there is nothing to understand - the system is just not making sense in the user's terms. Quite possibly, this is one of the millions of users who will eventually convince themselves that they, not the system, are stupid.

## Dialogue specification

Although the definition of a dialogue - as an open-ended series of interactions - seems to make for difficulties in encapsulating and formalising any particular dialogue, tools for formal expression are now quite highly developed, and in any case not all dialogues are complex; many are highly constrained:

```
Erase all files, Y/N (N)?
```

whereas in a complex multi-windowed application running with a WIMP system, the attempt to formalise the overall dialogue is probably futile (although some brave souls will try).

Basically, then, the problem of analysing and formalising dialogues could be seen as similar to the problem of grammar specification in natural languages - and this is not an intractable problem.

Alexander[3] has outlined a dialogue specification system (ECS - edit, compute, show) which can be regarded as an executable language, and indeed has the same basic set of *constructors* (the basic elements of many advanced languages and structured programming tools such as JSP (Jackson Structured Programming):

**SEQ** - a number of elements are executed in a sequential manner:

```
dialogue D consists of
          dialogue D1
then      dialogue D2
...
then dialogue Dn
```

**ALT** - a choice is made between two or more elements:

```
dialogue D consists of
          dialogue D1
and       dialogue D2
...
and       dialogue Dn
```

**PAR** - Two or more elements are executed in parallel, that is, simultaneously:

```
dialogue D consists of
          dialogue D1
or        dialogue D2
...
or        dialogue Dn
```

Using these elements, and some others, a basic cycle - the ECS cycle - is set up. The ECS cycle iterates repetitively through a number of *states*:

- **Edit:** the user performs some input, probably in response to a prompt

- **Compute:** the system analyses the input and performs the appropriate actions

- **Show:** the results of the *compute* state are output to the user.

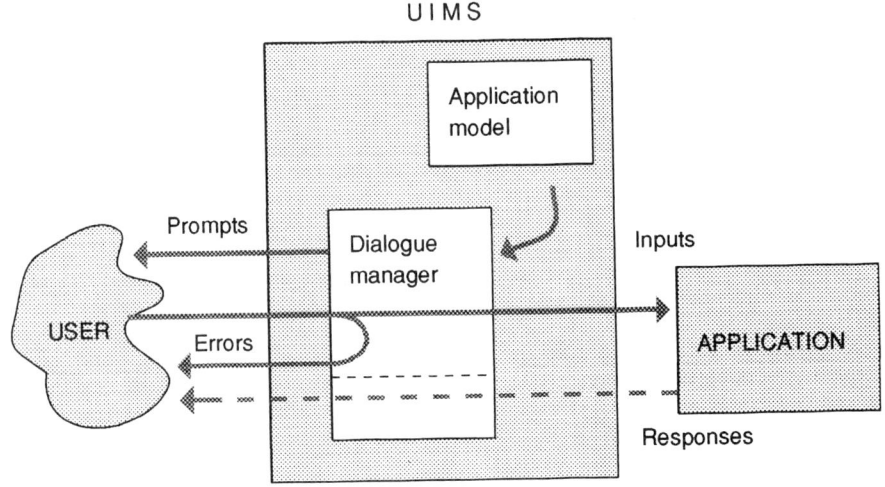

UIMS

*Figure 9.1 User Interface Management System for dialogue control (after Alexander, 1986)*

Figure 9.1 shows a dialogue manager, running an ECS 'engine', embedded within a user interface management system (UIMS). Imagine that the desired dialogue was a menu of choices for various file operations - deleting, listing etc., each choice being followed by further selection menus of the following form:

```
LISTFILE - lists the named file

        name of file to be listed? mydir/file1
        number of copies required? 3
        keep file after listing? n
```

The ECS program running within the dialogue manager is shown in part below (reproduced from Alexander, 1986):

```
compute(st) =
        if st[ICMD]nil = nil
        then do-cname(st)
        else do-pvalue(st)
```

```
do-cname(st)  =
          let inp = st[INPUT]0
              cdb = st[DB]0
              st' = st ds {INPUT}
          in st' ⊖
                      if INPUT ∉ dom(st)
                      then { INPUT-REQD -> true,
                              OUTPUT -> menu-intro(cdb) }
                      else if inp = STOP
                      then { TERMINATE -> true }
                      else got-cname(cdb, inp)

got-cname(cdb, inp) =
          if not in-db(cdb, inp)
          then { OUTPUT -> "error: no such command" }
          else { OUTPUT -> display-menu(cdb, inp),
                 ICMD -> mk-cmd(inp, 0),
                 FORMAT -> p-menus(cdb, inp) }
```

ECS obviously shares many syntactic features with conventional procedural languages such as Pascal and C; so the question arises, 'why do it this way at all?'. It should be appreciated that the apparent simplicity hides some fairly complex operations going on underneath. Having to code these explicitly would mean that the language would lose its expressive power in this particular domain. In any case, the language is designed for the communication of dialogue designs between HCI workers as much as for 'running' these designs.

## Characterising dialogues

It is probably easier to identify a number of dialogue styles, and classify a real dialogue as being one of these, than it is to perform an exhaustive analysis of all dialogues.

Eason[21a] has described two basic kinds of task which are associated with the extremes of dialogue style: **Closed** tasks are prescribed, and minimise the amount of choice needed from the user. A typical closed task would be the filling in of a form on-screen. An **open** task maximises user choice, the path is not predetermined and the rules are not made explicit. The openness of a task is associated with the number of alternative 'states' which are reachable from any point in the task.

Shackel[60] has described a system, developed by Palme, which elaborates this idea further. The system is designed to encourage 'user growth', and 8 levels of task have been described (with 8 corresponding levels of dialogue): at level 1, the user is led by menus and questions; at level 6, the user can define groups of commands into macros; at level 8, the dialogue is entirely command-driven and user configurable. An example might be found in the new *hypertext* systems (such as Hypercard on Apple Macintosh machines, Toolbook on IBM-type PCs, and Genesis on Acorn Archimedes machines), where several levels of dialogue are offered to users within what is basically a WIMP applications generator. The simplest level (generally termed *reader* level) allows users to 'browse' around pre-written applications; the next level, *author*, allows users to generate their own packages; and the highest level allows users to write programs directly in the script language which underlies these systems.

### Consequences of different dialogue types

It is useful to try and develop the idea of *quality* in a dialogue. Quality does not depend upon simplicity or complexity of a dialogue, but is directly related to the appropriateness of the dialogue for a particular task. Depending on the way in which dialogues are selected or developed, a number of different situations may arise:

- The user may be expected to defer towards the machine, if a machine-like dialogue syntax is used, or be expected to learn a new (possibly arcane) language. The information requirements and formats, as reflected in the dialogue, may be couched more in terms of the convenience of the programmer than of the user.

- The user may be expected to learn an inappropriately complex interface; imagine what a command-driven interface to a spreadsheet would look like, in place of the familiar grid.

- The dialogue could encourage user growth and development, starting with a simple menu or window dialogue, but allowing the user to develop skills in using a command-driven dialogue.

## Aspects of a good dialogue

Earlier, we raised the issue of how 'natural' a computer dialogue is; accepting that users will always make some assumptions of naturalness about the computer (however misplaced), Pinsky has detailed a checklist which covers the major areas of violation of what has been termed the *cooperative principle* (Grice[30]). There is an expectation on the part of the user that the dialogue will follow 'natural' lines, which in spite of being ill-defined, are capable of being violated. This violation is termed, by Pinsky, *conversational incompetence*:

- Take account of all the information transmitted by the user; do not ask for parts of it to be transmitted again

- Be pertinent: ensure that responses have a bearing on what has been transmitted

- Be logical: ensure that the response continues the rationale of the dialogue

- Give all the information necessary in the exchange (for example, the classical `'Abort/Retry/Ignore'`) gives no indication of the consequences of taking any of these actions

- Be clear: avoid references to unknown objects or processes

## Adaptive dialogues

In the course of a natural dialogue, it is expected that some modification will take place - either within a session, or between sessions. For example, teaching a novice to use a computer is unlikely to be successful if the explanation is pitched at a highly technical level in spite of the student's incomprehension. A good tutor will alter the vocabulary, knowledge base and dialogue to suit. More subtly, it is known that slight alterations of accent, or partial adoption of a partner's mannerisms, can enhance the dialogue process. Is it too much to hope that these positive aspects of human-human dialogues could be mapped across to human-computer dialogues? Indeed not. A major project within the Alvey initiative in 1984 was concerned with the investigation of intelligent adaptive dialogues, and research is very active in this area.

Before discussing how dialogues (and necessarily interfaces) may be made adaptive, we have to be quite clear as to what we mean by the word 'adaptive' - how adaptive does a dialogue need to be? And it what areas? *Adaptive* must be distinguished from *Adaptable* in this context. An adaptable dialogue is capable of modification in the form of reconfiguration, customising or 'tuning' by a user; an adaptive dialogue adapts *itself* in the light of previous knowledge about the user's performance. Totterdell, Norman and Browne[69] have suggested a convenient taxonomy of adaptive interfaces, as described by Benyon and Murray:

> *Level 1 systems* - produce a change in output in response to a change in input.

> *Level 2 systems* - include an evaluation function which selects from a range of possible outputs.

> *Level 3 systems* - include a mechanism for monitoring the effect of the selected strategy on the environment and altering the evaluation function accordingly.

> *Level 4 systems* - possess an internal model of the environment in addition to an evaluation function and use the predictive capability of the model to select an appropriate response.

> *Level 5 systems* - inherit knowledge from previous generations and adapt before they come into existence (evolution). The designer of such a system needs, therefore, to concentrate on the strategies for adaptation in addition to the mechanism.

Benyon and Murray suggest that 3 aspects of the system need to be modelled before any attempt at adaptation can be effective. There must be a **user model**, a **task model** and an **interaction model**. A user model must take account of such factors as personality, cognitive style, and resistance to change. One way of coping with this degree of diversity is to assign each user to one of a number of stereotypes.

The task model defines the syntactic and semantic aspects of the functionality of the application, and is generally stated in the form of a grammar as discussed earlier in this chapter.

The interaction model is derived from an individual user's set of strategies, heuristics and knowledge about the system and its interface, and, depending on the user and the system, may exist at a variety of levels. For example, an experienced computer user will have a different interaction model with respect to a word processing package than will an experienced secretary, although they may quite often perform the same operations.

Clearly, building the interaction model is at the heart of implementing an adaptive dialogue; and eliciting knowledge about the user-system behaviour is central to this activity. This knowledge elicitation may be manual (e.g. employing a knowledge engineer to monitor the system behaviour and modify the knowledge base). However, the range of possible behaviour is great, and it is likely that one of the automatic knowledge elicitation processes (discussed in Chapter 2) would be suitable.

## Summary

A dialogue with a computer system should be like a dialogue with a good friend - or, at least, an understanding colleague. All to often, it is more like trying to placate a duplicitous tyrant. The main reason is that dialogues, by their very nature, are open-ended and variable.

Increasingly, HCI workers are realising the importance of characterising real dialogues, and using this knowledge to build computer dialogues. Many of the problems occur in building natural language dialogues - see Chapter 10.

# 10 Natural language processing

## Introduction

It is probably every computer user's dream (or possibly nightmare) to be able to converse with a computer using natural language - that is, everyday human language as *spoken* or *written*. We can also classify some pictorial languages as natural - for example, written Chinese or Japanese.

Unfortunately, human language exhibits much more variety than attributes such as height or hair colour, even across populations. It is also characterised by a great deal of *redundancy*, that is, the message can be degraded considerably, both physically and syntactically, without losing meaning. For example, the following messages are all acceptable syntactically, and more or less identical semantically:

"I'll See you on July the 23rd"
"I'll be seeing you on the 23rd of July"
"July 23rd. See you then!"
"It's the 23rd of July that I'll be seeing you, then"

However, a formal syntax analysis system 'tuned' to any one syntactic system would have difficulty recognising all the above phrases as legal. It appears that a higher level of abstraction than the purely syntactic is necessary. The kind of system capable of doing this kind of processing is unlikely to be a formally computational machine. It is more likely to have developed its processing power by learning heuristics, rules and skills over a long period of time. In short, a human brain.

Does this mean that attempting to emulate the brain's processes in a computer is a waste of time? Not at all. It only means that computer scientists need to think in radical ways, and possibly employ devices that they would not normally regard as computers, such as neural networks.

In the future, natural language processing (NLP) is likely to have a significant impact in at least the following areas:

- NLP interfaces to databases

- Machine translation from one natural language to another

- Text scanning and recognition and/or improvement

- Text generation - for example, automatic documentation

- NLP toolkits for building specific interfaces

- Improvements to voice I/O systems (see chapter 6).

## Some attempts at NLP

### Weizenbaum's ELIZA

This interactive system was designed to fulfil one of the prime requirements of the Turing test for whether a computer is 'understanding' a conversation in any real sense. Imagine that you are in a room with a keyboard and screen, and are communicating with a 'being' in an adjacent room. The logic of the Turing test is that if you cannot tell whether the 'being' is a human or a computer, then a computer in that room would have passed the test.

Weizenbaum's program, ELIZA, was written, possibly with semi-humorous motivation, to demonstrate that understanding (even if we knew what it was) is not necessary to pass the Turing test. ELIZA simulates a psychotherapist, of a type which has often been caricatured. Its main strategy is to reflect to the user his/her own phrases, modified in a way which demonstrates a spurious 'understanding' of the original message. Certain phrases will be retained and brought out at a later stage. The following is a typical interaction:

```
Eliza:    The doctor is in..
Patient:  Hello, I have a headache.
Eliza:     Why do you say that you have a headache?
Patient:  Because I am meeting my mother for lunch.
Eliza:    How long have you had family problems?
Patient:  I do not have family problems.
.

.

.

Eliza:    Earlier you spoke about your mother.
Patient:  Yes.
Eliza:    Please do not be so short with me
Patient:  I'm late, goodbye.
Eliza:    Goodbye
```

The tricks that ELIZA uses are obvious, and yet the interaction is strangely compelling. There is an apocryphal story that Weizenbaum's secretary came to prefer interacting with ELIZA to seeing her own psychotherapist (and presumably it was cheaper.)

## Restricted-domain NLP

As we have seen, natural languages are characterised by a great deal of redundancy and variation, so much so that a computer-based natural language understanding system needs to be very complex to achieve even a moderate performance. It is worth investigating ways in which we could simplify the task of the interface, while not losing any of its power. One way is to restrict the *domain of discourse* - that is, not to allow the dialogue to rove over all possible utterances, but to restrict it to the areas of, say, financial accounting or scientific laboratories.

## Bobrow's STUDENT

Bobrow [12], in the 1960's, devised a program STUDENT, which demonstrated the power of such a technique. A typical input to STUDENT would be:

```
    (TOM HAS TWICE AS MANY FISH AS MARY HAS GUPPIES. IF
MARY HAS 3 GUPPIES, WHAT IS THE NUMBER OF FISH TOM HAS?)
```

The brackets are due to the fact that the input sentence is in fact an expression in the LISP language, which is widely used for Artificial Intelligence work).

After some fairly complex internal procedures, STUDENT returns with the following output:

```
(THE EQUATIONS TO BE SOLVED ARE)

(EQUAL X0001 (NUMBER OF FISH TOM (HAS/VERB)))

(EQUAL (NUMBER OF GUPPIES (MARY/PERSON (HAS/VERB)) 3)

(EQUAL (NUMBER OF FISH TOM (HAS/VERB)) (TIMES 2 (NUMBER OF
GUPPIES (MARY/PERSON)(HAS/VERB)))))

(THE NUMBER OF FISH TOM HAS IS 6)
```

Without going into any of the details of the internal processing, it is evident what STUDENT's strategy is. The relatively informal, loosely structured input message is transformed into a set of equations which, while conveying the same meaning, are well-structured enough to be directly calculated by standard LISP functions like EQUAL. Put another way, there are many possible input messages which map onto the canonical form expressed by the equations.

## Winograd's SHRDLU

The *domain* of SHRDLU is a small world of blocks - *blocksworld* - which have to be manipulated according to certain commands. SHRDLU has to know about two things: the grammatical rules of the domain of discourse, and the operational rules of *blocksworld*. Figure 10.1 illustrates a typical situation in blocksworld..

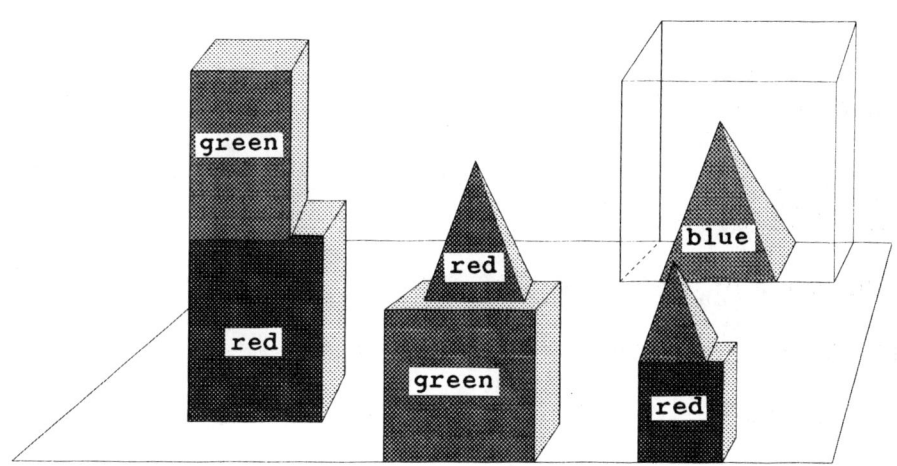

*Figure 10.1 'Blocksworld'*

## Interacting with SHRDLU

The following interaction illustrates the high degree of 'understanding' apparently exhibited by SHRDLU (from Gaines & Shaw[27]):

```
User: will you please stack up both of the red blocks and
either a green cube or a pyramid?
SHRDLU: OK

User: which cube is sitting on the table?
SHRDLU: the large green one which supports the red pyramid
User: is there a large block behind a pyramid?
SHRDLU: yes, three of them: a large red one, a large green
```

```
cube and the blue one

User: put a small one onto the green cube which supports a
pyramid
SHRDLU: OK

User: put the littlest pyramid on top of it
SHRDLU: OK

User: how many things are on top of green cubes?
SHRDLU: I'm not sure what you mean by 'on top of' in the
phrase 'on top of green cubes'
Do you mean:
1--directly on the surface
2--anywhere on top of?

User: 2
SHRDLU: Three of them

User: Had you touched any pyramid before you put the green
one on to the little cube?
SHRDLU: Yes, the green one
    .

    .

    .
```

and so on.

SHRDLU evidently provides a powerful simulacrum of understanding, and for many applications this would be adequate. Note that any ambiguities, or unknown relationships, are trapped by the system and a query made to the user. In this way, the system can build up its 'understanding' of the domain.

Clearly, for a domain in which objects undergo fairly simple transformations (such as a library or warehouse), a SHRDLU-type system could be employed. It would be particularly appropriate where untrained users would be interacting with the system. For example, most readers will have undergone the harrowing experience of queueing at a car dealer's spare parts counter, and being at the end of the queue. Apart from the usual frustrations (many people apparently regard it as a day out; many people do not appear to know what make or year or car they have got), the main problem is the identification of the offending part. The provision of public access workstations running a SHRDLU-like enquiry system (possibly with graphics) would speed up the process. The only contact between the public and the storeman would then be via a ticket with the appropriate part number printed on it. This would be greeted with enthusiasm by most storemen.

### DOS in English

Consider a user, sitting in front of a personal computer running MSDOS, and performing some housekeeping functions such as file backup from a hard disk to a tape backup unit.

The thought, as expressed by the user, might be:

> *"I'd like to back up all files in all subdirectories*
> *on the C drive which I modified after the 23rd of*
> *June 1988 to drive A"*

Many users would presumably regard it as ideal if they could directly input this message to the computer.

The reality is that the user has to enter the following command line:

```
BACKUP C:\*.* A:/S/D:06-23-88
```

(See also Chapter 2). To the casual user, the apparently simple syntax of this command hides a number of pitfalls:

- Should the *source* or the *destination* drive come first?

- Should the date qualifier be applied to the source or the destination?

- Is the date prefixed by a ':' or a '='?

Lane [41] has described a Prolog program which performs the appropriate transformations on a 'naturalistic' command message to turn it into something which is acceptable to the MSDOS command line interpreter (CLI). Assuming the input message *"Show all the files on drive B"*, the transformations are:

- Break the input line into tokens (*Show, all, the, files, on, drive, B*).

- Remove "chaff" such as *a, the, you*.

- Remove redundancies in the input (*every, all, complete* all map on to *all* or, further, to \*.\*).

- Look for a command (*kill, erase, remove, zap, wipe* all map onto *del*).

- 'Massage' the resulting message so that the word order fits a known syntax.

- If it is not possible to construct a plausible command, issue an error message and advise the user. Otherwise, issue the command. If the operating system does not recognise the syntax, the resulting error can be 'trapped' and a friendly error message given.

As Lane points out, this concept of error trapping could be extended to include the *likely* commission of errors (or, more accurately, mistakes). For example, on receipt of the command:

```
Kill all my .SYN files
```

it would be extremely helpful to have the response:

```
Do you really want to delete your only copy of NLDOS.SYN?
You've been working on it for hours.
```

This could be achieved by a simple process of checking the timestamp of the file(s) concerned, checking the current date, and finding out the last modification time of the file (all stored by MSDOS). Although this is reminiscent of the ominously friendly HAL computer in the film '2001 - a Space Odyssey' - or of the over-solicitous talking city Bellwether in Robert Sheckley's 'Dimension of Miracles' - it could save a great deal of time and frustration at the keyboard.

## Query languages

The interrogation and update of databases provides a perfect environment for the development of domain-specific NLP. After the proliferation of many different kinds of query language during the 1970s, a standard (structured query language, SQL) has been established, which follows largely the practice adopted by IBM.

SQL languages are invariably used as the interface to a *relational database* system. The technical details are beyond the scope of this book, but, briefly, a relational database comprises a number of *tables*, each table containing a number of *rows*. Each row comprises one record, split into a number of *fields*, and is uniquely identified by a *key* (which is, conventionally, the first field). Any field that is not the key is referred to as a *foreign key*. A foreign key can also be the key to another table. In this way, the various tables can be made to relate to one another.

### Syntax of SQL

By combining a (surprisingly) few keywords and operators, complex queries can be built up. The language is easy for the novice to learn, but supports 'power users' in their development.

The three main keywords are:

```
select      (column/s)
from        (table/s)
where       (row/s)
```

In addition, there are a number of qualifiers:

```
group by
having
order by
```

and a number of operators:

```
and or = != > >= between like
```

These can be combined into simple 'phrases' such as

```
select deptno, deptname from dept;
```

or quite complex ones:

```
select dept.deptno, deptname, job, empname
from emp, dept
where dept.deptno = emp.deptno and loc = 'chicago'
order by emp.deptno;
```

In the last query, two tables, *dept* and *emp*, were joined on the basis of the equality of the 'shared' key `deptno`.

For the kind of transaction common in database retrieval and update activities, it can be seen that SQL is an appropriate 'natural' language to use. For a skilled operator, the cognitive match is probably as good as any other kind of interface.

## More advanced NLP

Although the pattern matching of Eliza, the domain specific intelligence of SHRDLU and the utility of 'EnglishDOS' and SQL are undoubtedly useful in their own areas, we need more powerful techniques if we are to attain a more general NLP system. For this we need to look at the way truly natural - that is, human - languages are processed. Here we have a problem, because there is still much to be discovered about how this is done in the human brain.

There are several theories, each with its associated set of computer models, and they all seem to work quite well. We will briefly review some of them here, but the reader should note that this is an extensively researched area, and many journals exist.

### Transformational grammars

We owe the notion of transformational grammars to the linguist Chomsky. A grammar is a formal notation which describes a complex process, rather like a set of mathematical formulae. Additionally, it can be used directly as a 'template' against which to check the correctness of an input, when that input is correctly *parsed* (analysed). A transformational grammar establishes rules for *transforming* an input so that it can be rewritten as a set of grammatical rules. If the rules are in an acceptable form, then the input was correct. Note that the establishment of the *meaning* of an utterance is not the main purpose of a grammar, but is a useful side-effect. Figure 10.2 shows a (very simple) rewrite grammar using production rules.

```
S -> NP VP
NP -> DET NP1
NP -> NP1
NP1 -> ADJ NP1
NP1 -> NOUN
VP -> VERB ADV
NOUN -> bottles
VERB -> sink
ADJ -> furious
DET -> the
ADV -> slowly
```

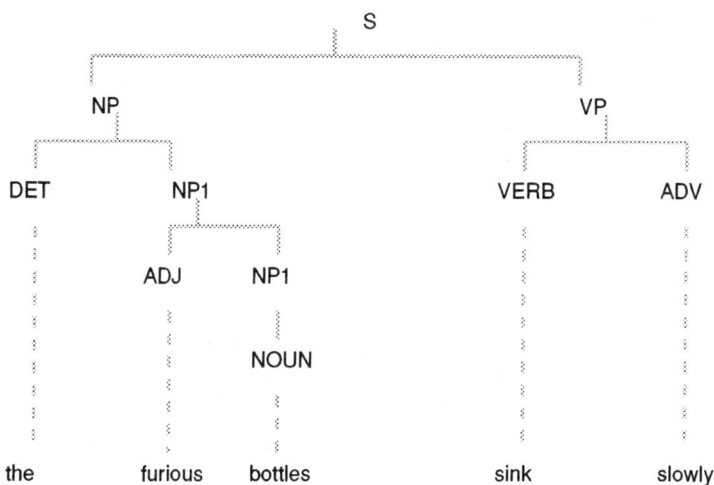

slowly, the furious bottles sink
the bottles, furious, slowly sink

*Figure 10.2 A rewrite grammar using production rules*

Although the sentences illustrated are patent nonsense, they are grammatically correct.

## Parsers

The grammars discussed above constitute the 'what' of language structure. We now need to consider *how* messages are analysed (parsed) for meaning.

There are two main types of parser - *deterministic* and *non-deterministic*. The distinction is concerned with when the decision on correctness is made. A deterministic parser will attempt to keep the analysis 'correct' all the way through the message. A non-deterministic parser will defer this decision until all the input has been received. Most practical parsers are non-deterministic, and there are two kinds: *Top-down* and *bottom-up*. The distinction concerns how the input message is analysed.

### *Top-down parsers*

These proceed by matching the portions of the input message against the grammar rules, starting with the top rewrite rule. If there is a failure in the match, the parser *backtracks* and retries the next rewrite rule. The main problem with top-down parsers is that a significantly ill-formed input upsets the analysis.

### *Bottom-up parsers*

A bottom-up parser proceeds by attempting to combine low-order elements in the input message into higher-order constituents according to the rules of the grammar. To avoid backtracking, a number of *stacks* are maintained to store intermediate results. When an analysis has reached the top level of a rewrite grammar, and there is nothing left on its stack, the message is deemed to be grammatical. A significant advantage of a bottom-up parser is that it is not upset by ill-formed input.

### *Transition networks as deterministic parsers*

Figure 10.3 illustrates a transition network for a simple language. The symbols of the language are *p,b,i,o* and the grammatical rules are embedded in the structure of the network. If a simple network such as this is enhanced with such features as look-ahead, global registers, conditions and actions, it is known as an *augmented transition network (ATN)*. An ATN is better able to cope with ill-formed input, and can parse more complex grammars.

## Definite clause grammars (DCGs)

Black[11] has described the DCG as a formalism for representing grammars in a rule format that has the power of a transformational grammar. The language Prolog is eminently suitable for implementing DCGs, because (a) the syntax of the formal statements conforms to the syntax of Prolog clauses and (b) when set out in this way, the DCG constitutes a runnable Prolog program. The following simple DCG corresponds loosely to the rewrite grammar of Figure 10.2:

```
sentence:- noun_phrase, verb_phrase.
noun_phrase:- adj, noun_phrase.
noun_phrase:- determ, common_noun.
noun_phrase:- common_noun.
verb_phrase:- verb, noun_phrase.
verb_phrase:- verb, adverb.

determ:- [a].
determ:- [the].
common_noun:- [bottle].
verb:- [sinks].
adverb:- [slowly].
adj:- [furious].
```

## Natural visual languages

Natural languages are not restricted to the written or spoken variety. We have in addition a rich repertoire of visual 'languages', from simple iconic representations (see chapter 8) to more complex ones such as cartoon strips.

Kindborg and Kollerbaur[40] have described the combination of lexical and visual presentation as 'lexivisual', and provide a number of rules

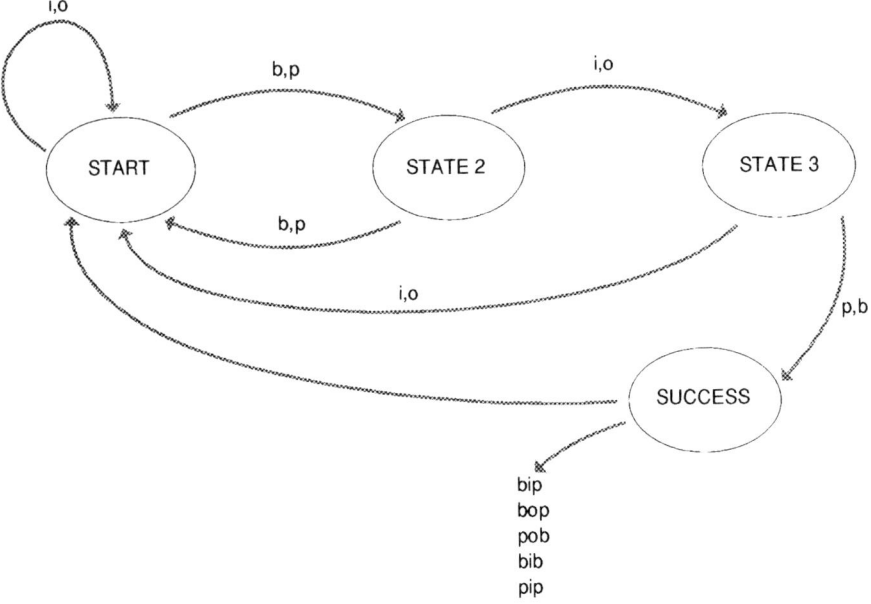

*Figure 10.3 A transition network for a simple grammar*

which determine good lexivisual presentation:

- Lexivisuals should have visual totality, be separate and self-contained

- They should give basic guidance, and limit presentation to primary facts and general aspects

- It should be possible to use lexivisuals as an aid to further studies

- They should make best use of the interplay between text and graphics to bring out the content of the presentation.

*Figure 10.4 Lexivisual and onomatopoeic presentations (from Kindborg & Kollerbaur 1987)*

## Summary

There is a variety of natural languages which people would like to use when interacting with their computer. Some are linguistic, and some are visual. It's even possible that computing may become enjoyable.

# 11 Usability

*"We have about 5 million pounds' worth of software sitting on the shelf, unused.*

*Why? Nobody can use it."*

*An oil industry executive*

## Introduction

The 'acid test' of a computer system is its usability, as judged by the user. This is more than just the quality of the interface or the colours on the screen; it embraces the quality of the dialogue design, the 'cognitive match' between the system and the user, and the quality of the documentation, online help (if appropriate) and general operating environment.

In this chapter we address the following questions:

- How do we define usability?

- How do we measure it?

- How do we ensure that it is 'built in' to every new system?

## Defining usability

Although people speak of a 'usable' package, the word is generally used in a casual way - if asked to elaborate further, users, even experienced one, become vague: "...it's just ...well... *usable*".

Shackel[60a] has analysed various usability measures and has proposed an operational definition of usability (i.e. as a set of goals), which can be incorporated into the requirements specification of a project:

### *Effectiveness*

- at better than some required level of performance (e.g. in terms of speed and errors)

- by some required percentage of the specified target range of users

- within some required proportion of the range of usage environments

### *Learnability*

- within some specified time from installation and start of user training

- based upon some specified amount of training and user support

- and within some specified re-learning time each time for intermittent users

### *Flexibility*

- with flexibility allowing adaptation to some specified percentage variation in tasks and/or environments beyond those first specified

### *Attitude*

- and within acceptable levels of human cost in terms of tiredness, discomfort, frustration and personal effort

- so that satisfaction causes continued and enhanced usage of the system

This is an interesting set of guidelines, and it begs several questions. How can early design decisions ensure enhanced usage of the system? And how do we cope with the enormous variation between users, and the interaction between satisfaction and learning? We also have a problem with newer, windowed systems, which seem to have solved all the usability problems at one stroke. Indeed, the 'look and feel' of such packages is now a legal 'hot potato'.

Useful though Shackel's definition is, perhaps we should pull back to a less operational, more theoretical stance to complement the picture.

Figure 11.1 is an attempt to illustrate the 'static' and 'dynamic' structures and processes due to the user, designer and computer. Ideally, there should be a shared understanding of facts and methods. The more the circles overlap, the more usable the system. In a sense it reflects principles that are more psychological than many computing workers care to admit.

It is, of course, anthropomorphic to regard the computer system as in any way 'understanding' in the way that humans do. However, to the extent that it is capable of transmitting intentions in a more or less transparent way, it is convenient here to confer the attribute of understanding upon it.

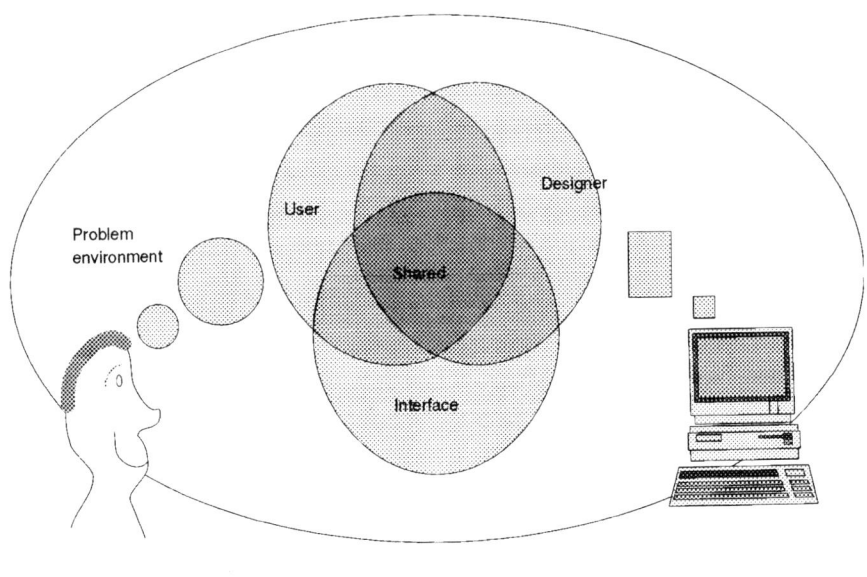

Human                                    Computer

*Figure 11.1 Shared 'understanding' between user, system and designer.*

It is convenient, however, to discuss each of these aspects separately, while bearing in mind that the user's experience is related to the totality of his/her experience.That being said, a major fault in the design or operation of a subsystem (such as a sticking key on a keyboard) can drastically influence the perceived usability of a system.

The goal of all HCI workers must be to establish a sufficiently strong and reproducible model of usability to enable it to be designed into a system from the very start.

### Gestalts

The concept of a *gestalt* is convenient in the context of usability - it implies that a system is understood as a totality, rather than as a collection of parts. Once the gestalt is grasped, operations with the system are better informed and more rapidly executed - a trivial example being the appropriate operation of accelerator and clutch pedals while moving off in a car. Some people never move beyond the early stage of independent operations on each pedal and hoping for the best. Many issues in usability may be interpreted as problems with gestalts.

### *Positive and negative transfer*

Possession of a gestalt can confer its own problems. Ideally, the gestalt can be used as a model to inform, for example, the learning of a new task. This has been termed *positive transfer* (of skills). However, if certain aspects of the task are fundamentally different, there can be *negative transfer* effects - previously well-learned and understood actions are now inappropriate to the new task. Such a situation would arise when, for example, an experienced user of the VAX/VMS operating system has to perform some work on a Unix system (or vice-versa). Whereas a novice would consult the manual for the correct syntax for a command, the experienced user is quite likely to become frustrated trying out known commands in the other system which either do not work or which work incorrectly.

In the worst case, aspects of the new task will have a spurious similarity to aspects of the old task, but have different consequences. A well known horror story among Unix users is the inadvertent deletion of all a user's files in all directories by inappropriate use of the *wild card* option in a **rm** (remove) command:

```
rm *.*
```

An MSDOS user who has just got used to the idea that **rm** in Unix corresponds to **del** in MSDOS will probably fail to notice the more extensive scope of the Unix command.

## Measuring usability

It is certainly useful to have an idea of what usability is, and to argue that it should be improved. But to convince software developers and purchasers we need more than fine words. We need some *metrics*. Having identified various indicators of usability, they must be measured in a controlled way and the results interpreted to provide a meaningful message.

## Monitors

An extremely convenient way of tracking users' behaviour is to interpose some measuring apparatus - a monitor - between the user and the machine (see also Chapter 4). The monitor should be transparent (i.e. undetectable) in operation, and will be able to produce a 'running commentary' on the following aspects of the interaction:

- Typed input from the user (e.g. commands, help requests etc.)

- Output from the system (e.g. error messages)

- Time delays between operations

With the advent of graphical user interfaces (GUIs) running on a common platform - such as X window - monitors can be constructed quite easily, and the following aspects of the interaction can be monitored in addition to those listed above:

- Mouse movement

- Menu and dialogue box selections

- Events such as a window being visited by the pointer

Figure 11.2 illustrates how a monitor in X window could be implemented. It is written as a normal X client, and functions by 'trapping' all Xlib calls generated by the application. It extracts the necessary information, such as timing, and updates its record file. The system call is then relayed, unchanged, to its original destination.

At a later stage, the report file is interrogated (this could be also done online via a separate window seen only by the investigator) and the results analysed.

The analysis could range from a simple list of events to a complex statistical analysis of the results.

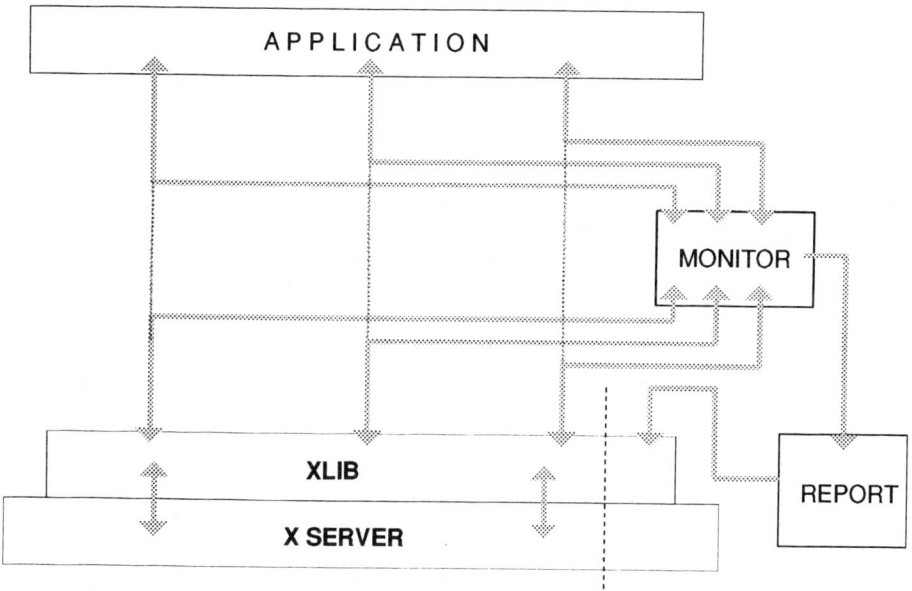

*Figure 11.2 A monitor running in the X window system*

The 'raw' output of a typical monitor session would look something like this:

```
Outer window is 0x700001, inner window is 0x700002

CreateNotify event, serial 7, synthetic NO, window
0x700001, parent 0x700001, window 0x700002, (10,10), width
50, height 50, border_width 4, override NO

ButtonPress event, serial 12, synthetic NO, window
0x700001, root 0x8006b, subw 0x0, time 660530112, (80,67),
root:(182,169), state 0x0, button 1, same_screen YES

MotionNotify event, serial 12, synthetic NO, window
```

0x700001, root 0x8006b, subw 0x0, time 660530272, (80,67),
root:(182,169), state 0x100, is_hint 1, same_screen YES

ButtonRelease event, serial 12, synthetic NO, window
0x700001, root 0x8006b, subw 0x0, time 660530272, (80,67),
root:(182,169), state 0x100, button 1, same_screen YES

### Structural maps

As we saw in Chapter 8, most people have a well-developed spatial sense. It would seem reasonable to assume, then, that anything that can strengthen the user's internal *cognitive map* of an application will assist in learning and understanding the package.

Certain educational theorists such as Ausubel [7] maintain that pre-structuring of material to be learned is useful if not essential to its ultimate retention. This concept has been stated in everyday terms as:

> *"You can't teach people what they don't already know"*

Patrick and Fitzgibbon [53] performed an interesting experiment in which this principle was put to the test. Performance (in terms of speed and error) of a computer-based editing task was tested in associated with the presentation of a map of the relationships between the functional elements of that task. The map was presented before (AD condition), after (PD condition) or not at all (ND condition). The results are shown in Figures 11.3 and 11.4.

It will be seen that the presence of the structural display enhanced both speed and error performance, particularly in the Advance Display condition. This is mainly due to the 'relevant ideational scaffolding' that the structure display provides.

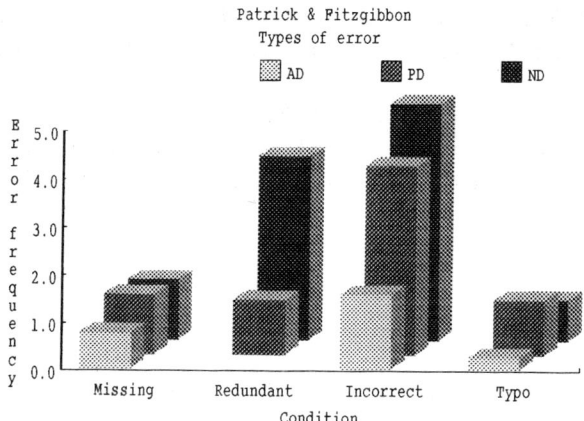

*Figure 11.3 Types of error committed in the Patrick and Fitzgibbon experiment. The conditions were: structure displayed in advance (AD); structure displayed afterwards (PD); no structure displayed (ND)*

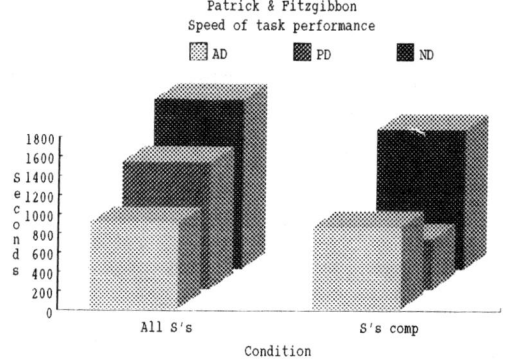

*Figure 11.4 Speed of task performance in the Patrick and Fitzgibbon experiment. The conditions were: data from all subjects (All S' s) and data from subjects completing (S' s comp)*

The difficulty of establishing certainties in this area is illustrated by an experiment conducted by Foss *et al*[25], again using computer manuals, which in some way contradicts Patrick and Fitzgibbon' finding. The Foss study used three independent variables: abstract versus concrete syntax; complex versus simple organisation; and presence or absence of a surrogate (mental) model. The results are illustrated in Figures 11.5a, 11.55b and 11.5c.

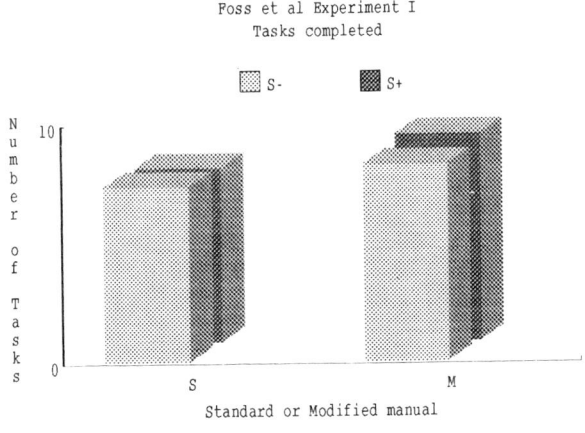

*igure 11.5(a)*

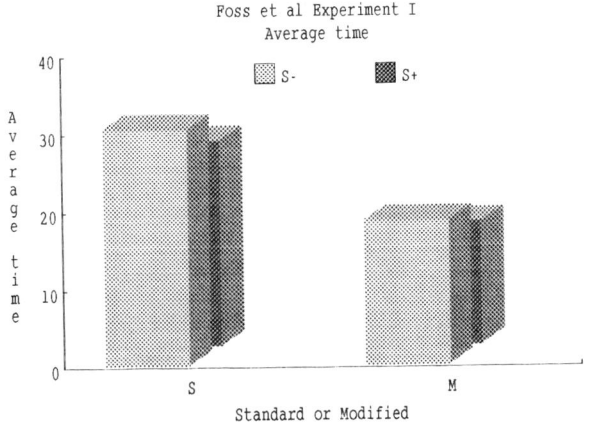

*Figure 11.5(b)*

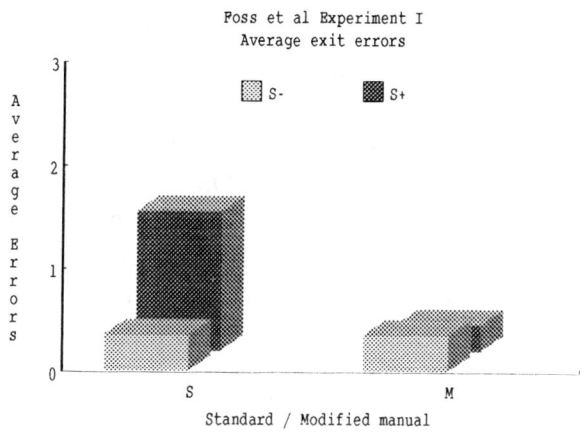

Figure 11.5(c)

## Documentation

Good documentation should provide more than an overview of the system and operating instructions. It should provide a 'safety net' so that any part of the system's functionality can be examined, and should attempt to provide paths for the solution of common problems.More subtly, it should in some sense enable the designer to 'stay with' the user. The aspects we will discuss are *structure*, *style*, and *content*.

### Structure

When a user refers to the hardcopy documentation for an applications package, it is rarely out of curiosity, or a search for pleasure. In the early stages, it may be to find out how to install the system; later, the user may wish to re-install parts of the system. Alternatively, it may be to seek information on one of the most commonly used functions in the system. Either way, the relevant parts should be accessible but this should not be at the cost of confusing the user.

**Style**
The following 'gem' is reported by Sohr [64]:

> *"The insert/delete key deletes characters to the left*
> *of the cursor position if operated in lowercase and*
> *if the Shift key is held down at the same time as*
> *pressing INST/DEL all characters to the right of*
> *the screen cursor are moved one position to the*
> *right with every keystroke and spaces created".*

Ironically, there are signs that the author of this piece was trying to be 'chatty', but it has gone very wrong. There is an inconsistent use of verbs - keys are variously 'operated' or 'pressed'. The key in question is referred to by different names, which would be confusing to a beginning user. The sentence is too long and the grammar is questionable, so that the user is not sure what 'every keystroke' refers to. Is it the INST/DEL key? Or some other key, like an alphanumeric key? Is the user expected to hold down the Shift key, press (or operate) the INST/DEL key, and press the new letter simultaneously, or does one press suffice?

This may seem like nit-picking. But first impressions tend to persist, so a user who eventually learns to experiment and develops self-help strategies will not forget the negative early experience that such badly-written 'help' creates.

The crucial function of any piece of documentation is to convey *information*, not just data. Sohr has suggested the following strategy for the documentation author:

- **Organize by Tasks** - A manual which takes the user through the various tasks in a *job-oriented* way, rather than in the order in which the tasks appear in menus, will be more rapidly understood.

- **Use Organizers** - These are 'links', possibly in a different typeface, which introduce the user to a new concept so that he/she is mentally prepared, and new terminology is likely to stick. (These are discussed later from a more theoretical stance)

- **Move from the Whole to the Parts** - The user will have substantial *domain knowledge* of the job that the application has to perform, so this should be capitalised upon. New information, such as how the application performs a task with which the user is familiar, can be introduced so that the user's knowledge and understanding are developed incrementally.

- **Repeat, Repeat** - Important points can be 'stamped' in by subtle use of repetition. Several examples could be given of a new feature, or an important concept - such as deletion - could be mentioned a number of times in a chapter.

- **Write Actively and Logically** - A warm, active style communicates information far better than a dry, 'technical' style. Unfortunately, the applications programmer is often the person who writes the documentation. The result is sometimes a kind of literary 'mugging' of the non-technical user.

- **Write Relevantly and Simply** - If a new concept is introduced, it should be explained simply. If a concept is not really needed, then it should be avoided altogether. A diagram can save many words of explanation.

- **Evaluate with the Eyes of a User** - This means going through a serious evaluation process with real users, taking the feedback seriously, and acting on it.

### Online help

The small experiment (detailed in Chapter 12) carried out as part of an HCI assignment at Bristol Polytechnic, illustrates the various problems of beginning users. A package (Turbo Pascal) was used for the first time by 32 people, and 'protocols' taken of their experiences as they entered, compiled and ran a small program.

One significant aspect that emerged was that users were confused as to 'where' they were in the integrated environment; just as importantly, they were often confused as to 'how they got there'. This concept of navigation seems to be central to most people's understanding of the system they are using, if it is anything more complex than  a simple menu-driven application. The user has to make choices from an early stage, and to make a choice people need information about the consequences of that choice (ignoring, for the moment, the benefits that can be obtained from serendipitous browsing).

Online help systems have been developed to assist the user in this 'navigation' problem at the point of delivery, as it were. Generally, pressing a key (commonly function key 1) calls up a help window containing appropriate information on the function currently in play. If the user is 'in' the editor section of an integrated package, for example, a table of keystrokes and their effects will be displayed. Further, more detailed, information is obtainable from a menu - e.g. keystroke shortcuts. In command line driven systems such as VAX/VMS, a similar facility is offered via the **help** command.

### MultimediaVideo, Cassettes etc.

In the more developed online help systems, the help text contains highlighted words which, when pointed at (using the cursor or mouse) and selected, provide more detailed information (possibly with further submenus). This is the simplest form of *active text,* or *hypertext*, which is becoming a highly developed area. There is in principle no limit to the kind of procedure which can be called up on the selection of an active text - sounds, animated images, interactive video from a compact disk, other applications - can be displayed in a separate window.

### Paper versus screen

Although the concept of a multimedia based context-sensitive online help system is very attractive, it is possible that in certain situations an old-fashioned document may be preferred. Books (or, for documentation, ring-bound manuals) still offer certain advantages over screen-based systems:

- They can be 'browsed' readily so that, depending on the purpose, access can be on a 'rapid scanning' basis or a more detailed examination made

- Notes can be made by the user (in pencil!) to assist understanding

- Parts can be photocopied for personal use

- They can be put into libraries

### Operating systems

Advances in operating system functionality have meant that the range of services available has extended beyond 'time of day' and 'file housekeeping' functions: many now incorporate tools and hooks so that applications developers can make use of operating systems 'primitives' (such as windows) to make help information available.

## General issues of Usability

We have assumed that the quest for usability is on a linear trend - the more we succeed in understanding usability factors, the more usable our systems will become. This is a dangerous assumption - although William of Ockham urged us not to complicate things unnecessarily, in certain cases the converse advice is useful: *Do not simplify things unnecessarily.*

In a paper entitled 'Ease of use - the ultimate deception?' presented to the HCI-86 conference, Thimbleby [68] argues that

> *"... if a system is sufficiently powerful to be 'easy to use' this implies it is sufficient to confuse."*

This assertion is borne out when we consider the everyday experience of users - trivial use of a package is often satisfactory, but once the user strays from this path, and attempts something rather more sophisticated, a 'Pandora's Box' (in Thimbleby's terms) is opened. He quotes the example of an intelligent user (a lecturer) who, after taking a considerable time learning a mathematical package, finds it ultimately unusable - the instructions are incomprehensible and the package uses little-known algorithms to achieve some results, which means that it cannot be used for teaching purposes, as the results cannot be verified.

*A personal experience...*

A little while ago, the author passed one of the personal computer laboratories in his department at Bristol Polytechnic. The unmistakable sounds of terminal confusion coming through the open door were heartrending. Always eager to help, (and possibly pick up any HCI snippets) he entered.

The scene was one of chaos. Piles of listing paper lay on the floor; students stared distractedly at the dot matrix printers, the lids of which had been removed (which added to the noise.)

What they were trying to do was simple - print out an assignment using an industry standard word processing package on an industry standard printer. The solution was, on the surface, simple. If you set up the applications package and the printer to make the same assumptions, all would be well. Collectively, the students were aware of the following facts:

- The assignment had to be printed on A4 paper, which is 297 millimetres ($11^2/3$ inches) long.

- The word processing package could be installed for 11 inch, A4 and 'other' paper sizes.

- The package could be set up to provide a Form Feed character at the end of a page, or to vertically 'fill' with blank lines for printers which do not have a 'top of form' operation.

- The printers (24 pin Near Letter Quality types) could be set up for a variety of paper sizes, including A4, by using a convenient setup dialogue.

- The printers could be set up for a 'top of form' operation which would feed the paper to the next perforation for the selected size.

The students were even aware of a very nasty 'gotcha' in the world of computer consumables, which is that A4 paper is not *exactly* 11.66" in length, which can lead to the bottom margin gradually shrinking throughout the document. The cure is to buy 'exact A4' which is, of course, more expensive.

After half a day of trying every possible combination, including some which apparently worked at first but went very wrong later, the students were ready to give up. Sadly, none of them had read any Sherlock Holmes stories. If they had, they would have remembered Holmes' Famous Dictum (slightly paraphrased): that if you have eliminated all but one of the possibilities in solving a problem, then whatever remains, *however unlikely*, is the solution. The improbable possibility, which comprised the solution in this case, was that they were using the wrong paper size. Due to a similar unfortunate experience in 1979, the author was able to point out, after a decent interval, that they were using 12" paper, which they had purchased from the computer centre, and which at first glance is indistinguishable from A4 paper. When approached, the computer Centre quite reasonably pointed out that they had been asked for "word processing" paper, which is what they had supplied (it was printed on the box). Although they knew the difference between A4 and 12" paper, they did not know that the students did not have this information. Moreover, neither party knew that the appellation "word processing paper" in this context is an American usage, and seems to refer exclusively to 12" paper.

The significant point here is that the *logical* thing to do was not the most *sensible* thing to do. Allowing the possibility of the paper size being wrong had been somehow ruled out by the problem environment - it was not in the rules of that game.

## Ensuring usability

Now that we have some terminology for, and metrics of, usability, it should be possible to think of some prescriptions for building it into new systems, and even into existing ones. However, it is unlikely that a stipulation of 'better cognitive matching' will be well received by a hardened systems analyst. The likely response would be 'what do you mean, exactly?'

The onus is on the HCI worker, then, to translate the high-level goals of usability into specific lists of requirements. This is a very important exercise, because to do it correctly means that HCI becomes more than a set of anodyne wishes. But what is the best way of conveying a 'usability checklist' which could be consulted by the design team?

It would be useful here to review the 'HCI model' outlined in Chapter 1. You will remember that we specified dimensions of 'depth' and 'strength'. For a system to be fully usable, it follows that the HCI should be as 'strong' and 'deep' as possible, within the limits of what we know about the cognitive ergonomics of the interaction. In other words, state-of-the-art HCI findings should be referenced and built in wherever possible. A sensible 'wish list' should stick to one level on the 'depth/strength' model.

As an example, we will track through a hypothetical development: a new system for the dealing floor of a medium-sized building society. Most building societies accumulate spare money during the day, which is made good use of by putting it on the international money markets for short periods, sometimes overnight. (If this seems to be a pointless exercise, the reader might care to work out the interest, at current rates, on £750,000,000 over 24 hours.)

A typical existing 'dealing station' comprises at least three screens: one holding a display of all major currencies at their 'buy' and 'sell' levels; one displaying other relevant financial information from the SEAQ Stock Exchange information system; and one screen for global financial information such as Dow Jones or Reuters. At the moment, each display has its own dedicated keyboard with special purpose function keys, and operators must know their way around all of them. The display quality often leaves much to be desired (on a system seen by the author, the displays were completely illegible due to bad focusing, and the dealers seemed to take a certain pride in being able to decipher what was on them.)

Given a free hand, what set of checklists would we produce?

## Ensuring usability

Although we have discussed in some detail a number of things that will ensure usability, we have to remember that system designers are human, and that human beings often need reminding of quite simple things to improve the quality of their work. (As a child, the author was fascinated by a small card carried in the driver's cab of all buses in Bristol: *Avoid*

*Prince Street Bridge*. Parents, aunts and bus conductors were submitted to a relentless inquisition regarding the reason for this injunction. The reason was never apparent, until a bus tried to drive across the bridge - it was one inch narrower than the bus). In a similar way, we need a few simple guidelines to assist us in the design of sociotechnical systems. Here are just two:

- Analyse the *human* and the *computer* tasks properly

- Design the system properly.

Wood-Harper et al[71] have summarised the important stages in the design of sociotechnical systems (figure 11.6)

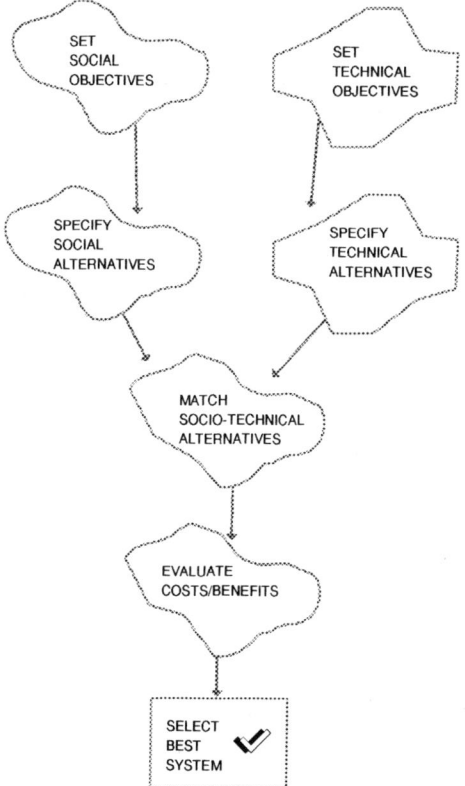

*Figure 11.6 Stages in designing for usability (after Wood-Harper* et al)

## Summary

If asked to sum up the main concern of HCI in one word, the word would be 'usability'. As we have seen, it is possible to offer working definitions of usability, to measure it and to offer advice to system designers. To this extent, it is a commodity, which may be to HCI what expert Systems were to Artificial Intelligence.

# 12 Experimental studies

> *When you can measure what you are speaking about, and express it in numbers, you know something about it. [Otherwise,] your knowledge is of a meagre and unsatisfactory kind.*
>
> *Lord Kelvin*

## Introduction

Part of the attraction of HCI is that it is a comparatively new discipline. which has not had time for all its domains of investigation to 'freeze' into different areas. One of the consequences is that good ideas, and their exploration, are not solely the prerogative of professional workers or researchers - students, workers in other disciplines, or even interested laypersons can follow through an interest in HCI without needing a large research grant (or, indeed, anything more than paper and pencil).

The experiments detailed in this chapter were all carried out by students pursuing an HCI option in the Department of computer Studies at Bristol Polytechnic. The experiments are simple in conception and execution, but demonstrate that useful things can be done on a limited resource budget. Experiment 1 was carried out in two 2-hour sessions (16 people in each session) and all the others were carried out as 'mini-projects' of 2 or 3 sessions of 2 hours duration.

# Experiment 1 - Using a new package

### Introduction
32 people participated in this study, which was designed to elicit information about users' experiences in a fairly free format. The scenario was 'getting to grips with a new package'. The package chosen, Turbo Pascal Version 5.5, is very popular in universities and polytechnics, offering as it does an integrated environment for program editing, compilation and test running. It is also used for running some of the experiments described elsewhere in this book. There is no doubt that it is friendly, robust and good value for money. But would the vendors claim that it is a perfect product?

This investigation sought to extract, in a fairly free form, information about what new, or naive, users think about a system, in this case an integrated programming environment.

The following *protocols* represent a condensed version of the raw data obtained in a 30 minute session. We present the raw data first because there were no preconceptions about what would emerge from the study.

### Method
The data was collected in the following way:

- The 16 people in each session were organised as 8 groups of 2. One member of the group acted as the 'guinea-pig', and the other member recorded the protocols. The experimental task was to enter, compile and run a simple program of the 'Hello World' type.

- The groups were asked to identify significant tasks, such as browsing around the menus, and identify problems, and solutions, associated with the task.

- Each group then compiled a list of the three most significant items.

- At the end of the session, all groups reported back verbally and the lists were recorded and discussed.

## Protocols

A selection of the protocols obtained is listed below, followed by a discussion. Note that they are unedited.

Task:      Getting help
Problem:   Opaque
Reason:    Assuming too high user knowledge
Solution:  a) Site enhancement; b) Online tutorial

Task:      Navigating menus
Problem:   Terseness; lack of clarity
Reason:    Cramping
Solution:  Bigger virtual screens

Task:      General familiarity
Problem:   Unclear meanings; 'Gotchas'
Reason:    Use of jargon ('Remove all watches')
Solution:  Analyse required knowledge levels

Task:      Getting to an item (in the menu hierarchy)
Problem:   Not obvious where we are
Reason:    Non-obvious indicators
Solution:  More plentiful/obvious status indicators (e.g. flashing)

Task:      Running the program (having compiled it)
Problem:   Keypresses not obvious - options not related to actions
Reason:    Cognitive mismatch
Solution:  Better English

Task:      Backtracking (through a menu hierarchy)
Problem:   Can't remember how we got here
Reason:    Cognitive mapping (to avoid 'sleepwalking')

Solution:    Online map - geographical?

Task:        Menu browsing generally
Problem:     How did I get here? How do I get to where I want to be?
Reason:      Spatial memory not being exploited
Solution:    Geographical mapping; Employ some psychologists!

Task:        General operations (editing, compiling etc.)
Problem:     What do to next
Reason:      Too many choices
Solution:    Ask user status

Task:        Loading/saving files
Problem:     Opaque user instructions
Reason:      Incomplete expansion
Solution:    More task analysis

Task:        General interface
Problem:     Claims to both 'logical' and 'intuitive' (is this possible?)
Reason:      Lack of thought/clarity
Solution:    More thought

## Discussion

Although no attempt was made at a statistical analysis of the data, one or two issues stand out as being worthy of further investigation:

- Users value highly a knowledge of 'where they are' in a package.

- A high degree of functionality is of little use if it cannot be accessed transparently (see Chapter 2).

On the first point, it is interesting to note that geographical data displays for databases, and topological displays generally, are coming under increasing attention from software developers.

Secondly, the various functions and operations within a package must be comprehensible to the user, especially if the package is 'user-driven' (that is, the user's choice of tasks is not predetermined, but comprises a sequence of optional selections).

## Experiment 2: Terminals versus workstations

### Introduction

Many of the advances in computing over the last few years have owed much to the exploitation of hardware and software technology, in particular in the area of visual interfaces (see Chapter 8). However, as in most things in life, an uncritical acceptance of new techniques is as inadvisable as an unreasoning Luddism.

The motivation behind this experiment was to test the assertion that visual interfaces improve the ease of task completion, especially where a highly interactive application is concerned.

### Method

#### Target Application

The application chosen was VAXNotes, which is a computer conferencing system running on DEC VAX minicomputers and workstations. The main rationale behind this choice was that:

- The VAXNotes application running on the host machine is the same, irrespective of the interface being used.

- The CSM Department at Bristol Polytechnic possesses a VAX cluster system, interfaced by conventional terminals and by workstations running the DEC version of X Window.

#### Subjects

19 subjects were tested, and the data from 18 used. All the subjects were familiar with the VAX environment.

***The task***

A simple task was required of each subject: to read a note in the VAXNotes system, and to reply to it. Each subject performed the task on both a conventional ASCII terminal, and on a workstation (DEC VAXStation).

***Data***

Data was again collected in the form of *protocols* - that is, transcripts of the subjects' responses to specific questions. (Strictly speaking, a protocol is an unstructured and open-ended monologue. In this context, the term is appropriate because subjects were allowed to 'ramble' as they answered the questions. Cynics have referred to this kind of data as 'psychobabble').

**Results**

The results obtained were astonishing. In *all* cases, the subjects preferred the terminal over the workstation. Some of the reasons were as follows:

- Users 'knew where they were' with the terminal version

- The prompts were more specific on the terminal version

- The use of the entire screen area on the terminal was preferred

- The terminal version was faster

- There were fewer keystrokes on the terminal version.

- Overall, the terminal version was simpler to 'drive'.

Some of the *raw data* of this study is listed below, in the form of quotes.

> *"I had no idea what to do [on the workstation]"*

> *"The workstation was aesthetically pleasing but*

*confusing"*

*"[The terminal] was clear, but uninteresting"*

*"[The workstation] was intimidating"*

*"There were too many possibilities for making a mistake [on the workstation]"*

*"I got lost in the middle of the task [on the workstation]"*

*"I wondered if the right things were happening while I waited [at the workstation]"*

*"I kept clicking, but nothing was happening [workstation]"*

*"The task was easier to grasp on a terminal"*

*"The keyboard gave better control, but the mouse was more fun"*

## Conclusions

The workstation is a prime example of what we have referred to as *technological push* (see Chapter 1). Typically linked to a powerful multiuser operating system such as Unix or VMS, it provides a 'virtual window' into several applications simultaneously. For a programmer or software developer, the benefits are significant. For example, the source code of a program can be displayed in one window while it runs in another under a debugger, with the output being displayed in a third window.

We now need to address the problem of why this enhanced functionality does not appear to map across well to the typical end user. Perhaps the significant issue is that of *multitasking* in the broad sense of the word. It seemed, overall, that users could not cope very well with multiple views on a single task if the various sections of the task were not easily discriminable.

It could be that a thoughtful use of, for example, colour could have served as an adequate disambiguator of the stages within a task. Certainly, once a number of windows were open on the monochrome screen, the impression was of a confusion of edges and corners, located all in one plane, rather than a set of overlapping *windows*. It is also worth noting that the 'Motif' interface definition (see Chapter 8) includes a 3-dimensional effect for window and button edges which might normally be considered fanciful (or, at least, optional). In the context of the study just described, the provision of such features could be regarded as essential.

## Experiment 3 - Screen colours

### Introduction

Sutcliffe [66a] has observed that properly designed colour displays can be more restful than plain monochrome ones, but offers the reservation that colour is a strong stimulus which is easy to over-use. Colour is commonly used for screen alerts, or highlighting menus, but what colour should a screen be when editing text, for example? Evidently a combination such as green on red (or vice-versa) is to be avoided; but is there any reason to suppose that grey on blue is better?

There is also a psychological factor - Western users prefer blue, red, green, purple, orange and yellow in that order. Moreover, many people suffer from a greater or lesser degree of colour blindness, and this should be addressed.

### Task

A simple timed editing task was chosen, in which a random string of letters was presented and the time from presentation until final keypress was measured.

### Method

A simple Prolog program was used. It was adapted from an example program distributed with the Turbo Prolog language, and is listed below:

```
predicates
  wait(char)
  equal(char, char)
  test(string)

goal
  makewindow(3,7,0,"",0,0,25,80),
  makewindow(2,7,7,"Key to press now",2,5,6,70),
  makewindow(1,7,7,"Accepted..",8,10,10,60),
  Word = "ejksopmcredkjgslows",
  write("Please type :\n\t", Word, "\n\t"),
  time(0,0,0,0), test(Word),
  time(_,_,S,H),
  shiftwindow(1),
  write("\nYou took ",S," seconds and ",H,"Hundredths").

clauses
  wait(X):- inkey(Y), equal(X,Y).
  wait(X):- shiftwindow(2), write(X), wait(X).
  test(W):- frontchar(W,Ch,R), wait(Ch),
               shiftwindow(2), write(Ch), test(R).
  test("").
  equal(X,X):- !
  equal(_,_):- beep, fail.
```

## Results
The timing results are summarised in the bar chart in Figure 12.2. The individual results are also shown to indicate the variability.

## Discussion
Although no statistical test was carried out on the data, some interesting results emerged. Firstly, although pink/purple was the slowest combination for 9 of the 11 subjects, yellow/blue (the preferred combination) was fastest for only 5. This suggests that poor screen colour has a greater effect on bad performance than good screen colour has on good performance. On the other hand, some subjects reported that the pink/purple combination made them 'concentrate' more.

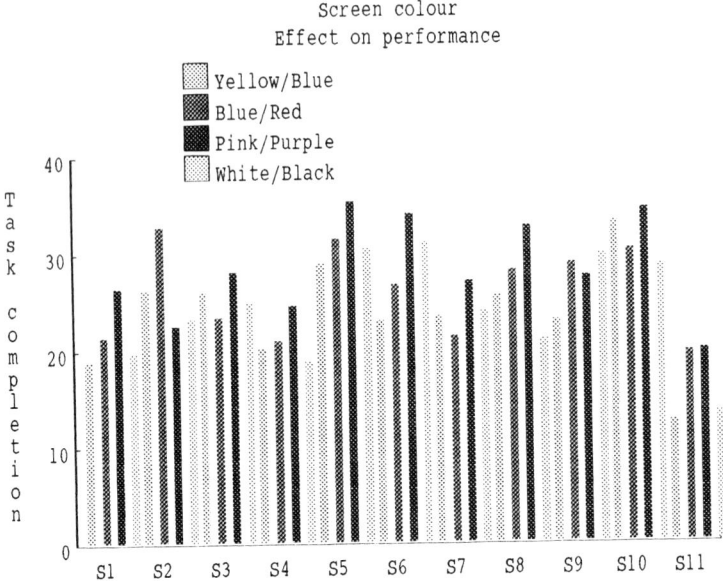

*Figure 12.1 Screen colour versus performance by subjects*

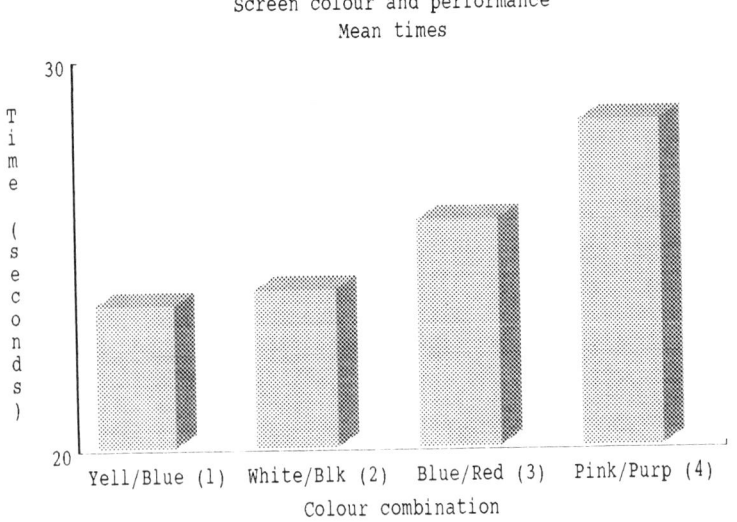

*Figure 12.2 Screen colour versus performance*

# Experiment 4 - Screen text attributes

## Introduction

Although many computer vendors would like it to be the case, reading from a visual display unit (VDU) is not the same as reading from paper. Ideally, it should be - the bulk of data held in computers is textual, it is being input in great quantities, and generally ends up on paper in one form or another.

Dillon *et al*[20a] have carried out a study comparing reading from paper and reading from a screen. They report these findings:

- Reading from screen is up to 30% slower than reading from paper

- Reading from screen is more fatiguing

- Reading from screen gives rise to more errors

- Reading from screen is rated by most people as inferior

In attempting to find the causes underlying these findings, Dillon et al reported the following factors as being significant:

- The orientation of the screen

- Eye movement across the screen

- The visual angle subtended by the screen (i.e. the distance from eye to screen)

- Aspect ratio (height/width ratio)

- The dynamic aspects of screen filling and refresh rates

- Flickering due to the refresh rate

- Image polarity - colour of foreground versus colour of background

- Display characteristics (font size, inter-line spacing etc.)

- Anti-aliasing

- The users (e.g. were they habitual computer users?)

(Readers would find it useful here to refer to the discussion of visual interfaces in Chapter 8.)

The major conclusion was that it was the display quality, and colour polarity, which had the most significant effect on the performance. It was unclear from the study, however. whether proportionally spaced (typeset) fonts, where each letter occupies a space proportional to its width, were more readable than fixed space (typescript) fonts where the character pitch is fixed; and whether there was an interaction with the display polarity.

This study investigates these aspects.

**Method**

A piece of text (a short story) was split into six fifty-word sections, separated by half-screens so that only one section could be seen at a time. The text was displayed using Microsoft Windows 2.03. This has the advantage of possessing an online clock which was used to time the experiment.

Two fonts were chosen - a Times Roman type (TimesRmn) to represent a proportionally-spaced font with serifs, and Courier (a standard typewriter font). When displayed on the screen, the Courier font appeared to be larger, so the point sizes were scaled to correct for this anomaly.

The experiment proceeded in two phases:

- The screen was set to a positive polarity (black text on white), the timings taken for each condition, and the subjects asked to provide an opinion on the readability of the text.

- The screen was set to a negative polarity and the procedure repeated.

The order of presentation was reversed for half the subjects in order to balance out any practice or fatigue effects.

## Results

The timings for each condition are shown graphically in Figure 12.3. Generally, the smaller fonts were read more slowly.

Secondly, the reading speed of the smallest font is the same irrespective of screen polarity, apart from the smallest Times font.

Thirdly, the Times font was judged by all subjects to be the least readable (but, on this system, the fonts were not displayed in an anti-aliased form. This would tend to favour less 'ornate' fonts such as Courier.

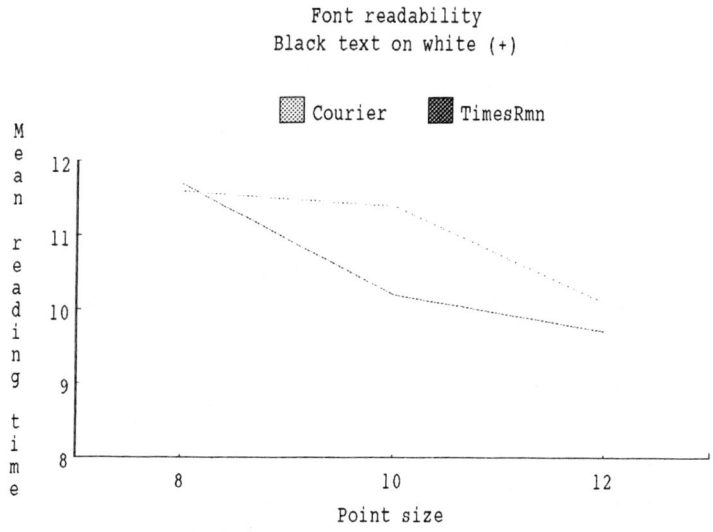

*Figure 12.3 Font readability versus font style and point size - dark text on white*

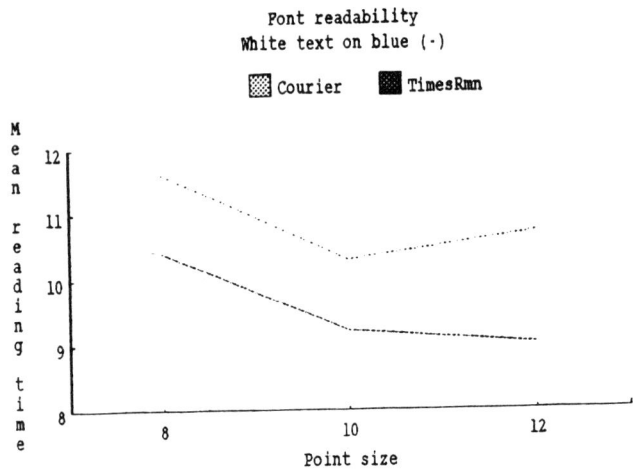

*Figure 12.4 Readability versus font style and point size - white text on dark*

## Discussion

The readability of text is becoming increasingly important as more people use computers for activities in the area of 'personal productivity', particularly desktop publishing. Displays that were adequate for form-filling are generally inadequate for text-intensive tasks, but users do not always appreciate this.

This study indicates that, overall, light text on a dark background is more efficient in editing tasks, with an improvement on larger point sizes. This is at variance with the judgment of many computer vendors, who provide 'paper-white' monitors as the default display. From Dillon et al's findings, the superiority of the light-on-dark is to be expected: in the absence of the very sharp print contrast obtainable with paper, a dark-on-light display provides much less contrast. With the additional problems of low resolution screens, we are forced to the conclusion that the empirical evidence does not support the manufacturers' preference, suggesting that marketing considerations may have taken precedence over consideration for the user.

## Courier 8 point

A typical prairie dog hole goes down almost perpendicularly from ten to twenty feet, extends horizontally an equal length, and has side chambers. It is protected against surface flow of water by a tunnel-shaped mound from six inches to a foot high. There is a roomy side-tunnel not

## Courier 10 point

a great distance below the mouth, where the owner and his family can remain clear of any water that does enter. The inhabitants keep their grounds cleared of weeds that enemies can lurk behind, and they refuse to burrow against brush and trees. They are strictly diurnal in habits. They

## Courier 12 point

are always on the look-out and warn each other of danger by incessant barking and chattering. When pursued, a prairie dog will dive into a neighbour's fortress if it is more accessible than his own. The animals are always in the vicinity of their holes. The enemy that catches

## Times Roman 12 point

one on top of the ground must exercise surprise and strategy. Coyotes have devised many strategies for catching them. One day we were hiking through the scattered brush on a mountainside overlooking a valley well populated with prairie dogs. The sky was dark and threatened rain. While looking and

## Times Roman 14 point

listening, the noisy barking of prairie dogs was heard. Soon, a coyote was noticed on the edge of the prairie-dog town, close to the base of the mountain. He had not seen us. He went scratching at a prairie-dog hole into which his approach had sent the owner.

## Times Roman 18 point

all neighbours having retreated into their holes. We wondered if the coyote was crazy enough to think he could dig down to the bottom of a prairie-dog hole? By now, thunder was rolling around the mountain. Even someone without coyote weather-sense could tell it was going to rain.

*Examples of fonts used in the text readability test*

## Summary

These simple experiments show that interesting and useful results can be obtained with a little effort, and that the conclusions are not always intuitively obvious.

# 13 HCI and design

*A designer is someone who creates an agreeable environment.*

*Terence Conran (Designer)*

## Introduction

The computer industry has always been aware of the need for good design. Many major methodologies have been developed to ease the task of translating a complex, 'rich' picture of reality into models suitable for programming a computer-based system. Arguably, however, the emphasis has been on the problems of the computer rather than the human. To do more than pay lip service to the needs of the online user has been, until recently, to exceed the capabilities both of the target system and of the chosen design methodology. Those methodologies (e.g. ETHICS, as outlined by Enid Mumford[50]) which sought to address the human problem often divorced the human domain from the computer domain if they were not properly understood, leading to an uneasy symbiosis between two different kinds of system.

More recently, advances in hardware and software design have led to two developments: better and more powerful graphical displays (leading to direct manipulation systems as discussed in Chapter 8); and more flexible, adaptive software design methodologies. We will concentrate in this chapter on one example of the latter, object-oriented programming systems (OOPs). Further, certain aspects of interface design have been eased by the maturation of a number of task analysis procedures, either as useful models or as direct prescriptions for interfaces.

Finally, and most importantly, there has been an increasing awareness of the relationship between system design and the kind of errors committed by the system (in combination with the human operator / user).

## Analysis and Design principles

Figure 13.1 illustrates the conventional view of systems development (formalised into an often-used model known as the Systems life-cycle), reflecting the conventional wisdom that systems are conceived, developed and decay into senescence much like living organisms. The cynical observer might conclude that this 'planned obsolescence' benefits the computer industry rather than the user. Certainly, the onset of the *maintenance* phase, which accounts for a large proportion of time and money in complex systems, is often used used as a diagnostic indicator that a system is coming up for replacement.

In an ideal world, maintenance work should not be necessary if the original analysis and design work has been adequate; and yet it is one of the major computer industries, which provides a livelihood for hundreds of thousands of people.

The increasing influence of HCI has meant, amongst other things, that users are asking more questions about the systems that they have to use, and are less reticent (or timorous) in doing so. The consequences are that:

- The maintenance phase is being moved forward in time

- Increasing attention is being given to radical methods of systems analysis and design.

Also refer to Task Analysis, Chapter 4.

## Formal methods

In recent years, the importance of designing 'correct' systems has been highlighted by a number of factors, possibly the main one being the increased use of computers in complex applications such as aircraft navigation systems and 'fly-by-wire' aircraft such as the Airbus A320.

If such systems had always worked perfectly, then it is possible that the need for *formal proofs* of the correctness of the design would not have achieved such importance. But for systems which have to perform flawlessly in a well-bounded  (but not always predictable) set of conditions, some kind of formal design methodology is essential.

As far as the human-computer interface is concerned, the argument for formal design methodologies for non life-critical systems is harder to make; if the consequence of a badly thought through dialogue design is that the user gets irritated, not killed, then we can probably tolerate it. But there are also reasons why we should pay attention to formal methods in HCI:

- A robust and comprehensible interface is increasingly likely to determine whether a package will sell or not, bearing in mind the growing population of 'user choosers'.

- Certain aspects of the design cycle can be made more efficient.

- The formalization of parts of the system mean that the resulting procedures are re-usable and better documented.

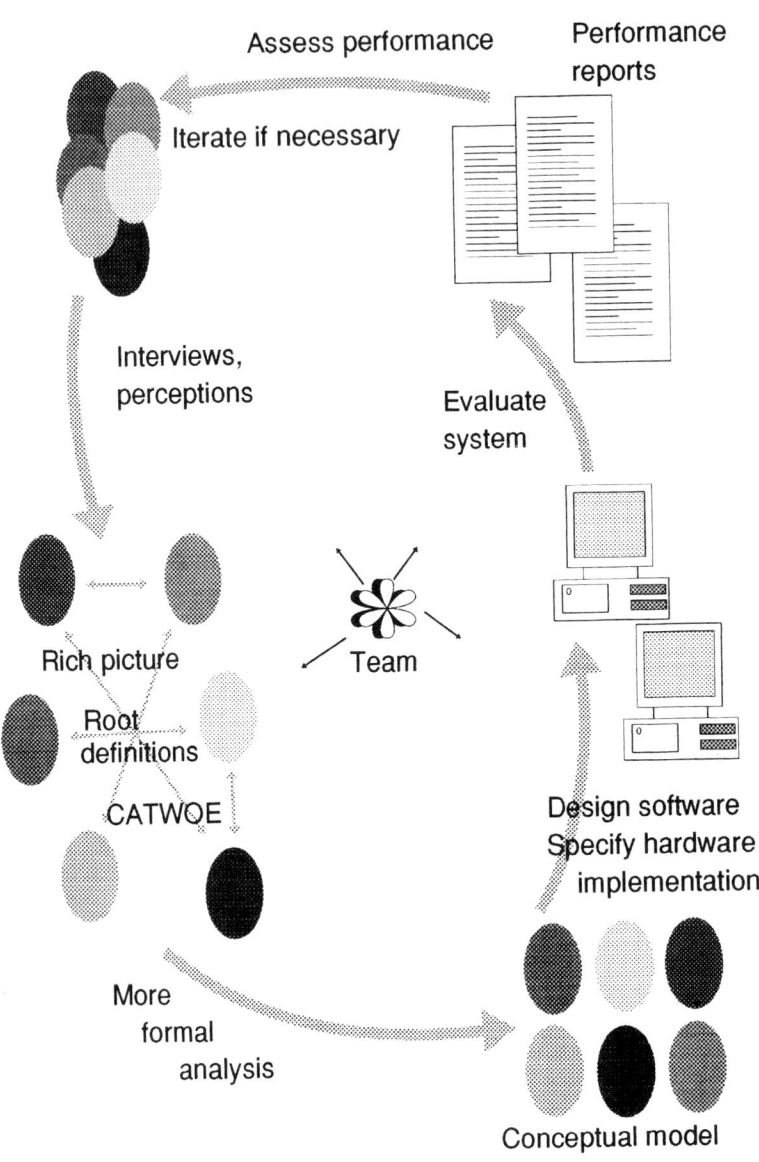

*Figure 13.1 Systems life cycle - conventional approach*

Certain important formal methodologies have come into prominence recently; we will concentrate on those that are capable of addressing themselves to the issues of dialogue design and interface design. Irrespective of the particular methodology employed, there are shared features to formal techniques, as described by Alexander [4]:

- Formal specifications concentrate on the 'what' rather than the 'how' of what the software in the system is designed to do.

- Formal systems employ a mathematical notation to convey the specification.

- Use of a mathematical notation gives a formal meaning to the specification, which is easier to convey and reason about than informal specifications.

- There is no ambiguity in the specification, as may happen with natural languages.

- The method is amenable to automation for such activities as syntax checking and type checking.

As Alexander points out, the specification can either be regarded as complete in itself, with the concomitant advantages of clarity and consistency, it can be used as part of the wider process of software development. For example, it can be repeatedly transformed by a mathematical process until it is an executable program; it can be used as a benchmark against which the final software is checked; or it can be 'run' as an emulation of the final system, and its performance assessed.

**Design problems**

Most systems analysts and designers set out with the best of intentions to provide comfortable systems for people to use. Unfortunately, all to many of these systems fail in this objective. Why should this be so?

The main problem seems to be that system design is, in the early stages, a 'person-centred' activity, where a 'rich picture' emerges via modelling, structured walkthroughs and so on; but in the later stages,  as implementation approaches, the activity becomes much more 'computer-centred' (for the consequences of this, see Chapter 1). Knowledge of user characteristics is lost, or deemed irrelevant, leading to systems which behave in a 'brittle' manner, that is, they fail to respond flexibly to unforeseen situations.

In the final stages, the operation of the planned system is almost entirely computer-centred, with little opportunity for adaptation or flexibility in the user interface. As Shneiderman [62] has pointed out, systems, generally,

- require users to remember too much

- are intolerant of minor errors

- are confusing to novices

- use inappropriate command modes

- force users to perform tasks in undesirable ways

**Lessons to be learned**

Much HCI information comes from sources other than the study of human-computer communication in conventional systems. As we saw in Chapter 2, general models of HCI can be developed; and the utility of a model is in its generality of scope. This works the other way too: lessons learned from different domains can contribute to HCI understanding, and hence to HCI models. At a certain level (the one we are interested in), a complex system can be an aircraft, a nuclear power station, or a spreadsheet running a financial forecasting package - the difference is due to the consequences of the error, not with the combination of conditions that led to the commission of the error.

In any case, the magnitude of the consequences of an error is a relative factor as far as the operator / user is concerned - a hard-pressed manager who has just lost his spreadsheet data for that afternoon's business review is unlikely to get very upset reading about a nuclear reactor accident in the Soviet Union, catastrophic though that event may be.

The HCI interest in human factors in complex control systems is due, also, to the enormous amount of data examined and analysed by the investigatory authorities after an incident. It is beyond doubt, as Reason [58] states, that

> *"...system catastrophes are rarely caused by one factor, either mechanical or human. Rather, these...analyses show that they arise from the unforeseen and usually unforeseeable concatenation of several diverse and often trivial events, each one necessary but singly insufficient."*

### Nuclear power plant emergencies

In the much-documented Three Mile Island incident, where a combination of 'impossible' events led to the near meltdown of a nuclear reactor, the human factors aspect of the situation was investigated in great detail. Some of the outcomes were intuitively obvious - for example, if several hundred audio alarms go off simultaneously, it is likely that the cause of the problem will be difficult to determine due to information processing limitations in the human operator.

More interesting was the finding that the operators inadvertently made things worse by responding immediately - a certain amount of time spent in thought, rather than action, might have improved the situation that developed. These findings, albeit applied with hindsight, do seem to indicate that the original interface was planned without adequate empirical input as regards the relevant human factors.

Figure 13.2 shows a chart of the relative contribution of various factors to nuclear power plant emergencies.

Recent work on NPP (Nuclear Power Plant) operation has resulted in the following guidelines:

- Control system design should be fault-tolerant of human idiosyncrasies

- There should be feedback from the system if the wrong button is pressed

- The control system designers should carry out a human error analysis as the first stage of a design

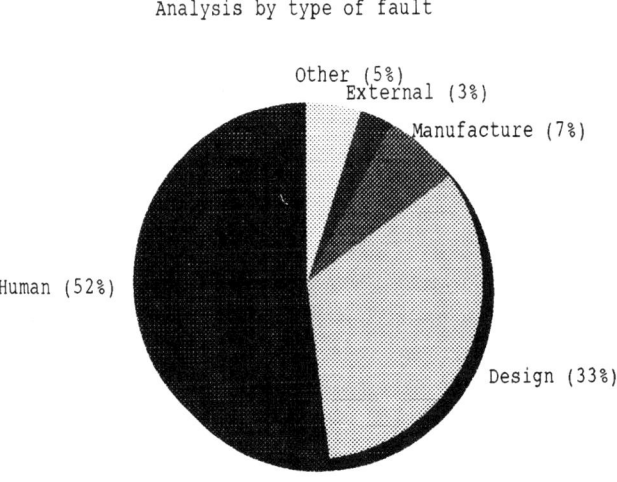

NPP Emergencies
Analysis by type of fault

Other (5%)
External (3%)
Manufacture (7%)

Human (52%)

Design (33%)

*Figure 13.2 Contribution of various factors to nuclear power plant emergencies. From Reason, 1987.*

In practical terms, new control systems are increasingly adopting the following features:

- A 'half-hour' rule is adopted, whereby the essential controls are disconnected in a critical situation, and the plant is guaranteed to be stable for about 30 minutes. During this time, the operator has to regain control in a systematic manner.

- Full automation is increasingly seen as inappropriate for normal running; the flexible input of the skilled operator is now seen as vital for the correct operation of the system.

- Failsafe systems are being designed where the lack of operator input for a significant time leads to an orderly closedown of the system rather than uncontrolled behaviour of a less desirable kind.

Overall, a correct balance should be struck between machine-driven processes and human-driven processes in the system. The corollary to this is that the operator should be much more involved at all stages; just as the pilot of a modern airliner is not just the driver, but a flight systems manager and part designer.

This leads inevitably to a greater *understanding* of the system on the part of the operator; if there is no understanding, then there is no point in continuing to interact with the operator (it is significant that, once the critical phase of the TMI incident had been reached, the operators freely admitted throwing the rule book on to the floor and hitting buttons more or less at random - it was arguably as useful as trying to interpret the rules in an unknown situation). If this state is reached, the the system must at least 'fail safe'.

### Operator psychology

One factor which cannot be ignored in safety-critical systems is the psychological suitability of the operator for carrying out such tasks. There is a considerable onus on the operators of such systems to maintain alertness while maintaining a capacity to think analytically and to respond at great speed should the occasion demand. Is this reasonable?

There is some evidence that people who emerge as *introverts* on tests such as the Eysenck Personality Inventory (EPI) are better at tasks which involve quiet, analytical thought; whereas people who tend towards *extraversion* are better at controlling complex systems. This would seem to indicate conflicting requirements in the operator; by definition, one cannot be both an introvert and an extravert. One solution might be to ensure that, within the operating *team*, there is an appropriate balance of 'thinkers' and 'doers'.

### *Consequences for design*

Although the above discussion concerns NPPs and their operators, the major points map across very well to the normal HCI situation; the consequences of failure are not generally so extreme, but they may be costly in terms of money or human well-being.

Finally, returning to the theme of operator psychology, there is no reason to suppose that different psychological types have the same experience at the interface, and yet the system design generally takes no account of this.

Overall, it seems that the early application of adequate task analysis procedures would have saved many problems.

## Designing for WIMP systems

(Thanks are due to Digital Equipment Corporation for allowing the author to paraphrase parts of their XUI Style Guide in this section.)

### DEC's XUI style

The Digital Equipment Corporation has defined a 'style checklist' for use by applications writers who wish to exploit the full windowing facilities of DEC Window (a proprietary implementation of X Window; see Chapter 8 for a discussion of visual interfaces generally):

- **User control** - The user feels 'in control' of the application if error messages are clear; if potentially destructive situations are warned against; if interfaces can be customised to some extent; and if some redundancy is built in (for example, allowing 'hot keys' to select a function in addition to a drop-down menu).

- **Direct manipulation** - The user's actions and the behaviour of logical objects are well-coupled; the results of an operation should be signalled immediately and unambiguously.

- **Progressive disclosure** - The more common functions should be presented first, with more subtle and sophisticated functions being revealed after more extensive navigation or experience on the part of the user. A minority of the functions available may account for most of the usage; these should be given prominence in the opening windows of the application.

- **Aesthetics** - "The XUI Interface presents the user with a work environment that is pleasing but never distracting. The appearance is clean and free of meaningless decoration and flashiness. It is an interface design that respects the professional who works with it daily.

  The XUI interface is almost transparent. Each screen object has a distinct appearance that the user can quickly recognise and easily understand. At the same time, the style of the interface graphically unifies these elements, and ensures a consistent and attractive appearance at any screen resolution."

- **Consistency** - The operations should be consistent across applications, so that (for example) saving a spreadsheet should involve the same logical and physical operations as saving a report. Applications developers are urged to use the standard mechanisms (widgets) such as dialogue boxes, menus etc. Experience in designing such systems is thus incremental.

- **Design process** - "From the user's perspective, the interface *is* the product". User involvement is identified as being vital, even to the point of role-playing - "be a user".

- **Avoiding common design pitfalls** - These are identified as: *premature closure* (too early an assumption that the design is complete); *deductive designing* (from abstract principles, lacking validation by checking with users); *copying an existing application* (windowed interfaces generally require a complete re-think of the design); and *showing implementation details* (they should not 'show through' the interface. Although the user's understanding requires, to a certain extent, knowledge of how the application is structured, this structure should be presented by the interface, and not depend on a knowledge of how the internal procedures are related).

## Object-oriented design and programming

Traditionally, software has been designed by teams of people, each working on a different part of the project. The eradication of errors was thought to be largely a function of careful design and testing. Some kinds of 'bug', however, were worrying by their persistence and unpredictability. Analysis of this kind of bug revealed a number of things:

1 The separation of data areas from code areas in large programs led to a certain slackness in checking for the correct usage of procedures

2 There was often evidence of a duplication of effort in defining data structures

3 There was often no control over the choice of variable names by different teams

The solutions to the above problems are:

1 Procedures and data are combined together into a package (an object). PROCEDURES + DATA = OBJECT

2 A generic type for each class of objects is defined, and new variants are generated by concentrating on the differences with the parent class. This is termed *inheritance*. inheritance

3 The same name can be shared among different objects within a hierarchy, the result depending on the type of object (overloading, or *polymorphism*). For example, a different method might be employed for printing a string or a real number, but this should be the concern of the object, not the programmer.

The consequences for computer systems design have been considerable.

The robustness of objects, once defined, means that:

- they can be used and re-used as building blocks without rewriting them

- the consequent speed improvement in system development means that rapid prototyping techniques can be considered

- the complexity of human-computer interfaces can be captured and modelled in a way which earlier methods have failed to do.

There is another, major advantage to the use of an object-oriented methodology: the components of the developing system can be viewed from the outset as independent, co-operating elements which map directly onto the processes in the real-world domain. This is in direct contrast to what we may term the traditional view, where the richest and most complex of systems has ultimately to be mapped onto a sequential processor.

Many workers argue that this step involves an unacceptable change in focus of the modelled system, and introduces undesirable side-effects such as *brittleness* - the inability of the system to respond gracefully in unforeseen error situations.

By contrast, the object-oriented view preserves the original 'rich picture' as far as possible, and the design process is seen much more as a successive refinement and formalization of a complex system rather than its translation into arbitrary sequential processes and remote data structures.

At one time, object-oriented languages were termed *actor* languages, the metaphor being that the system comprised a number of actors on a stage, who would repeat their lines (methods) on receipt of a cue (message). The metaphor is thus of an active, self-directing collection of intelligent agents.

This notion resonates very strongly with HCI workers, who find that they can think of systems design in ways which do not 'write out' the human user as an unfortunate necessity, a source of errors and complaints; but as an object with interesting methods and attributes which it is challenging to try and model.

**Typical design methodology**

The following methodology has been described by Booch. It is one of many approaches, but is typical, as the nature of object-oriented design leads to a natural convergence of approaches.

- Identify the *objects* (by a partial life-cycle approach)

- Identify the *operations* for each object - that is, their 'dynamic behaviour'.

- Establish the *visibility* of each object - what it 'sees', and what sees it

- Establish the *interface* for each object. Work out its static representation and define its *boundary*.

- Implement the object and its interface. Express in the form of *code*.

Note that no specific mention is made of HCI in this methodology, but it is easy to see where it would be incorporated - at the very beginning. If the users, and their likely demands, are accommodated at the very beginning of the exercise, then the dialogues and interfaces they have to use will benefit from a more prolonged exposure to the environment of the growing system.

More specifically, the visibility of the objects can include the user interface so that the functionality of each object can be made visible to the user as well as to other objects.

**Object-oriented programming - an example**

In addition to the best-known 'pure' object-oriented programming languages, such as Smalltalk or Actor, most conventional programming languages can be enhanced to include object-oriented extensions. The most common are the enhanced C languages (C++, Objective C) and Pascal (Microsoft and Turbo Pascal 5.5). Each implementation expresses the object-oriented philosophy in its own syntax, as far as possible. Rather than go through all the variations, we will study an example of object-oriented programming in one language, C++.

```
Class Window  {
Private Part:
  bitmap:array[1..1024][1..1024] of bits;
  Xsize, Ysize : integer;

Public Part:
  create();
  redraw(LowerX,LowerY,UpperX,UpperY);
  resize(x,y);
DrawText(text,x,y);

}

/* Later, an application calls... */
Window w;
w:redraw(10,10,30,30);
.
.
```

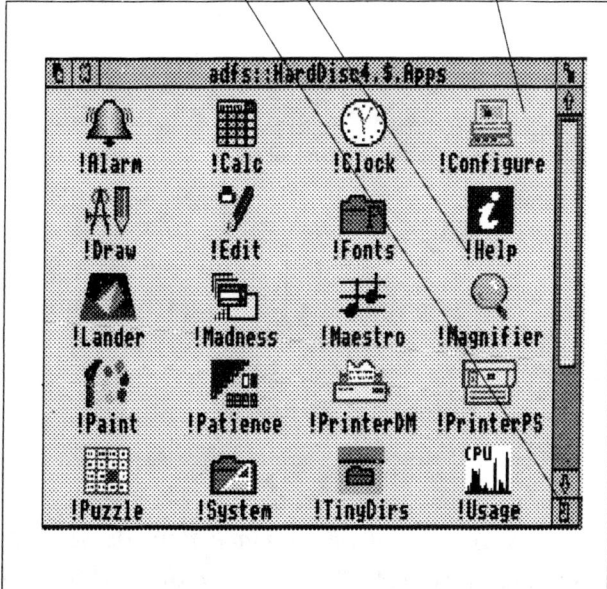

*Figure 13.3 Object oriented programming in C++ with windows (after Collins-Cope, 1988)*

### Designing user interface management systems (UIMS)

The combination of the techniques described above would seem to offer great promise for the effective design of UIMS - not just an interface specification, but a complete interface building and management system, developed according to established HCI principles. Unfortunately, as Hartson and Hix [33] have stated,

> *"Despite advances in human-computer interface development, no accepted methodology exists to guide development of the complex structure of an interface."*

Hartson and Hix carried out a study, over a two year period, of how three people developed the interface to a document retrieval system. Their major finding was that interface development proceeds in alternating 'waves' of top-down (analytic) and bottom-up (synthetic) activities. To the extent that no commonly used major design methodologies encompass both approaches in a single design cycle, Hartson and Hix developed a *star* model of interface development and design (Figure 13.4).

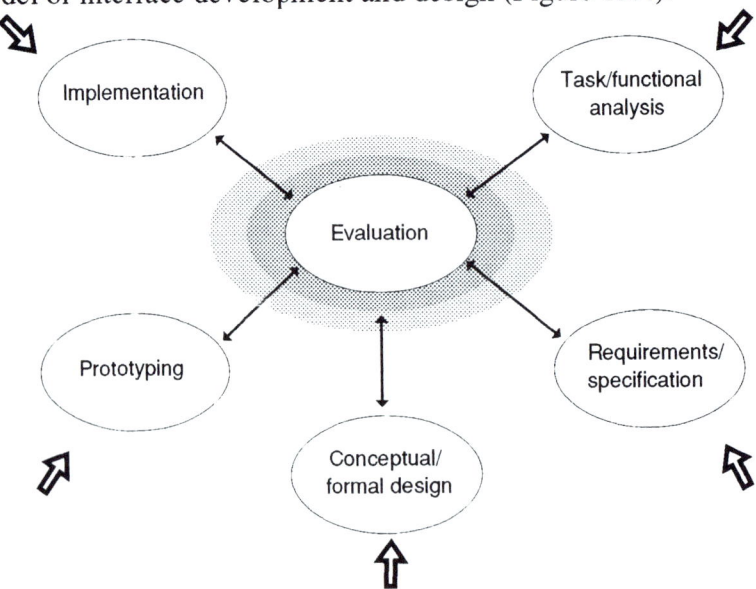

*Figure 13.4 'Star' model of interface development developed by Hartson & Hix (1989). This model allows maximum flexibility in alternating analytic and synthetic modes of design.*

## LENS - logical evolution of new systems

The LENS philosophy - which is an approach, not a methodology - is offered as an attempt to pull together various prescriptions and checklists which address themselves to the design of computer-based information systems, and particularly to interface and dialogue design.

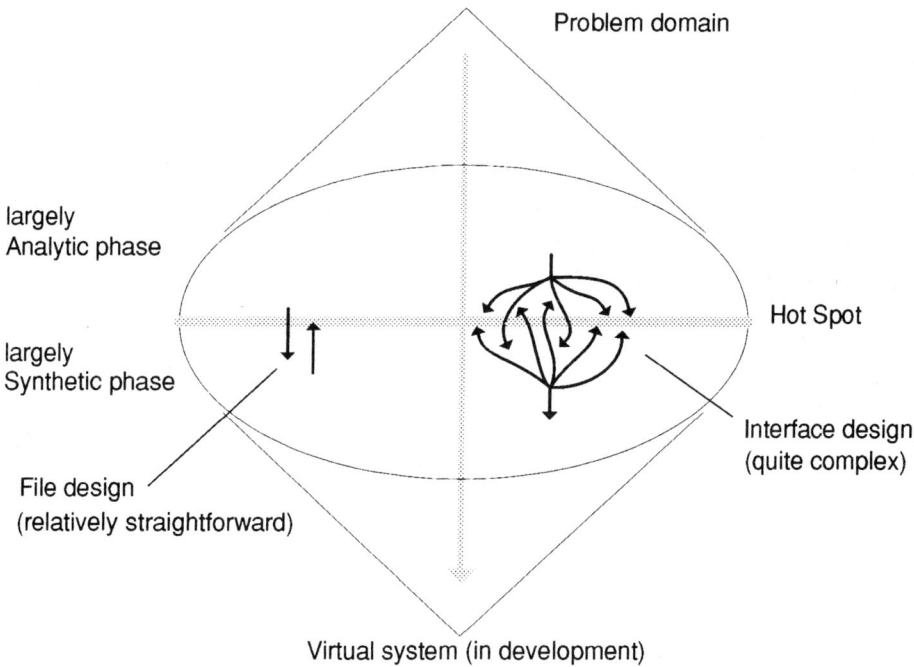

*Figure 13.5 The LENS approach illustrated graphically*

The LENS philosophy attempts to address the following points:

- The goal in designing all systems is to achieve transparency (and hence good cognitive matching etc.)

- System design is rarely a straight-line process - in the same system, certain points of implementation can be 'seen' from an early stage, and others must be painfully worked through

- At any one time, both analytic and synthetic activities are proceeding concurrently

The following should be true of the system as it approaches its 'focal point':

- The 'lens' should not obscure the view of the original problem domain, although it may act as a magnifier / reducer of some parts of it

- Any areas of obscurity in the lens can be identified and avoided

## Summary

System designers are the people who must be convinced that attention to HCI principles results in better software, with better 'user reviews'. Designers, generally, pride themselves on products that have a coherent 'look and feel' (such as the Apple Macintosh and its associated software). A good furniture designer talks to anatomists and ergonomists, as well as fabric designers; but cognitive psychologists are not usually at the top of the system designer's contact list.

This is a pity, as they would probably discover they had a lot in common.

# 14 Special Issues

*"We're all created equal. But we're not all created the same"*

*Martin Luther King*

## Introduction

As stated in the Preface to this book, the aim of HCI is to make computer-based information systems compatible, both physically and cognitively, with their human operators. But people vary immensely on an individual and collective basis, and they also vary within themselves - the confident and competent brain surgeon may be reduced to a querulous and confused state when expected to interact with a computer keyboard (the author has seen it happen, and it is a tragic sight). By the same token, an arbitrary collection of people display a different kind of collective behaviour at a supermarket than if they all work together at an office.

Disabled people, whether their disability is of hearing, sight, or mobility, form a special kind of group - one to which the benefits of technology appear to have been apportioned in a particularly mean way by their able-bodied (or unchallenged) colleagues. HCI should be able to make significant improvements in this area, considering that, as far as interacting with computers is concerned, we are all disabled in one way or another. Even from a stance of enlightened self-interest, there is much to be gained by computer users generally if the HCI community make much more of an effort in improving interfaces for disabled people.

This chapter addresses the issues of:

- How interfaces may be adapted to suit changes in a user, or between different users

- How the HCI community can ensure that better systems and interfaces are provided for disabled users.

### Individuals

One of the certain things which can be said about people is that they vary. The variance can be in inherited or acquired characteristics. This is not salient in certain areas - hair colour, height, etc. In other areas it is highly significant - keyboard skills, position on a learning curve, etc. Other factors are less obvious but certainly significant: attitude, emotional state, time of day, arousal. The only thing a designer can say for certain is that the user will probably be unlike anything he/she has imagined.

So how is it possible to design an application for a single user? Certain assumptions must be made about literacy, knowledge of the application domain, etc.

If the interface itself could take some responsibility in this process, and make modifications which were related to aspects of users' behaviour, then we would have an *adaptive* interface. These are discussed in Chapter 7 and 9.

### Disabled users

A recent estimate gave the number of people who, while suffering some disability, were potentially ready and able to contribute in the IT area, as well over half a million. Of these people, 108,000 have a disability which puts them into categories 7-10 (moderately physically disabled) with a further 418,000 suffering 'some dexterity problems'. This represents an enormous reserve of untapped talent. Moreover, these figures do not include blind people or deaf people.

Of course, there is no reason to suppose that a disabled person should be more attracted to computing as an occupation than anyone else; but a computer is very often a more accessible tool for people who have restricted mobility. It is transportable, adaptable and provides a 'window on the world'.

It is increasingly evident that HCI, while gathering information about the situation of 'able-bodied' users, is thereby providing an increasingly large knowledge base about disabled users; but arguably there is a need for specialist research to be done in the various categories and kinds of disability - or *challenge* (which is the favoured term nowadays).

(In the three sections that follow, references will be made to the British computer Society's Disability Special Interest Group, and to a meeting which was held on HCI and computer systems for users with special needs. The author was privileged to be the chairman of this meeting).

## Physical disability

Physical disability is the most obvious because a loss of muscular function or control generally means that the sufferer becomes dependent on a wheelchair for mobility. It is important to distinguish between various types of paraplegia, as the choice of interface will vary. Some people (for example muscular dystrophy sufferers) may have limited movement in their arms and wrists, but finger movement may be precise enough to control a switch or knob. Other people (for example accident victims) may have normal use of their arms and hands, but be paralysed elsewhere.

### Voice I/O

The distinction between input and output must be kept clear: many people with motor problems may not be able to articulate well enough verbally for a voice recognition system to perform adequately. The same problem means that voice output is an appropriate medium as long as there is sufficient dexterity (not necessarily manual) to drive the system.

Voice I/O is discussed in detail in Chapter 6.

### Keyboards and touchpads

As indicated in Chapter 5, there is a great variety in the design of keyboards, and there are no fixed rules. If any purposeful movement can be captured as a result of a surface being touched, hit or stroked, then a keyboard can be designed around the user.

A well-known example is the **concept keyboard**, which is a flat sheet with no particular demarcations visible. It returns an X-Y position on being touched, the significance of this position depending on the type of *overlay* which is placed on the keyboard.

The concept keyboard can emulate a conventional keyboard with the appropriate overlay; or, if the user cannot make such fine motor movements, the overlay can divide the keyboard into as few as 2 areas.

In the case of a user with no voluntary motor movement at all, adequate information rates can be achieved by sucking and blowing on a tube according to a particular pattern (protocol). Such a device (possum) has been available for a number of years, and updated versions are becoming available for interfacing with personal computers.

## Other devices

### *Doppler effect devices*

These are particularly useful for users who do not have effective limb movement, but who can move their heads. A sensor/transmitter device is placed on top of the computer monitor, and the user wears a pair of acoustic reflective devices on his/her head. The device operates in a similar way to the sonar on a submarine: an ultrasonic sound is emitted, and the reflections are picked up by the receiver and interpreted as movements. Usually, these movements are interpreted as mouse movements. The mouse emulation is completed by simulating a button using a puff of air in a tube.

According to the vendors of the system, most conventional software can be driven with a little practice. The main advantages for the challenged user of these systems are:

- They are transparent

- They are consistent

- They are adaptable

• They are suitable for a wide range of applications

**Direct brain input**

> "*Eight years ago Dr. Lance Meagher, a physician living in Oregon, was stricken with amyotrophic lateral sclerosis...Today he is unable to move his head, hands or legs; he cannot talk, eat or even breathe on his own. Nevertheless the forty-year-old physician and ex-pilot one day plans to be placed in the cockpit of an aeroplane to fly solo around the world.*"

The device, a Brain Response Interface (BRI) that could make this possible was constructed by Erich Sutter of the Smith-Kettlewell Institute of Visual sciences in San Francisco, and has been described by Ward [70]. Making use of the fact that different visual stimuli (such as patterns of flickering dots) produce different wavelike responses from the visual cortex of the brain, Sutter constructed an 8 by 8 grid in which each element contained a letter or symbol together with a unique dot pattern.

When Dr. Meagher focuses his eyes (the only part of his body that he can move) on a square, the BRI analyses the resulting waveforms which are transmitted to it via scalp electrodes. A match is made, and the relevant square identified. An appropriate action is then performed, which varies from a control action (such as switching on a light) to composing text. Further arrays can be called up by using a sequence of 'control' squares. There are 2048 user-programmable commands that this system can perform.

The possibilities of such a system are far-ranging, for both disabled and non-disabled users.

## People with a visual impairment

To the layperson, blindness may seem to be the most debilitating of conditions, and yet it is probably true to say that more blind people are employed in 'normal' jobs, as a proportion of the population, compared with other disabled groups. For example, there are many blind computer programmers, lecturers and authors. We must distinguish between various degrees of sight loss - there are many more *visually challenged* people, who possess some degree of vision, than totally blind people.

This could have something to do with the comparative recency, in evolutionary terms, of vision as a sensory modality - we depend on our other senses quite highly, but this dependence is quite subtle and 'overlearned', so we possibly overestimate the importance of vision in our daily life. Certainly, it is not essential for maintaining a conversation, or enjoying a piece of music, or even for finding your way around a town.

There is no reason, therefore, for blind people to have inferior powers of communication, and it is this factor that enables blind people to continue to be able to communicate at a high level, with other people and with computers.

## Voice input
The capability of voice input devices, as discussed in Chapter 6, does not yet render them suitable for connected speech; but in certain domains they will be as useful as they are in other applications.

## Voice output
This is much easier to handle than voice input, as we saw in Chapter 6. It is also a much more useful facility for blind people. For example, a blind touch-typist can monitor his/her input by arranging that each word is 'spoken' by the package as text is entered, either continuously or on a signal from a spellchecker.

Devices exist that can 'read' the screen display of a conventional word processing package and speak the words or individual letters.

## Braille
To people who have been blind from birth, braille is the natural form of non-verbal communication. It comprises an alphabet of special symbols in the form of patterns of raised dots. Devices have existed for may years

which enable a tape to be embossed automatically: the **perkins brailler**. 'Soft-copy' versions of this device, on which raised pins simulate the braille images.

Packages (such as Pia's **braillemaker**) also exist which are capable of translating text files into braille and outputting them to a brailler. At the time of writing, the author is not aware of any packages that enable braille text to be edited directly.

## Other interfaces

### *Large displays*
For people with visual impairment, it may be sufficient to have a large display for text or numbers. In this respect, the more recent personal computers and workstations have much to offer - the ability to scale the displayed text from, say, 14 points to several hundred points (1 point = 1/72nd inch) renders it readable even to people with very restricted vision.

### *Special purpose computers*
A (small) number of personal computers exist which are specially designed for (and by) blind people. The **Eureka**, for example, possesses a braille keyboard for input and a voice synthesiser for reading the 'screen' and echoing commands. The screen exists as a virtual array of text, which can be navigated with a 'cursor' which signals its position acoustically.

The operating system is an 8-bit system (CP/M) which, although it was developed in pre-IBM PC days, can run industry standard software such as WordStar (TM) and SuperCalc (TM). Although the screen display cannot of course be seen, it can be accessed in the normal way, and the display output as words or as single letters. An experienced (blind) user can perform as well as a sighted person on a conventional machine.

## Deaf people
It is important to distinguish between *pre-* and *post-lingually* deaf people (that is, deaf from birth or *adventitiously* deaf), because the problems of each group are quite different. Prelingually deaf people have not had the

linguistic input which would enable them to develop conventional communication skills - including speaking, reading and writing. Most prelingually deaf people in Britain communicate using British Sign Language (BSL), an entirely visual means of communication.

Possibly as a result of using BSL, the spatial and graphical awareness of deaf people is good, and so direct manipulation systems would seem to provide a good platform on which to build applications for deaf people, especially for communication purposes.

### *A personal experience...*

In 1988 the author helped to organise, jointly with the University of Bristol, a 'new technology' week for deaf people at Bristol Polytechnic. We were slightly concerned that the learning curve for packages such as desktop publishing would be steep, as prelingually deaf people tend to have unconventional literacy skills, as you might expect.

We need not have worried. Without exception, the group mastered all the main features of the DTP package, and in addition the associated painting and drawing packages. They also mastered the principles of spreadsheet operation, data import and export, and setting up a laser printer. All this was achieved within an afternoon - a performance well ahead of our expectations for *hearing* students.

## Summary of issues in disability

There is no doubt that there is a vast resource of untapped talent represented by people with special needs. We now need to consider how we can meet two aims:

- How people with special needs can have their disability functionally diminished or abolished in the work situation

- How people with special needs can use computers in a life-enhancing way in their domestic and social lives.

The BCS conference, mentioned earlier, reached a number of conclusions on these issues. Firstly, a number of interest groups were identified: *Industry*, who could provide resources and operate from the point of view of enlightened self-interest, if not altruism; and *Users / developers*, who were nett consumers of resources until such time as useful products were developed. *Government* was identified as the agency which translated basic rights and social needs into policies and resources.

The interaction, so far, was judged to be imperfect in relation to what has been achieved in countries such as the United States and Denmark. In an effort to articulate what was needed to sting the various agencies into action, the **WASP** model emerged:

- **W**illingness - on the part of government, industry and society generally, to recognise the problem, and to resolve do something about it

- **A**wareness - of what needs to be done, and of the precise needs and aspiration of various groups of people with special needs. Also awareness that a co-operative, rather than a patronising, approach would be better received

- **S**tandards - there are many emerging international standards for computer interfaces for non-disabled users. Standards committees may need reminding of the existence of the special needs population. Additionally, conformance to standards such as X window (see Chapter 8) would save a great deal of work for special needs software developers.

- **P**ortability - a great deal of  work is machine-specific, leading to costly and inefficient conversions where porting is undertaken to different hardware.

# 15 The future

*By logic and reason we die hourly. By imagination we live.*

*W.B. Yeats*

## Introduction

The partnership between people and computers is now permanent and embedded in our business and domestic culture. Advances will occur in technology, some of them difficult to comprehend from our current perspectives. People will also advance, assisted in this advancement by the computer culture we have created. Strains will also be created: the vast majority of the world's population do not benefit directly from any of the issues discussed in this book, and to some extent the same is true of disabled people in Western cultures.

If HCI does nothing more than foster an attitude of vigilance, care and attention to standards within the computer vendor and user community, then it has succeeded in its aims. But as we will see in this final chapter, many new techniques will emerge, and new challenges will arise for individuals and organisations. HCI will help us to formulate appropriate coping strategies.

## Computers

There can be no doubt that the recent advances in technology, particularly in the area of data fusion and knowledge acquisition, will radically alter the very way in which we look at the world itself. It seems that the human brain likes to play with models; this is not really surprising considering that reality itself has to be modelled in order for the brain to make sense of it. The actual image on the retina of the eyeball, for example, is reddish, out of focus and suffers considerable barrel distortion. The nice sharp coloured pictures we see are largely a result of interpretive processes applied by the brain.

It cannot be unreasonable, or unnatural therefore, to make use of what we know about these processes to further amplify the brain's capacity for modelling the world in order to make certain activities more efficient.

Additionally, it is likely that new kinds of human-computer interface will be found that not only mimic reality but go beyond mimicry to total synthesis. For example, the 'Tomorrow's World' programme on BBC TV recently featured a unique *sculptural* output device, which comprised a tank filled with a special heat-sensitive gel. When laser light, modulated by a computer, was focused to a spot in the gel, it solidified. Scanning the laser beam through the gel enabled a solid object to be built up. The possible applications are left to the reader's imagination.

## Humans

Humans design, manufacture, sell and use computers: the machines cannot yet do this for themselves. There seems to be no reason, then, why people should continue to have bad experiences at the keyboard; yet we suspect that they will do so. Evidently some of the solutions are, at the moment, out of peoples' control - the problems being too tied up with other faults in the infrastructure of commerce and industry, or in the society in which we live. It is useful to speculate what could be done at the individual and collective levels.

## Individuals

If the *goal* of HCI is to improve the user's comfort at the interface, then its ultimate *aim* must be to make users feel better about what they are doing. From a personal point of view, this is justification enough; from a more pragmatic perspective, a happy user is a more productive user - the overtones are no more sinister or Orwellian than the provision of, say, better workplace conditions for the population generally.

Related to this is the possibility of enabling a far greater amount of personal influence and style to migrate, via the interface, into the working situation. This can be partly achieved by providing interfaces and applications architectures which are *resonant* with the user's knowledge and skills (see also Chapters 7 and 14).

Human beings also like to explore - or *browse* - while working, and it is often this activity, usually officially frowned upon, which enables many people to arrive at more optimal (better) solutions to a problem than if they had employed a purely 'straight-line' approach. Generally, creative people have always found this to be the case. The sad fact is that although the majority of people are creative, given the chance, their employment allows them no chance to develop creative strategies which could benefit both them and their employers.

## Left brains and right brains

A further aspect of psychological functioning which does not seem to have been directly addressed either in conventional or IT-supported environments is that human beings have two halves to their brain, which function in radically different ways.

Generally, the *left* brain is known to support logical, concrete operations and the right brain to support creative and abstract functions. Computing (of the conventional kind) is almost entirely a 'left-brained' activity - systematic, logical and deterministic. The more recent direct manipulation systems, however, encourage a more open-ended kind of activity. This could, in principle, lead to a more integrated use of the whole brain in computing activities, and, as a consequence, less stress and *anomie* in the user.

### *Maslow's hierarchy of needs*

The paragraphs above express more than just a pious hope that things will improve psychologically for the computer user. In the 1970s, Maslow, a psychologist, proposed that people survive physically and psychologically by maintaining, and satisfying, a *hierarchy of needs*. At the lowest (physical) layer, we need warmth, food and shelter. human beings denied even this basal level are unlikely to survive for long.

As we ascend the hierarchy, the needs become increasingly related to the psychological aspects of life - culture, employment, leisure. The top of the hierarchy is represented by *self-actualisation*, which is the target state for beings that do more than just consume food and keep warm.

In a sense, a user exploring a new applications package is working at quite a high level in Maslow's hierarchy - the need to discover, explore and understand a new territory. By the same token, providing a user with powerful tools for interface development or adaptation allows him/her to actualise some high level needs - the need for a good interface, for example.

## Organisations

If the classical 'pyramid' model of organizational structure and information flow is examined (Figure 15.1a) it will be seen that two

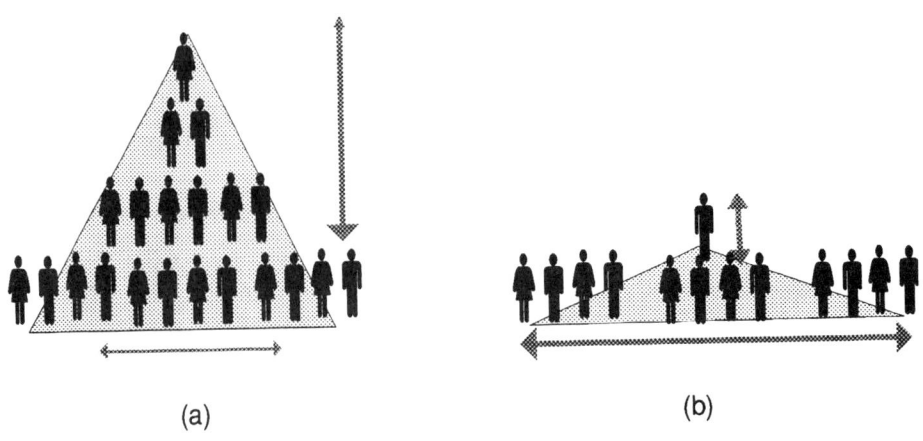

(a)                                        (b)

*Figure 15.1 Evolution of management style.*

features characterise it:

- The vertical flow of information and commands

- The relative lack of horizontal communication between elements of the pyramid

It is increasingly evident that the mode of operation of automated offices in the future will favour horizontal communications, and a consequent 'flattening' of the pyramid. There are a number of reasons for this:

- Important management information is often inaccessible, and there is undue disruption when it is called for on a demand basis.

- If the information has to pass through 'layers' of people, there is an opportunity for misinterpretation or error.

- Most corporate procedures work quite well without any intervention, yet management often feels impelled to intervene, possibly from a lack of firm objectives.

The consequences could be quite profound for the management of organisations:

- Decisions will be taken at lower levels, probably assisted by automated decision-support systems

- Several layers of management will disappear

- A new organizational unit, the *workgroup*, will come into prominence. The workgroup is characterised by its collective mission rather than by the personalities or permanency of the people comprising it.

- The linkages between people, both individually and in workgroups, will become stronger and more formalised with respect to the tasks they are engaged on

- There may be rôle conflicts and identity problems as the new ways of working 'shake down'.

Overall, this process should be viewed as an opportunity for organisations to improve the status and aspirations of their grassroots workforce, rather than as an attack upon middle management - although we have to face the fact that many middle managers will face a diminution of rôle. Certainly, those organisations where the resistance to change is due to status preservation strategies will have greater difficulty in adapting. In terms of the pyramid model: whereas in (a), information flows were mainly vertical, and organisation was by edict, in (b), the information flow is mainly horizontal, there is a greater devolution of responsibility downward, and there is a degree of self-organisation - into, probably workgroups.

Argyle[6] has listed the problems caused by the persistence of inappropriate workgroup structures after the introduction of new technology:

- *Oversized working groups* - status differences become too marked, communication is muddled

- *Lack of cooperation between sub-groups* - communication difficulties and lack of opportunity for interaction result in failure of cooperation

- *Indirect access to information* - individuals needing access to information may find that it has to be channelled through other group members, producing delays, distortion etc.

- *Inappropriate communication structures* - for simple missions, a 'hub' - type structure is more efficient, with all members accessing the centre for information; for more complex missions, a 'ring' or 'fully connected' model is more efficient.

To put it bluntly, the organisation that is incapable of responding to changing patterns of work and practices among its members is doomed to failure. In the Information Technology industry especially, the skills shortage will be with us for some time, and, increasingly, employees will expect to work in a way which gives them flexibility, outlets for good ideas, a high degree of connectivity with fellow information workers, and so on. Employers will be expected to respond with appropriate amounts of imagination and resourcefulness. If they do not, they will lose their employees.

### *Workgroup computing*

Stefik *et al*[65] have described a system, **cognoter**, that facilitates group decision making and problem discussion. It was developed at the Xerox PARC (Palo Alto research center) and works rather like an intelligent electronic blackboard.

### *An alternative view*

It would be wrong to have an uncritical acceptance of the assertions made above, namely, that the adoption of new technology would fundamentally reshape our organisations. For a variety of reasons, the scenario may not develop in that way. In a paper entitled *Are new technologies* really *reshaping our organizations?*, Taylor and Katambwe [67] take the view that there is no evidence that organizations are adapting to IT solutions. Rather,

> *"...several studies conclude that the introduction of new technologies usually end up supporting the* status quo.
>
> *Therefore, it is not so much that technology shapes the users' practices and structure of decision-making, as that users shape the technology to fit their preconceptions of organizational practice and hierarchy of authority."*

Taylor and Katambwe identify the existing power structure as the main factor in determining the course of IT development: in the large, well-established organizations that formed the basis of most of the studies they quote, radical new working methods would be unlikely to survive. They conclude:

> *"If so, the rate of founding of new organizations to replace old must be seen as a critical variable mediating the influence of technology."*

Thus, technology itself is seen as an agent for change, but only when incorporated during the early growth of the organization. This idea may also have consequences for when we teach young people seriously about computing - 11 or 12 years of age may be too late!

## Growing up with the computer culture

It is beyond doubt that the typical personal computer will, by 1992, possess the following characteristics:

- Extremely light weight and compact size (less than 3 lb. weight, A4 size and ½" thick).

- Powerful CPU (10-20 million instructions per second)

- Handwritten input as the norm, with optional keyboard; voice input and output optional. The display, input surface, microphone and loudspeaker functions will all be supported by the same membrane.

- Built-in modem and possibly radio link; automatic background processes to perform various 'housekeeping' functions such as database update etc.

- Built-in opto-magnetic drive (for multimodal data and programs); built-in high quality printer.

- Large amount of memory (4-16 megabytes), some of this non-volatile so that important data can be retained.

- Operating system which supports co-operative working with other machines, by sharing files or even procedures.

By this time, it is to be hoped that HCI has made much more of an impression on system designers, so we could expect to see the following features:

- Operating system support for such operations as context-sensitive help, adaptable interfaces etc.

- Operating system support for *domain-specific* functions (for example, font control for desktop publishing (DTP), special palettes for art programs, etc.)

It seems as though the problems of interfacing people with computers, having been successfully attacked, may give rise to further interesting problems of interfacing *societies* with computers. For by this time, there will be a global dependence upon information technology; the computer culture will be as pervasive as the car culture, but hopefully less destructive to the environment. In many cases, possession of appropriate computer facilities will render journeys to work unnecessary unless there is a real need to meet people (this may mean that meetings will be better planned and more productive - although this is probably a vain hope).

It is possible that we may be seeing the beginning of a *post-industrial* era, which to some extent reverses the effect of the Industrial Revolution by permitting people to work in less deterministic ways. This is certainly reflected in the style of computing services, which are moving to a more distributed *client-server* approach which eschews the need for a large, central mainframe. There is no longer any need for geographical proximity to affect the quality of work. It is possible that the cities we have developed to serve the traditional needs of manufacturing and service industries will lose those functions, but persist in a new form which recognises the importance of 'city life' for its own sake - community activities, cultural activities etc.

In a situation where data storage will be made both much more extensive and long-lived (typically, thousands of megabytes for hundreds of years), it will be quite realistic, for example, for children to carry their educational record around with them for life. This will undoubtedly have a profound effect on the next generation, who will come to regard their personal computer as an intelligent assistant and library combined rather than as a computer *per se*. Improvements in interfaces (as a result of applying good HCI practice, of course) will ensure that these machines are natural to use.

The author's three year old daughter, for example, certainly has no fear of the keyboard of her father's personal computer; the main emotion she displays is disappointment that the machine is not delivering what she expects of it in terms of performance or functionality. (Why does it take a whole twelve seconds to copy daddy's book (2.5 megabytes) to a backup file? Why are there only 256 colours on the screen? Why does it take so long to rotate a picture through 90 degrees? and so on.) It is interesting to note that, ten years ago, a machine of comparable power - 4 million instructions per second, 2 megabytes of memory, 42 megabytes storage capacity - would have needed a whole suite to itself, along with two or three attendants.

## New realities

Throughout this book, there have been hints that, using computers, we can create and explore alternate realities which may be helpful to us in visualising and manipulating data in the real world. Is it possible that, using computers, we will be able to transcend the boundaries of what we consider to be normal, and create and explore realities for ourselves that we cannot yet imagine? The answer must be made in philosophical terms, because we do not really *know* - but we can make a fair guess: Yes.

To a very great extent, we draw conclusions about the universe we live in by making abstractions and intuitive leaps, which become formalised into further systems. The languages we use to convey these ideas are Mathematics (for formal, testable ideas) and Philosophy (for more tentative ideas). Very often we have no direct knowledge of what bounds our ideas and consciousness, in the same way that a fish has no concept of water.

### Ouspensky's strange worlds

The philosopher Ouspensky[52] has attempted to explain the difficulty we have with reality by positing a number of strange worlds, and the problems of the creatures which inhabit them.

### A one-dimensional world

Imagine a world comprising only one dimension, which we could visualise as a straight line. A being inhabiting this world could move along the line, but would not have any concept of it. Anything happening to this world, such as other lines or planes intersecting it, would be perceived only as a point. All phenomena would therefore be seen in an identical way, differing only in time. The inhabitants of this world would never be able to develop the concept of a higher-order dimensionality.

### A two-dimensional world

A two-dimensional world is more interesting, both to us and to its inhabitants. The plane surface defined by the two dimensions has two sides, and the inhabitants can see (and move) around it.

An event in this world would have a richer set of metrics with which to characterise it: a line intersecting it would be seen as a point; a moving line would be seen as a point that disappeared and reappeared somewhere else. A coin, dropping side-on through this world, would be seen as a line which appeared on one side, and then disappeared on the other. A coin dropped edge-on would appear as a line which appeared, expanded and then shrank again. Observant inhabitants of this world would be able to compile a catalogue of interesting phenomena, from simple (such as the coin) to complex (imagine what they would make of a cow blundering into their world). They would be able to develop the concept of a surface, but would not know what it was.

Finally, imagine that a child's windmill (with a transparent hub) is placed in this world and rotated (figure 15.2). After their initial shock, the inhabitants would report that the following phenomena had occurred: An oblong object appeared on one side, and disappeared on the other. This kept on happening. The phenomena were related in some way by their regularity, but no further structure could be deduced. The concept of time might then be developed as some regular event that was associated with one side of the world or the other, continually appearing *from* one side (the past) and disappearing *into* the other (the future). The unity of the windmill as an entity could not be conceptualised in 2-D World.

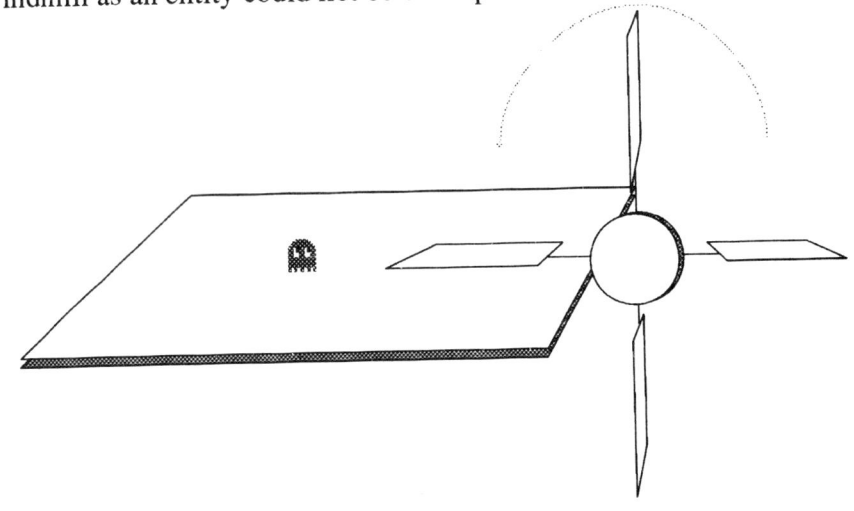

*Figure 15.2 Events in a 2-dimensional world*

What is the point of all this? Simply that we could argue that, in our world, we are in the same position as Ouspensky's 2-D Worlders. In Newton's time, we had a concept of the universe that was fairly consistent until Einstein developed his theories of Relativity. Now, physicists are asking fundamental questions about the relationship between energy, matter and time that our current scientific framework cannot explain (they may be, for example, different manifestations of the same thing, as the Unified Field theory sets out to prove).

If a computer, via its interfaces and dialogues, can offer novel ways of representing and manipulating the various manifestations of reality that pass through it, then it is possible that we can develop new 'handles' on reality. Just as a genius born into the 2-D World could possibly have made an intuitive leap into the third dimension, and thus given a satisfactory explanation of the structure (if not the purpose) of the windmill, so a corresponding genius in our world could gain insights into corresponding problems.

We do not need to look very far for justifications for this idea. The spreadsheet, developed in the 1970s, is now an almost indispensable tool for a wide range of financial and scientific activities (see also chapter 7).

Using it, any non-programming domain specialist can perform useful work, and gain insights by doing a variety of 'what-if' projections. Calculations can be made to repeat automatically, and so simple simulations can be developed. With advanced spreadsheets, 3-dimensional data spaces can be explored and graphs or surfaces plotted; the concept of the spreadsheet, however, is simple, and not too difficult to program. Users can grasp basic operations in half an hour, and soon be writing macros for their own use and the use of others. Hardly any of these users would claim to be 'programming a computer', and yet that is what they are doing, functionally.

There is no reason to suppose that equivalent gains in productive power would not be conferred by advanced interfaces of the kind discussed earlier in this book. Using a datasuit, 3-dimensional display and direct manipulation techniques, a user will be able to visualise and transform complex data spaces, and directly display the results to an interested audience. Moreover, users could share the experience of travelling through this data space, with different users taking different views according to their special interests.

## Conclusion

Many people sitting in front of a computer would rather be doing something else. Let's change that.

# Appendix A References

[1] Abbott, R: "Knowledge Abstraction" *Comms. ACM, 30*, 8, p.664 (August 1987)

[2] Abstracts: *Abstracts in Human-Computer Interaction* Ergosyst Associates Inc.

[3] Alexander, Heather: "ECS - A technique for the formal specification and rapid prototyping of human-computer interaction" *In: BCS Workshop Series: People and Computers: Designing for Usability* CUP, 1986

[4] Alexander, Heather: "Formally-based tools and techniques for human-computer dialogues" *Ellis Horwood Series in computers and their Applications* (1987) ISBN 0-7458-0298-2

[5] Anderson, Ray: "Holo-Scope" Personal Computer World, November 1988 p.168

[6] Argyle, Michael: "The effects of Technology" in: *The Social Psychology of Work*, Pelican Books 1974

[7] Ausubel, David P: "Schemata, Advance Organizers, and Anchoring Ideas: A Reply to Anderson, Spiro and Anderson" *Journal of Structural Learning, 7*,1 (1982) p.63

[7a] Baddeley, A: "The Psychology of Memory", *Harper International*

[8] Benyon D & Murray, Dianne: "Experience with Adaptive Interfaces" *The Computer Journal* **31**,5 (1988) p.465

[9] Bench-Capon, TJM and McEnery, AM: "People interact through computers not with them" *Interacting with Computers*, **1**,1 (1989) pp. 31-38

[10] Bjørn-Andersen, N: "Are 'Human factors' human?" *The Computer Journal*, **31**, 5 (1988) pp.386-390

[11] Black, WJ: "Intelligent knowledge-based systems" *Van Nostrand Reinhold (UK)* (1986) ISBN 0-442-31772-7

[12] Bobrow (Student)

[13] Bolter, J. David: "Turing's Man" *Penguin Books* 1986

[14] Cantwell-Smith, Brian: "The limits of correctness" *Symposium on Unintentional Nuclear War*, Budapest, 1985

[15] Card S.K., Moran T.P. & Newell A. "The Psychology of Human-Computer Interaction" *Lawrence Erlbaum Associates*, Hillsdale, N.J.

[16] Carroll, John M. & Carrithers, Caroline: "Training Wheels in a User Interface" *Comms. ACM*, **27**, 8 p.800, August 1984

[17] Cater, John P: "Electronically Speaking: Computer Speech Generation *Howard W. Sams & Co.* (1983) ISBN 0-672-21947-6

[18] Chang, Shi-Kuo: "Icon semantics - a formal approach to Icon system design" *International Journal of Pattern recognition and Artificial Intelligence* **1**,1 (1987) pp. 103-119

[19] Choukri K & Chollet G: "Adaptation of automatic speech recognisers to new speakers" *Computer Speech & Language*, Vol.1 No.2 (Dec 1986), p.95

[20] DeWilde, Greg: "A Programmer's Approach to Users' Manuals" *Computer Language* July 1986 p.39

[20a] Dillon A, McKnight C & Richardson J "Reading From Paper versus

Reading From Screen, *Computer Journal* **31,** .5 p.457 (May 1988)

[21] Dixon, F.J: "Simplifying Screen Specifications - the 'Full Screen Manager'" *The Computer Journal*, **28**, 2, p.117 (May 1985)

[21a] Eason K.D. "A task-tool analysis of manager-computer interaction" *In: Shackel B (ed.) The concept of usability - Proc. IBM software and Information Usability Symposium, 1981*

[22] Edwards, Elwyn: *Information Transmission*, Chapman & Hall, 1964

[23] Edwards, Elwyn: "Human factors in Aviation" *Aerospace*, June/ July 1985 pp.13-17

[23a] Fogel, L.J., Owens A.J. & Walsh M.J. "Artificial Intelligence through Simulated Evolution" *John Wiley* 1966.

[24] Foley, James D: "Interfaces for Advanced Computing" *Scientific American special issue on Advanced Computing, 1988*

[25] Foss, D.J., Smith-Kerker, P.L. & Rosson, M.B: "On comprehending a computer manual: analysis of variables affecting performance" *International Journal of Man-Machine Studies*, **26**,3 (1987) p. 277

[26] Frankish C.R, D.M. Jones, C. Madden, K. Waight and J. Stoddart "Parcel Sorting by Speech Recognition: Human Factors Issues" *BCS Workshop Series: People and Computers III*, CUP 1987

[27] Gaines, B & Shaw, M: "The Art of Computer Conversation" *Prentice-Hall International* (1984) ISBN 0-13-047332-4

[28] Goodwin, Nancy C: "Functionality and Usability" *Comms. ACM* p.229 (March 1987)

[29] Goodwins, Rupert: "Voice Recognition" *Personal Computer World*, p.178,Oct 1988

[30] Grice, H.P.: "Logic and conversation" In *Syntax and Semantics*, P.Cole & J.L. Morgan (eds.) Volume 3, Academic Press (1975)

[31] Gwei, Godwin M & Foxley, Eric: "Towards a consultative on-line

help system" *Int. J. Man-Machine Studies,* **32**, 363-383 (1990)

[32] Harrison MD & Monk AF (eds.): "Designing for usability" *HCI-86 proceedings, CUP / BCS*

[33] Hartson, H.Rex and Hix, Deborah: "Towards empirically-derived methodologies and tools for human-computer interface development" *Int. J. Man-Machine Studies* (1989), **31**, 477-494

[34] Hoeber, Tony: "Open Look Design Goals" *Sun Technology,* Autumn 1988 p.63

[34a] Holland, John H: "Escaping Brittleness: The Possibilities of General-Purpose Learning Algorithms Applied to Parallel Rule-Based Systems" In: *Machine Learning II,* (Michalski et al, eds.)

[35] Houghton, Raymond C. Jr: "Online help systems: a conspectus" *Communications ACM,* **27,2** *(February 1984)*

[36] Jagodzinski AP & Clarke DD: "A Multidimensional Approach to the Measurement of Human-Computer Performance" *Computer Journal,* **31,** 5, p.409 (May 1988)

[37] Jerrams-Smith, J: "SUSI - A Smart User-System Interface" *HCI-85 Proceedings* CUP / BCS

[38] Johnson, Jeff: "Modes in non-computer devices" *Int. J. Man-Machine Studies (1990),* **32,** pp.423-438

[39] Kavaler Robert A, Lowy Menahem, Murveit Hy and Broderson Robert W: "A Dynamic-Time-Warp Integrated Circuit for a 1000-Word Speech Recognition System" *IEEE Journal of Solid-State Circuits,* **SC-22**, 1 (February 1987)

[40] Kindborg M & Kollerbaur A: "Visual Languages and Human Computer Interaction" *BCS Workshop Series: People and Computers III,* CUP 1987

[41] Lane, Alex: "DOS in English", *Byte,* Dec 1987 p.261

[42] Maass, Susan: "Why Systems Transparency?" in *The Psychology of*

*Computer Use,* (TRG Green, SJ Payne & GC van der Veer, eds.) Academic Press Computers and People series (B. Gaines, ed.) 1983

[43]   Maddix, F J and Morgan, G: "System Software: an introduction to Language Processors and Operating Systems" *Ellis Horwood 1989.*

[44]   Maller, V A J: "HCI - ephemeral fashion or fundamental shift?" *Computer Bulletin,* September 1986 (Editorial)

[45]   Martin, Anne & McAleese, Ray: "How to help Experts to 'Give up their Secrets': the experience of Notecards" *University teaching centre publication, University of Aberdeen (1987)*

[46]   Monk, Andrew (Ed.): "Fundamentals of Human-Computer Interaction" *Academic Press Computers & People series (B. Gaines, ed.)* 1984, ISBN 0-12-504580-8

[47]   Moran, T P "The command language grammar" *Int. J. Man-Machine Studies,* **15** (1981)

[48]   Moore, Roger: "The art of talking to a computer" *Sensor Review,* October 1983

[49]   Morris D, Theaker CJ, Phillips R and Love, W: "Human-computer Interface Recording" *The Computer Journal,* **31,** 5 (1988) 437 - 444

[50]   Mumford, Enid: "Defining System Requirements to meet Business Needs: a Case Study" *The Computer Journal,* **28,** 2 p.97 (May 1985)

[51]   O'Reilly, Tim: "The Toolkits (and politics) of X Window" *Unix World,* February 1989 p.66

[52]   Ouspensky, PD: "Tertium Organum - a key to the enigmas of the world" *Routledge & Kegan Paul* (1957)

[53]   Patrick J & Fitzgibbon L: "Structural displays as learning aids" *Int. J. Man-Machine Studies* (1988) **28,** 625-635

[54]   Payne, S.J. "Task Action Grammars" In: *Interact-84 Proceedings,* B. Shackel, ed. , North-Holland, Amsterdam

[55] Pinsky, L.: "What kind of 'dialogue' is it when working with a computer?" *The Psychology of Computer Use* (Academic Press Computers and People series, B.Gaines (ed.)) 1983

[56] Rasmussen, Jens: "The Human as a Systems Component" *Human Interaction with Computers*, H.T. Smith & T.R.G. Green (eds.) Academic Press (1980)

[57] Rasmussen, Jens: "Skills, Rules and Knowledge; Signals, Signs and Symbols, and Other Distinctions in Human Performance Models" *IEEE Transactions on systems, man and cybernetics*, **SMC-13**, 3 (May/June 1983) pp. 257-264

[58] Reason, James: "The human contribution to Nuclear Power Plant emergencies" *Human Reliability in Nuclear Power Conference* (1987)

[59] Runciman, C & Hammond, N: "User programs: a way to match computer systems and human cognition" *BCS Workshop Series: People and Computers: Designing for Usability* CUP (1986)

[60] Shackel, B: "Dialogues and language - can Computer Ergonomics help?" *Ergonomics*, **23**,9, pp.857-880 (1980)

[60a] Shackel, B: "Ergonomics in design for usability" In: *BCS Workshop series People and Computers: designing for usability* CUP (1986)

[62] Shneiderman, Ben "Designing the User Interface" *Addison-Wesley, 1987* ISBN 0-201-16505-8

[63] Sime, ME & Coombs, MJ: "Designing for Human-Computer Communication" *Academic Press, Computers & People series (B. Gaines, Ed.)* ISBN 0-12-643820-X (1983)

[64] Sohr, Dana: "Better Software Manuals" *Byte*, May 1983 p.286

[65] Stefik Mark, Foster Gregg, Bobrow Daniel G. et al: "Beyond the Chalkboard: Computer Support for Collaboration and problem Solving in Meetings", *Comms. ACM*, Jan 1987 p.32

[66] Sutcliffe, Alistair: "Using JSD for Human-Computer Interface

Design" *Michael Jackson Systems*

[66a] Sutcliffe, Alistair: "Human-Computer Interface Design" *Macmillan Computer Science series (1988)* ISBN 0-333-42899-4

[67] Taylor, James R & Katambwe, Jo Mulamba: "Are new technologies really reshaping our organizations?" *Computer Communications,* **11,** 5 (October 1988) p.245

[68] Thimbleby, Harold: "Ease of use - the Ultimate Deception" *Proc. 2nd Conference of BCS HCI SIG, September 1986*

[69] Totterdell P.A., Norman M.A. and Browne D.P "Levels of adaptivity in interface design" in: *Proceedings of Interact '87,* H.Bullinger and B. Shakel (eds.) Elsevier-North-Holland, Amsterdam (1987)

[70] Ward, Darrell E: "Gaze Control" *Omni,* December 1988 p.30

[71] Wood-Harper AT, Antill Lynn and Avison DE: "Information Systems Definition: The Multiview Approach" *Blackwell Scientific Publications (1985)* ISBN 0-632-01216-8

.

# Appendix B HICOM examples

The HICOM computer-assisted conferencing system is run by Loughborough University for the benefit of the HCI community. It runs on a VAX minicomputer and uses a standard conferencing system, VAXNotes.

These transcripts were downloaded by using the 'capture' feature of a typical communications package running on a (real) IBM PC-AT. The reader will note several things about the tenor of the notes:

- There is no undue reverence for things, ideas or people

- Conferees are not reticent in expressing their views

- Contrary to what might be expected in a computer-based environment, the messages are highly 'conversational' in tone.

Overall, the philosophy for contributions is best summed up by the moderator for the ACM Public Risks conference:

FORUM ON RISKS TO THE PUBLIC IN COMPUTERS AND RELATED SYSTEMS
ACM Committee on Computers and Public Policy, Peter G. Neumann, moderator

The RISKS Forum is moderated. Contributions should be relevant, sound, in good taste, objective, coherent, concise, and nonrepetitious. Diversity is welcome.

Some editing has been done, as in the original interactions the rate of typographical errors is high; but this is understandable bearing in mind that (i) people are typing quite rapidly (ii) The 'echo' is often delayed and (iii) the need to get a message across rapidly often takes precedence over exactness.

The first discussion, 'How open are toolkits?' is a personal view on certain aspects of Open Look, one of the standard GUI toolkits. Although it may seem like a fairly strong indictment of this particular standard, it should be remembered that discussions on these standards are still in a fairly fluid state - it would be surprising, and possibly ominous, if the spokespersons of the user community settled prematurely into an unquestioning acceptance of the various committees' recommendations.

## How open are toolkits?

```
Note 37.0                    How open are toolkits?           4 replies
HICOM::BROOKE "John Brooke, DEC UIA A/D Group"    93 lines  15-SEP-1988 09:54

Here's somebody's view on OPEN LOOK (tm) and, by implication, on toolkits
and style guides in general. It could equally well apply to mac interfaces,
X-windows, DECwindows, NeWS or anything else.

What are the views of HICOMers on this?

From:    REOVTX::ROLL::USENET  "USENET Newsgroup Distributor  14-Sep-1988 1715"
14-SEP-1988 22:18:01.76
To:      @SUBSCRIBERS.DISCC:
Subj:    USENET comp.cog-eng newsgroup articles
Newsgroups: comp.cog-eng,comp.software-eng
Path: decwrl!ucbvax!pasteur!ames!amdahl!pacbell!well!shf
Subject: OPEN LOOKPosted: 14 Sep 88 01:29:55 GMT
Organization: The Blue Planet
Xref: decwrl comp.cog-eng:659 comp.software-eng:854


I recently had the opportunity to listen to Tony Hoeber from Sun
Microsystems speak about OPEN LOOK(tm) (capitalization is correct) and
what it is designed to do.

I don't like it.  I don't like it at all.

The goals are good, and some of the problems they address are real, but
OPEN LOOK is not the answer as far as I'm concerned.  OPEN LOOK is not a
windowing system, it is not a toolkit, it is not software at all -- it
is a *specification* for the "look and feel" of graphical user
interfaces which fully details the appearance and function of the
elements of the interface.  The idea is that if different applications
running on different window platforms on different hardware all have the
same "look and feel," then users will be more comfortable and more
proficient quickly.
```

While this valid in principle, and OPEN LOOK does provide some good
guidelines to work from, it goes too far in specifying exactly what the
interface must look like.

Scroll bars are a good example.  OPEN LOOK specifies exactly what scroll
bars are to look like almost at the bitmap level and how they are to
behave.  The only user preference is what side of the scrolling area the
scroll bars normally appear.  Now, there are lots of interface toolkits
out there which provide scroll bars, and although they all look and
behave somewhat differently, the basic concept is the same.  I have used
many different styles and looks of scroll bars, and while I like some
better than others, I have never had any trouble figuring out how to
operate them.  Switching styles has never really slowed me down.

Scroll bars are a little like door handles.  There are lots of different
styles of door handles in the world but they all have some basic
similarities.  They are typically a hand-sized object set about halfway
up the surface of the door which, when turned, pressed or lifted operate
the door latch.  If you encounter a door handle which varies too much
from what you expect, it might slow you down a bit, but for the most
part, variations in door handle style don't pose a significant
impediment to productivity.  In fact, doors with different purposes can
require different types of handles.  Can you imagine if the door to your
office, your car and your shower were required by law to use the same
standard door handle?

I object most strongly, however, to how OPEN LOOK has already made all
of the aesthetic decisions.  Sun hired a graphic designer and he set
forth the look of OPEN LOOK.  The appearance of windows, buttons, scroll
bars, even the colors allowed are part of the specification.  There is
no room for innovation, no room for creativity.  It's like requiring
that everyone wear designer clothes from the same designer -- any other
style of clothes are "non-standard."  Like an other artist, I want full
control of my media.  OPEN LOOK takes this away.

All of this attention on minor details actually fails to address the
real issues behind user interface standardization -- that of how a
particular application maps into the controls presented to the user.
This very difficult issue is still left up to the programmer.  Although
OPEN LOOK provides some guidelines as to how certain common operations
should be handled, at the level of detail at which it's concerned, it
cannot hope to address all of the possible needs that an application may
have of its user interface.

User interface design is a difficult craft often poorly done.  OPEN LOOK
attempts to address standardization, but instead imposes dogmatic and
arbitrary limitations on the interface designer.  What user interface
designers need is not a standard "look and feel," but rather a careful
look at the art of user interface design, perhaps a definitive reference
work on the subject so that programmers can create their own user
interfaces that are clear, simple and attractive.

Stuart Ferguson        (shf@well.UUCP)
Action by HAVOC         (shf@Solar.Stanford.EDU)

End of note

I too have seen OPEN LOOK and, like our correspondent, don't like
the idea of standards at this level. For one thing, I don't like
the look of OPEN LOOK! It's a horrible, ugly art deco - inspired
look. I don't like the "elevator" (I don't like the terminology).
I don't like the mouse button arrangements. Etc., etc.. If I don't
like it, I don't suppose everyone else will - so what's the point
of having this ugly, awkward style-guide when, as was said, there
are plenty of similar-style interfaces and the differences don't
usually cause a problem? I agree entirely with the implied suggestion
that a UI standard should be somewhat deeper.

Actually, I quite like DECwindows. But then I like the Mac Interface
too.

End of note

The interesting thing is that this "Common look and feel" myth
persists. I have come across many product managers and software
engineers who believe that making things look the same is enough
to ensure good human factors. This goes hand in hand with the myth
of consistency - ie that consistency in itself is a good thing.
How does one get across the message that it doesn't matter about
the look, it's logical structure of the UI and how it maps onto
what people do with it that is important?

End of note

It's clear that there is a strong move towards achieving a standard
interface across Unix software with things like X-Windows and Open
Look. No doubt this desire is being duplicated in the MSDOS - OS/2
(do I have OS/2 right?) world. It seems to me that this is an issue
which ought to be of vital interest to all Hicomers. We could do
with a regular update of what's happening and perhaps a special
conference. I wonder if there are any HCI people in the UK working
in this area?

End of note

My understanding is that:

    ISO standards for WIMP interfaces will come from
    IEEE standards for POSIX, which will come from
    work on X-windows (by the self-elected X-Open group?), from
    /USR/GROUP Technical Subcommittee on usability, chaired by
    Al Weaver at IBM Austin (who I am trying to contact!)

```
Any other information or clarification appreciated!

End of note
```

## "Verdi was a Green"

The motivation of starting this topic was not levity, although there is no reason why HCI should not be fun. The author had a concern that HCI should be regarded as a conservation area, for reasons of enlightened self-interest apart form anything else.

As you can see, some interesting exchanges ensued.

```
Note 24.0                    Verdi Was a Green                13 replies
HICOM::FRANK_MADDIX "Frank Maddix, Bristol Polytech" 14 lines  12-JUL-1988 11:13

    I wonder if any incipiently verdant colleagues might like to start
    a conference on GreenNet.

    I think HCI is an essentially conservation-oriented activity.

    After all, we are dealing with people's sense of well-being and
    fulfilment at work, with optimising resources and reducing waste.

    OK, so it's information not whales or trees, but the principle's
    the same.

    I have a student working on a related project, and would be interested
    to talk to anyone about it.  We're talking open information here!!

End of note
```

(This was the initial note, stimulated by a conversation with an M.Sc. student about his placement work.)

```
Note 24.1                    Verdi Was a Green                  1 of 13
HICOM::JV_EARTHY "JONATHAN_EARTHY"              4 lines  28-JUL-1988 17:44
                      -< interested response... >-

    I am slightly confused as to what you are saying but keep talking.

    And, how would HICOM fit into conservationist policies? what is
    the species count at the moment?

End of note
```

(The respondent was not the only one who was confused. The author hadn't really expected any replies).

Hello Jon.

I think I was mainly concerned with the QUALITY of the human-computer
experience (from the human point of view), bearing in mind that
'computer' is generally a symbol of a wider system; and that ideas
of quality can come from divers sources.

I suppose HCI specialists are an endangered species - they favour
spending loadsamoney on improving system design, and this is not
a popular activity with those who just want to get the product out
of the door.

I actually think that intelligent application of HCI makes a BETTER
product, but cost accountants need convincing.

I'm thinking up some more parallels.

End of note

Yes, hello,

This sounds like a good one for HCI'88, I'll have to think of a
good pub in the city centre.

Before the moderator steps in and suggests that a two-person
conversation belongs on Email there are two very good books on the
philosophy (?) of technology which should guarantee some sleepless
nights, both are by a character called Langdon Winner:

Autonomous technology, 1977, To the Lighthouse Press (may be University
of Chicago Press now). ISBN 0-262-23078-X (this is hard going with
one of the largest reference lists I have seen in a book)

The Whale and the Reactor, 1986, University of Chicago Press.  A
more mature and toned-down version but without any justifying theory
- not as much use for arguments! sorry no ISBN.

    JV
End of note

Done it again: for 'To the Lighthouse press' read 'MIT press'.

End of note

Note 24.5                    Verdi Was a Green                    5 of 13
HICOM::SH_HOLMES "Steve Holmes, Plymouth Polytechni" 20 lines  10-AUG-1988 12:14
                        -< Interested >-


    I think I understand what you're on about when you talk about
    quality, waste and resource utilization.

    For me, I suppose this means issues such as taking into account
    users' attitudes and preconceptions (or misconceptions) as well
    as wider organizational aspects such as job and task issues;
    minimizing the destructive kind of change which leads to a loss
    in usability (in an identifiable and measurable way); ensuring
    good correspondence between interaction and user-understanding
    in terms of striving for the ever elusive ideal man/machine
    symbiosis.

    But what do you mean by 'conservation-oriented'? This suggests
    something to do with ownership and hence responsibility of some
    kind, maintaining an operable state, some form of preservation
    (perhaps), and protection from external (detrimental) factors
    ... a kind of ecological approach to HCI.

    Is this what you had in mind?
End of note

Note 24.6                    Verdi Was a Green                    6 of 13
HICOM::G_STORRS "Graham Storrs, Logica Cambridge"    27 lines  22-AUG-1988 14:55
                 -< How Green Was My Silicon Valley? >-

    I can't help thinking that this is the silliest thing I have yet
    read on HICOM. HCI is about people interacting with computers.
    In my experience, the people who interact with computers most are
    people with loadsamoney, lots of vested interest in such matters as
    using fossil fuels, pulping forests, blowing people up, building nuclear
    bits and bobs and so on - not really conservationists if you
    get my drift. I can't really see how HCI could, with its hand on
    its heart, properly associate itself with "green" movements.

    I *can* see what Frank is getting at though. I think most of us
    in HCI have a vague motivation at the back of our ids to do something
    vaguely nice for people. Unfortunately, it is probably also true
    that, as a breed, we love techy, whizzy, futuristic, spacey, gee-whiz
    gizmos like computers too. There is no conflict here, as long as
    we don't mind restricting ourselves to making marginal improvements
    in the quality of life of the best-fed, best-cared for people in
    the history of the world (us) but I think we are on very shaky
    ground if we start telling ourselves we are likely to make more
    than this marginal difference or help anyone other than this group.
    As for how our support for the industrial nations, industry, the
    war machine etc. may or may not make the world a better or worse
    place, I'd best keep my views to myself ...
End of note

Note 24.7                    Verdi Was a Green                    7 of 13
HICOM::FRANK_MADDIX "Frank Maddix, Bristol Polytech" 32 lines  23-AUG-1988 11:38
                     -< Not so sili... >-

    Graham.

    Imagine that you are deaf.  The only means of communication you
    have with your peers (deaf) is Sign Language (when you meet) or

via an incredibly cumbersome, expensive user-hostile system like
Vistel.

You observe your hearing colleagues chattering away electronically,
and you can't help feeling left out of things. You can't even ring
up a deaf colleague to discuss the situation. You generally don't
make much sense to hearing people either.

You would value any development which enhanced communication with
deaf or hearing people. Your whizz-tech colleagues don't seem to
be able to help. Why not? Because they are suffering from the same
problems with regard to lousy interfaces, inflexible systems etc.

The point being: (1) Not all users (or potential users) of IT are
IT professionals.
(2) We are *all* disabled in a not-so-extreme way when it comes
to interacting with technology. Perhaps if attention was paid to
the problems of disable users, we might get some insights into our
own condition (after all, verbal learning research has done OK out
of deaf people).
(3) The 'greening' process is really an attitude. When applied
to whales, it saves them. When applied to computer interaction,
it improves it by cutting waste and enhancing quality, which improves
productivity.

I'll try and give some more coherence to what was, initially, a
bit of serendipity.

End of note

Note 24.8                        Verdi Was a Green                    8 of 13
HICOM::G_STORRS "Graham Storrs, Logica Cambridge"    19 lines   23-AUG-1988 16:21
                 -< you can't save a whale with an improved HCI >-

If I'm understanding what Frank is saying, he seems to have taken
the view that I'm talking only about computer professionals. This
is not so. Our whole society is based on killing, burning, pulping,
irradiating, poisoning and generally behaving rather badly towards
everything else that lives. The computer and its attendant technologies
(HCI for instance) seem so deeply embedded in this culture that
I find it hard to see what we could possibly offer a conservationist
anything but a belly-laugh.

However, from Frank's last reply, I get the impression that I'm
not quite following the argument or something since he seems to
associate "green" with a sort of general disposition to do good.
Well, if that's so, I'm afraid the opportunities are inherently
limited. computer users (even genuinely disabled ones) live in a
world of money and comfort and privilege unheard of in the history
of the world. Anything we can do for them in the way of making
interfaces easier to use will, of course, be of some help in making
their lives even better - but the difference must be seen in context
and I think it has to be judged as marginal.

End of note

Note 24.9                        Verdi Was a Green                    9 of 13
HICOM::NIGEL_BEVAN "Nigel Bevan, NPL"                6 lines   23-AUG-1988 16:34
                 -< Spin-off? >-

In general economic terms I suspect that the more you do to make
the rich richer (via improved HCI?) the more well disposed they
are to spend some of their surplus income on the poor, thus making

the poor richer as well.  Alternative social systems striving to
achieve something more approximating to equality seem to have been
less successful.
End of note

```
Note 24.10                    Verdi Was a Green                10 of 13
HICOM::BROOKE "John Brooke, DEC UIA A/D Group"    12 lines  23-AUG-1988 17:14
                  -< We do HCI because otherwise there'd be no market >-
```

The cynical view (and I am of course a well known cynic) of HCI
is that as the market for computers amongst technophiles and propeller
heads becomes saturated, then you must make it easier for people
to use computers otherwise you're limiting your areas of potential
expansion.

Actually, why should we be especially concerned with computers?
I can think of lots of other tools we use which could do with increased
usability. I suspect they're just too boring for most people to
be bothered about.....


End of note

```
Note 24.11                    Verdi Was a Green                11 of 13
HICOM::NIGEL_BEVAN "Nigel Bevan, NPL"           8 lines  23-AUG-1988 17:26
                      -< HCI and Design >-
```

I think bridging the HCI/designer gap is just as important as the
HCI/computer science gap.  Denis O'Brien has stimulated some interest
in the are, and the Design Council Support for Design: human Factors
might help - but I suspect that designers (the "creative" type)
are as ignorant of HCI as computer scientists were 5 years ago.

Just as HCI embraces all product development, design embraces all
HCI.
End of note

```
Note 24.12                    Verdi Was a Green                12 of 13
HICOM::R_TAYLOR "Richard Taylor - BTRL"        14 lines  24-AUG-1988 11:14
                     -< designers and the HI >-
```

> might help - but I suspect that designers (the "creative" type)
> are as ignorant of HCI as computer scientists were 5 years ago.


Nigel, you might be interested to know that over the last year I
have been working with Alec Robertson of the School of Graphic Design
at Leicester Poly and one of his MA students exploring how graphics
designers can contribute to User Interface design.

There is a sense of deja vu when you here the arguments of why they
should be involved.

   Richard

End of note

```
Note 24.13                    Verdi Was a Green              13 of 13
HICOM::STEPHEN_TAGG                       23 lines  25-AUG-1988 13:01
                       -< political flame >-
```

In Note 24.9, Nigel says.....
    In general economic terms I suspect that the more you do to make
the rich richer (via improved HCI?) the more well disposed they
are to spend some of their surplus income on the poor, thus making
the poor richer as well.  Alternative social systems striving to
achieve something more approximating to equality seem to have been
less successful.

This argument (or thatcher-tenet) is certainly suspect. If improved
HCI makes the rich richer, that increased richness is only marginally
targeted towards making the poor slightly less poor. With equally
suspect suspicions perhaps the rich only spend on the poor when
not to do so would threaten their ever-increasing richness. Certainly
patronising/charity is not an efficient way of making the poor less
poor. The fact that every pink government since 1950 has not had
half the gumption of Ms Thatcher to pursue its beliefs may explain
the apparent lack of success of non-market strategies.
    In other words I guess I agree that HCI workers are compromised
with Multinational Market-capitalism, and that green-conservationist
ideas are yet more liberal attempts to tidy up the disastrous effects
of multinational market-capitalism, without addressing the cause.
    political flames off


End of note
No more replies

# Index